DOUGLAS McCALLA is a member of the Department of History at Trent University, Peterborough.

Based in Glasgow and Toronto and later Hamilton, the trading business of Peter and Isaac Buchanan became one of Canada's largest. The crash of 1857, which abruptly ended an Upper Canadian boom, brought its growth to a halt, and increasing financial problems led to its failure in 1867 and again in 1872. This history of success and failure reveals much about the Anglo-Canadian trading system and the Upper Canadian economy of the period.

The Buchanans' timing was excellent; in 1834 they began operations in Glasgow and Toronto, early in the prolonged era of growth which by the mid-1850s had transformed Upper Canada from a frontier wilderness to a relatively developed agricultural society. In 1840 they added a large branch in Hamilton. Over the years a number of new partners were admitted, and branches were established in Montreal, New York, Liverpool, and London (Canada West). By 1845 the firm dealt in all the major categories of the colony's imports. By 1856 Peter's and Isaac's initial capital had increased sixteenfold, and the total capital of all partners exceeded £ 360,000.

The business's rapid rise indicates something of the processes, extent, and timing of Upper Canadian business and economic development. It also exemplifies the workings of the British export trade, notably Glasgow's role, and it clearly illustrates the significance of the metropolitan rivalries of the era. The workings of the international credit system are central to the story. And its failure is equally indicative of the changes in the commercial environment after the boom years.

The Buchanans were also significant historical figures. Isaac Buchanan is well known for his career in politics and his many writings on economic issues. His brother played a vital role in promoting the Great Western Railroad of Canada in Britain. Drawing on the voluminous Buchanan Papers in the Public Archives of Canada, this book illuminates a key period in Canada's economic and historical development.

'Isaac Buchanan M.P.P.' from his *Relations of the Industry of Canada with the Mother Country and the United States* ... (1864)

DOUGLAS McCALLA

The Upper Canada Trade 1834-1872: A Study of the Buchanans' Business

UNIVERSITY OF TORONTO PRESS
Toronto Buffalo London

© University of Toronto Press 1979
Toronto   Buffalo   London
Printed in Canada

Canadian Cataloguing in Publication Data

McCalla, Douglas, 1942-
   The Upper Canada trade, 1834-72
   Bibliography: p.
   Includes index.
   ISBN 0-8020-5442-0
   1. Ontario – Commerce – History. 2. Wholesale
   trade – Ontario – History. 3. Buchanan, Isaac,
   1810-1883. I. Title.
   HF3229.05M32   382'.09713   C79-094097-3

The maps on pages 111 and 120 were drawn by Geoffrey J. Matthews

Contents

Contents vi

Acknowledgments

This book is a revised and much shortened version of my Oxford D PHIL thesis, which was completed in 1972. In the course of my work on this subject, I have accumulated many obligations, the most important of which at least I would wish particularly to acknowledge here. I have to thank Dr R.M. Hartwell, who supervised the thesis, and Dr A.F. Madden, both of Nuffield College in Oxford, for their criticism and their encouragement. In Canada I have benefited especially from the advice of Professor J.M.S. Careless, who prompted and ably directed my first researches on questions of business organization and development in nineteenth-century Canada. Alan Wilson and Elwood Jones both subjected an earlier draft to most thorough and helpful readings. And I have been stimulated and inspired on numerous occasions by conversations on the themes of this book with Bill Downes and with Viv Nelles.

The facilities and the kind assistance of the staff of the Public Archives of Canada greatly expedited my researches in the voluminous Buchanan Papers. The courteous and friendly staffs of the Scottish Record Office and of the reference departments of the Mitchell Library in Glasgow and the Hamilton Public Library offered much assistance. Else Irvine typed the thesis version and Marian Morgan the condensed one; Barbara Soldera and Cathy Brunger have quickly done all the requisite typing of revisions and additional material. Jean Houston's and Jean Wilson's editorial work has greatly improved this final version. Nancy Macmillan's help with the index has been invaluable.

The financial assistance which permitted the initial research for this book was largely provided by the Rhodes Trust, to whom I am deeply grateful for the privilege of studying in Oxford. Trent University has provided small grants as needed and, more important, a year of leave during which the present work was largely completed. This book has been published with the assistance of a grant from the Social Science Federation of Canada, using funds provided by the Social Sciences and Humanities Research Council of Canada, and a grant to University of Toronto Press from the Andrew W. Mellon Foundation.

My wife Anna has borne with this book for a long time, and it owes much more to her than perhaps she realizes.

To all of these, my thanks and appreciation.

THE UPPER CANADA TRADE 1834-72

1
Introduction

This is the story of a business, founded by Peter and Isaac Buchanan in 1834. Based in Glasgow, where their father had been a merchant before them, and in Toronto, newly incorporated as Upper Canada's first city, they would export British dry goods to Upper Canada for sale at wholesale. By 1856, the business had grown to be one of the largest in Canada, a general wholesale house with as many as seven partners and six branches, annual sales of up to $2,000,000, and a capital approaching $1,500,000. In their first twenty-two years of trade, Peter and Isaac saw their own capital increase at a highly satisfactory rate, an annual average of almost fourteen per cent. But despite its success and its scale, the business suffered a severe setback in the crisis of 1857, could not adapt to the end of the age of extensive growth in Upper Canada, and went bankrupt in 1867. Isaac Buchanan refloated the business, but again failed in 1872.

How had such growth been possible? Why did the business fail to consolidate its position at the head of the Upper Canadian business world? While answers to these and related questions depend, in part, on personal factors, an account of the business's rise and decline also offers perspectives on questions of more general interest, for the Buchanans' history can only be understood when viewed in the setting of the North Atlantic trading world in which they operated. In particular their experience illuminates the development of business in western Upper Canada in its era of rapid extensive growth, from about 1830 to the mid-1850s, and it is at least suggestive of the structural changes that followed that age of expansion. It serves also to illustrate the processes of the British, and especially the Scottish, export trade in their period; marketing, after all, was a vital aspect of the industrial revolution.[1]

This account is based on the Buchanan Papers, a large collection gathered primarily by Isaac Buchanan and now in the Public Archives of Canada. Although the papers contain few of the formal business records, such as account books and routine correspondence, they do cover comprehensively the partners' major decisions in the business, and they provide statistical material on which to base a detailed chronology of the business's development. The size of the collection and its relatively peripheral relationship to what have been the major concerns of Canadian historians have meant that, until the last few years, limited use has been made of them.[2]

The importance and influence of business and businessmen in Canadian history have long been recognized, and have led recently to a welcome and substantial increase in the study of Canadian business history.[3] Indeed, one observer has urged a move away from studies of individual firms to more comparative studies.[4] But this advice is difficult to follow in the many areas of Canadian business history where the first scholarly or even, in many cases, popular firm histories have still to be written. Comparative study will proceed at its peril if it does not draw effectively on the limited number of good collections of business records that we have, yet such records tend to be bulky and time-consuming to explore. Hence one justification for this study is simply that it opens up an important source for the history of Canadian trade in the nineteenth century.

Although the Buchanans' business was larger in sales and capital and more complex in its branch system than almost any other in Upper Canada, its structure, development, and problems serve to indicate and reflect those of business as a whole. The Buchanans were import-export merchants in what proved to be the last age when such merchants were the pre-eminent figures of the North American business world.[5] The success of their generation of merchants in Canada in founding banks, insurance companies, railroads, and the like would transform the institutional structure of the economy and deprive later merchants of many of the roles that men such as the Buchanans had.[6] Looking backward, however, historians may tend to exaggerate the importance of corporations and more modern forms of business in the first half of the nineteenth century. How else, for example, can one explain Toronto historians' persistent interest in the ephemeral 'stock exchange' of the 1850s?[7] In fact, until sometime after 1850, private partnerships were the normal form of business organization, and trade, in a staples dependent economy, was much the most significant area of business opportunity.[8]

We already have some valuable studies pertaining to the organization of early nineteenth-century Canadian trade, such as the classics by Creighton and Buck, but they have been based largely on public records.[9] It is important, however, to set private experience against public documents; in business, as in politics, appearance and reality, public statement and private action, might diverge widely.[10] For example, the Buchanans' most profitable years included years when the public records speak of deep depression; there are reasons for the contrast, but it is valuable to draw them out. Businessmen were quick to lament publicly, yet they could often adjust privately, as the Buchanans demonstrated when the Corn Laws were repealed. The Buchanans' experience thus offers an inside view of the Upper Canada trade and of the private business sector, a vital one in any age of Canadian history, not least the nineteenth century.[11]

The prosperity in this era of the western Upper Canadian economy, and hence of the Buchanans, depended ultimately on the success of Upper Canadian wheat as an export staple. Such Canadian dependence on staples may, however, have led historians to focus too narrowly on the export trades, by comparison with importing, in the process of staples development.[12] Before wheat exports could increase, a long period of frontier expansion was required. In that period, the import merchants played a vital role in the operation of the credit mechanisms by which new territory was brought into production. Fowke surely was right: there can have been few 'self-sufficient pioneers.'[13] In effect, imports preceded exports, and the import merchants and the cities in which they operated acquired a precedence in the business world. British credit, nominally short-term, was relayed through the commercial system to the frontier and through store credits financed a great deal of the capital investment required to bring new areas of staple production into being.

As Professors Careless and Lower in particular have reminded us, metropolitan viewpoints were very important in nineteenth-century business.[14] These views reflected the reality that locational considerations were vital ones in trading success. The trader's prosperity was normally closely intertwined with the trading fortunes of the city or town in which he had chosen to operate, and the gains of one centre were often the losses of another. Because the Buchanans had constantly to consider this reality, their strategy illuminates some of the locational factors that were important in business growth and survival in their era. They sought to meet the problem, in part, by opening branches in a number of cities, but their business came to be most closely linked to Glasgow and Hamilton, two cities that later lost much of their trading importance and became, instead, industrial centres. The Buchanans' history illustrates the growth of each in trade and indicates something of the sequence of changes by which the trading roles of the two cities ended. It is noteworthy that through firms like the Buchanans' such relatively tiny frontier communities as Hamilton and Toronto were directly linked to the British metropolis at a time when the American import trade, and hence American inland cities, were becoming heavily dominated by New York.[15] The imperial connection and the active search for new markets by British merchants, notably those in Glasgow, account for this difference. Those who have seen it as a reaching out by colonial Upper Canadians, to bypass Montreal for example, have seen the process backward.

Such business connections were important informal links between Britain and British North America. The Buchanans' business provided a conduit through which flowed not only British credit and goods but also individuals and their ideas and values. How, for example, did Canada's business world acquire its strong Scottish tinge? The Buchanans' hiring and credit-granting practices suggest reasons. The Buchanans played an important role in the English promotion and the Canadian development of a major Canadian railroad, the Great Western, and this too illustrates the vital informal links of metropolis and colony.[16] It has, of course, been known that such links existed, but it is interesting to see how they operated in a particular instance.

Thus this study may be seen in the light of general business community studies. Charles Wilson has pointed to the role of the 'known community' in economic activity, and this is particularly evident in the operation of the credit structure that underlies any visible trade structure.[17] Personal knowledge by the lender or the endorser of the borrower was essential to the system's operation. Credit tied metropolis and hinterland together and was the basis of the whole structure of middlemen. Yet preoccupied by visible commodity flows, we may tend to neglect the relatively invisible role of credit and finance. In the Buchanans' business, credit was fundamental; their operations show how the British and Canadian financial systems operated and were connected. Their experience demonstrates once again that the British credit system proved most flexible and responsive to the expanding needs of business.[18]

At the risk, perhaps, of obscuring some broader changes, this study traces in considerable detail the firm's year-to-year fortunes, for the partners' decisions can only be understood in the setting of their experience and of the imperfect information that they possessed. Hence, attention is given also to some of the economic, business, and political indicators that influenced their thinking, such as movements, often quite short-term, in grain prices, bank discounts, and the like. The broad changes and trends that give history its patterns are not, it is hoped, slighted by this, but such changes are often clear only in hindsight, with information that the people of the period did not have; and in any case, they can often fruitfully be seen as the ultimate outcome of a process of many smaller changes.[19] Such is the case, for example, with Hamilton's rise and decline as a trading centre or Glasgow's demise as an entrepôt in the North Atlantic trade.

Thus this study examines the Anglo-Canadian business world of the mid-nineteenth century through the narrative of one business's rise and decline and the analysis of the functioning of the business's system, its controls and operation, strengths and weaknesses. Inevitably the experience of one firm is more suggestive than conclusive on the many wider questions that define the context within which the firm is set, but that is perhaps for the best at this stage of research in nineteenth-century Canadian business and economic history. This study does not offer full-scale lives of any of the partners in the business; Isaac Buchanan's immense range of activities alone would preclude that. A focus on the business cannot, however, neglect entirely the careers of its partners outside the warehouse and counting house. These careers were very much based on the business, and in turn had many implications for it.

Finally, the Buchanans' bankruptcy reminds us that failure was anything but atypical for the businessmen of the pre-corporate age.[20] Business history may well tend to emphasize success stories, for it is firms that survive that tend to have kept, by design or luck, old records and that may wish to commemorate their growth and survival with company histories. Insecurity's place in history should not be forgotten.

2
Founding the business

When the Buchanans opened their business in 1834, Peter was twenty-nine years old and had been in business, with his father and then another partner, for fourteen years; Isaac was twenty-four and had nine years of business experience. They had about £12,000stg in capital, inherited from their father. The character of their business was conditioned by their capital, experience, and connections, and by their Glasgow location.

By 1707, the Irish and coastal trades and the Scottish domestic trade had made Glasgow Scotland's leading port. The Union fully opened the colonial trade to Glasgow's merchants, who at once sought a place in the Thirteen Colonies' greatest trade, the tobacco trade, which was dominated by merchants in London and Bristol.[1] The Glasgow traders had only limited success until the 1740s, yet by 1768 Glasgow had become the leading British port in the trade, handling fifty per cent of Britain's tobacco imports. This extraordinary success was aided by the Navigation Laws, which forced all colonial tobacco to be shipped via a British port, and by Glasgow's northern location: the northern route was safer in wartime, and the voyage from the Clyde to Virginia usually took two or more weeks less in each direction than that from more southerly ports. But it was the result above all of the French tobacco monopoly's decision about 1740 to buy more of its requirements in Glasgow, where the price was somewhat lower than in London, and of the distinctive commercial system employed by Glasgow merchants to secure tobacco.[2]

Traditionally, the tobacco trade had been organized on a commission basis, merchants in England selling consignments received from the Chesapeake planters. London merchants had agents and warehouses in the colonies, but used these mainly to control advances and secure consignments. Ownership of the tobacco remained with the planter, who bore the risk on his produce until it was sold in England. This system persisted despite Glasgow merchants' efforts to break the hold of the established houses on the trade of the Tidewater plantations. The Glasgow merchants chose, or were forced by the dominance of London, to operate on their own account, buying tobacco in the colony and bearing the risks themselves. This system enabled them to respond quickly to rising French demand by moving over the fall line into the inland areas of Virginia and Maryland. Glasgow firms set up stores throughout the region, bypassing the London agents in the ocean ports, and supplying the credit needed to open it to cultivation. Like frontier general stores throughout North America, these stores retailed European and West Indian goods on long credits and purchased produce from the grower. Profits in the trade in fact came primarily from retail sales, because the French were powerful enough to exact the lowest remunerative price for the tobacco. Glasgow firms required many stores to gather large amounts of tobacco, and in contrast to the London firms in the Tidewater trade, which had relatively small numbers of large accounts, the Glasgow firms had large numbers of small accounts. To pay cash for tobacco, to sell retail goods at long credit, and to operate many stores all involved major management problems and heavy commitments of capital. Accordingly Glasgow's traders created larger firms than were common in London; they were also strongly supported by Glasgow's private banks, several of which were dominated by tobacco merchants.

Thus the Glasgow merchants, in a manner quite different from the traditional practices of the sedentary merchants, extended metropolitan finance and organization directly to the American frontier. Theirs was always an entrepôt trade: over ninety per cent of the tobacco entering the Clyde was destined for re-export, while the largest part of the goods sold in the colonies were not of Scottish manufacture. But profits from the trade accumulated in Glasgow, the city developed a more complex trading and financial structure, and Glasgow's leading bankers and merchants became known in and connected to the London financial structure.[3] After 1775, however, the American Revolution destroyed the trade; Glasgow's merchants, fortunate to escape without a total loss, were forced to seek other sources of profit. Some merchants renewed trade with the United States after 1783, while others looked to Europe or even Canada and Nova Scotia, but many who chose to remain in trade looked to the West Indies. They were the leading single source of Britain's imports, and Glasgow's traders had long sought a share of their produce. Although London, Bristol, and Liverpool dominated this trade, Glasgow's merchants began to make gains. By 1790, the West Indies had become the most valuable overseas market for Glasgow's merchants.[4]

Thus Glasgow in 1800 retained a significant overseas trade despite the loss of much of the staple trade on which its trading fortune had first been built. During the 1780s, cotton manufacturing began to grow rapidly in the Glasgow area. It drew on the capital and skills of the traditional linen industry, and much of it was located outside Glasgow, but the industry was organized around Glasgow and depended on the credit and marketing facilities that trade had given the city. Reflecting the city's continued rapid population growth and its successful accumulation of capital, Glasgow burst its medieval boundaries in the 1790s and a major building boom ensued.[5]

By the 1820s, when Peter and Isaac Buchanan began their business careers, a large and diversified business community had developed in and around Glasgow. It consisted of new wealth and old, large firms and small, traders and manufacturers; a part of it was most concerned with cotton, another with the domestic and coastal trades, and another with the overseas trade; and each group was further subdivided.[6] Although there was much overlapping of interest and membership among various groups, divisions did exist; no one businessman could know closely a very large proportion of the city's business community.

At the heart of the business community were the banks, which, through their control of credit, their management of the community's capital resources, and their links to the national credit structure, linked the widely varied economic activities of the city into one coherent system. In the 1820s and 1830s, Glasgow's banking structure, already well developed, continued its rapid expansion. There were branches of all five Scottish chartered banks, including the newer and more aggressive Commercial and National banks. Complementing these were the locally based private banks, most of which remained more oriented to the demands of trade than were the chartered banks. Reflecting the continuing expansion of banking competition, four major new banks were founded in Glasgow in the 1830s.[7]

Despite its diversity, the Glasgow business community shared something of a common outlook, perhaps best reflected in the Glasgow Chamber of Commerce, established in 1783. The Chamber emphasized the city's continuing interest in trade, its developing enthusiasm for manufacturing, and above all its optimism. Having lost the tobacco trade, Glasgow's businessmen had found new growth and prosperity in the West Indies and in cotton manufacturing. They had put to work the city's new population pouring in from the countryside and from Ireland. Now they promoted more ambitious business schemes. The swift rise of the iron trade after 1830 could only enhance their confidence. Glasgow had become the centre of Scotland's economic development and one of Britain's most rapidly growing cities.[8]

Peter Buchanan Sr, father of Peter and Isaac, was a member of this Glasgow business community. Several authors, writing about business in Glasgow, refer to 'the Buchanans,' but there were many Buchanans in Glasgow, at every level of society. Peter Buchanan Sr was not closely related to the great Buchanan families, the tobacco lords, the bankers, the provosts. He was the son of a farmer and maltster in Buchanan Parish, Stirlingshire, and in 1800, at the age of forty, he married Margaret Buchanan, whose father was also a farmer (Figure 1, p 12). Both sides of the family were of the middle rank of farmers, neither well-to-do gentry nor impoverished crofters. Margaret Buchanan's sister married Andrew Buchanan, a merchant in Jamaica, and her half-brother became a shawl manufacturer in Glasgow; Peter's brother was a storekeeper in Glasgow.

By 1807, Peter Buchanan was settled in Glasgow, where he manufactured either cotton or linen textiles.[9] He prospered in business during the Napoleonic Wars and either purchased or took over in settlement of a debt owed him by Andrew Buchanan the 1378-acre estate in Buchanan Parish known as Auchmar.* This estate, valued at about £10,000, was part of the historic Buchanan lands, and its ownership entitled Peter to add 'of Auchmar' to his name.[10] He joined Glasgow's Merchants House in 1812, giving his occupation as 'home trader.' From 1816 to 1821, he was a director of the Buchanan Society, a Glasgow-based genealogical, charitable, and social society. He became an Elder of the Church of Scotland, and the family found many of its friends outside business – in medicine, teaching, and the church.[11] By 1820, for reasons that are not spelled out, he had turned almost entirely from manufacturing to trade. He was, perhaps, going into semi-retirement; he might have been trying to develop a business for his sons; he had perhaps found trade more profitable than manufacturing during the war; his domestic market might have disappeared; or it is even possible that he aspired to the higher prestige that commerce still held in a city where the leading figures had achieved success in trade and continued to be active in overseas trade. At any rate, like many others in Glasgow, he was deeply involved in the West Indies trade.

By 1820, however, the West Indies trade was in difficulty. After 1815, trade in the West Indies' staple exports, sugar and coffee, fluctuated in volume, while prices fell significantly. Within the West Indies, an increasing share of these exports was supplied by the colonies Britain had captured

---

* It is unclear precisely when he took over the estate fully; evidently he had held a bond or mortgage from Andrew Buchanan for some years. He was certainly in full possession before 1815. Isaac Buchanan attached great importance to this estate's having been in the family and twice named Canadian properties he was developing 'Auchmar.' Sketches of his life referred prominently to the original Auchmar, 'an ancient family seat.' See Morgan, Sketches of Celebrated Canadians 553; and Notman and Taylor, Portraits of British Americans 382.

Figure 1
Partial genealogy of the Buchanan Family

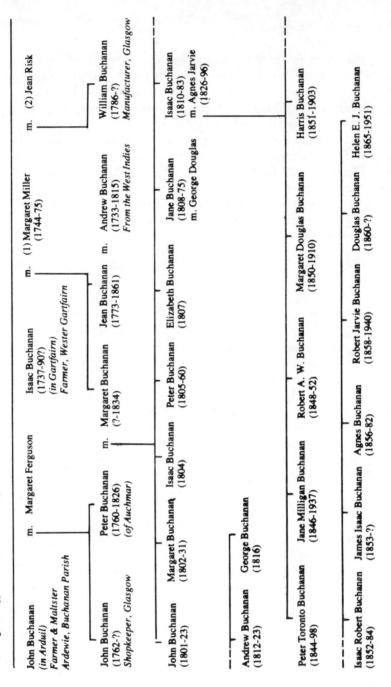

Sources: R.M. Buchanan, *Notes on Members of the Buchanan Society* 96, 102, 131; Mary H. Farmer, 'Calendar of the Buchanan Papers, 1697-1896'; Hamilton Public Library, Reference Department files, 'Hamilton, Biography, Buchanans,' photocopy from a Buchanan family Bible.

during the war, Demerara, Berbice, Essequibo, St Lucia, and Tobago; and other areas, notably Brazil and Cuba, now competed in European markets with the British West Indies. Sharply falling land values during the twenties reflected the ruin that these changes spelled for many West Indies planters. While some new mercantile opportunities were created in the new colonies, so many firms were competing for the West Indies trade that, for most, profits must have diminished or vanished.[12]

Peter Buchanan's involvement in the West Indies trade was of two types. The first was his partnership with one Duncan Buchanan in a firm known as Peter Buchanan and Company in Glasgow and Buchanans and Company in Demerara.[13] Duncan Buchanan, not a near relative, had lived in Demerara, and was on a visit to Scotland in 1820 when Peter first met him. Peter soon agreed to support Duncan in a retail dry goods store in Demerara. This was a new type of business for Peter, who had previously dealt only in goods of his own manufacture. It was planned to revive his fortunes and to provide an opportunity for his eldest son John, aged nineteen, who was being exiled to Demerara for some misbehaviour. Peter Buchanan agreed to invest £6000 and Duncan £3000 in the business, and Duncan and John then left with a shipment of goods to open the store.

Almost immediately the business met difficulties. John and Duncan fell out, John returning to Glasgow. Duncan put money from the firm into a plantation, despite an agreement not to withdraw funds. Sales were not easily made even on credit, so profits could not be large, and Duncan proved an unreliable judge of credit in the deteriorating economic climate of the 1820s. Remittances fell behind, Peter refused to send further shipments, and the partners began to quarrel openly. Peter named an agent in Demerara to intervene to save his funds; at the end of 1821 he gave the required twelve months' notice to dissolve the partnership. The matter went to court, and although Peter changed agents several times, money continued to be lost.

It is not clear how much Peter Buchanan lost in Demerara. The agent who finally proved satisfactory reported in 1829 that the firm's chief assets, a claim against Duncan Buchanan and 137 planters' accounts, were almost valueless.[14] Peter Buchanan's initial investment and sums invested in goods in 1821 and 1822, for which he had had to pay when remittances did not come, had all been lost. The loss could well have exceeded £10,000stg. Peter Buchanan had badly misjudged the character of Duncan Buchanan, whom he scarcely knew, and the chances for profit in Demerara. Distance and the problem of finding a reliable agent had further complicated matters.

In the same period, Peter Buchanan had sought to spread his risks by sending consignments to at least seven other markets, mainly elsewhere in the Caribbean. These consignments, many of which consisted of handker-chiefs and gingham, were perhaps largely goods of his own manufacture. In total value, they might have equalled his shipments to Demerara. Goods were sent to local branches of Glasgow mercantile houses except in Berbice, where he consigned to Charles Lyle, whom he met at about the same time as he encountered Duncan Buchanan and with whom he met little better success. All but one of the consignments of which there is record were sent between 1820 and 1823, but he could have begun this business earlier. In every market his goods sold slowly, and any profits must have been consumed by interest.[15] His business was running down rapidly, as a result of heavy competition in world markets and of his own poor selection of goods. In 1822 he gave up his extensive Glasgow premises in Hutcheson Street, and there began even to be talk of selling the Auchmar estate when the extent of the lock-up of his capital in the West Indies became apparent.[16]

Peter Buchanan died on 17 April 1826. His executors placed the realization of his estate primarily in the hands of his son Peter, who was now the eldest son, John having died, heavily in debt, in Demerara in July 1823. Under the will, Mrs Buchanan was to receive £500 plus an annuity of £200 per year; her sister, Mrs Jean Buchanan, was to receive £300 plus an annuity of £120 per year. The residue was to be divided equally among the four surviving children.[17] Peter Jr, only twenty-one, was responsible for six persons, and it was clear that his father had not left enough money to provide for them all in accustomed style. Yet the younger Buchanans were scarcely penniless; they had quite enough capital to secure good business positions for the two surviving boys.

Peter Jr had entered his father's business in 1820. By 1822, his father was leaving him in charge of the office at times, letting him handle more of the correspondence, and allowing him to send occasional consignments on his own account.[18] By 1826, Peter realized that his father's business offered no opportunity for growth, and he therefore sought to liquidate it as rapidly as the depressed conditions in the Caribbean allowed.

At this time he was perhaps in partnership briefly with one Edward Walkinshaw of Glasgow, but by 1827 he had entered another partnership known as Laing and Buchanan. Peter's partner, Robert Laing, a slightly older man, had operated his own business as a dry-salter in Glasgow since at least 1825. He and his brother Seton, who was already in the grocery and dry-saltery business in London, were friends of the Buchanan family. Robert Laing invested £3000 and his stock of goods in the new firm, and Peter invested £2000. While it sent occasional consignments overseas to Canada and Rus-

sia and imported ashes from Canada, its primary business was the purchase
of indigo and other dyestuffs, usually in London, for sale to the growing
Scottish textile industry.[19] Peter, who knew something of textiles from his
father, could learn much through this business about the Scottish textile
trade and about business in England too; for example, in 1830 he visited
London for the first time, to buy at an East India Company sale. The business grew slowly and sought to take few risks. Sales in ten months of 1831
were £29,490, and there were almost no bad debts, but profits on this volume struck Peter as low.[20]

Isaac Buchanan had meanwhile begun his own mercantile career. Later in
life, Isaac claimed that after leaving the Glasgow grammar school he had
begun to train for the professions or an academic career, only to turn aside,
on a spur-of-the-moment decision and without even consulting his parents,
to enter business; but it is also possible that the decision was caused by the
decline in family fortunes. At any rate, in October 1825, a friend arranged
for him to join William Guild and Company, a Glasgow firm trading to
Jamaica as Guild, Woodburn and Company and to Honduras as A. Woodburn and Company. William Guild and Peter Buchanan Sr must have known
of one another from their similar trading interests, but they do not appear to
have been close friends. As in virtually every project he ever took on, Isaac
threw himself into his apprenticeship whole-heartedly. Soon he had completely won the favour of William Guild.[21]

Guild too was finding the Caribbean trade unsatisfactory. Hoping soon to
retire, he began to look for new opportunities for his son and finally settled
on Canada as an area to explore. It was a sensible choice for a moderately
sized Glasgow mercantile house at this time. It was natural for a merchant to
look first for other mercantile opportunities or for respectable opportunities
in finance, because these more than manufacturing were areas in which his
skills and experience were most directly applicable. The range of trading
opportunities in a port depended above all on development in and extension
of the city's hinterland, although ports could sometimes develop entrepôt
trades using capital or legal and locational advantages. Underlying any established trading structure were these factors, and, in addition, a foundation of
credit, tradition, trust, and knowledge that made it difficult for new firms or
new cities to break into such a structure.[22] Thus, traders generally looked for
growth or change of some sort to provide new opportunities; in the mid-
1820s, to a Glasgow trader, their number was limited. Glasgow's west coast
location hampered its competitiveness in the fast-growing trade with conti-
nental Europe. The Asian market attracted much attention, and traders from
all of Britain's west coast ports participated in the campaign against the East

India Company's monopoly.[23] Those looking to the overseas trade, however, had good reason to look first across the Atlantic, for the west coast ports had their greatest locational advantages over London in the Atlantic trade, and the volume and value of the Atlantic trades were far greater than those to Africa and Asia. After 1815, much attention was given to the trade of the former Spanish colonies, but if many firms found roles in this trade, the potential of these markets proved greatly overestimated. After 1825, Central and South American markets no longer seemed so attractive.[24]

The United States was now the greatest of Britain's Atlantic export markets, especially for goods other than low-priced cottons, and was the source of Britain's raw cotton imports, whose volume and value rose tremendously after 1815. During the 1830s, the United States was the chief destination for Britain's capital exports, an indication that the reputation in Britain of the United States as a centre of opportunity was high.[25] But the Anglo-American trade was showing signs already of focusing on just two ports, New York, now the chief centre in the American import trade and in American finance, and Liverpool.[26] Although Boston, Philadelphia, and Baltimore handled rapidly increasing volumes of trade, all were being reduced to regional centres and their direct trade with Britain did not increase as did New York's; initiative in the American import trade was, moreover, shifting increasingly to American-based houses, which had better knowledge of their market. New Orleans handled a growing share of the great cotton staple, but its links with Britain were limited by its financial dependence on New York.

Of all Britain's outports, since Bristol had long been in relative decline, only Glasgow could after 1815 still hope to compete with Liverpool for a major share of the North Atlantic trade. Glasgow's locational advantages in relation to the North Atlantic rivalled Liverpool's, but Glasgow's hinterland, despite its industrialization, was far less developed. In the 1820s, though, it was still possible for Glasgow's traders to anticipate that the city's cotton trade would develop along lines parallel to, if some years behind, Liverpool's; even so, some Glasgow firms, taking no chances, opened Liverpool branches.[27] Glasgow mercantile houses in these years secured some share of the American trade, but such houses had to be relatively large to compete for a share of the staple cotton trade at least. This was one further factor that must have influenced William Guild not to look to the United States, despite its prospects, in the years after 1825.

The St Lawrence River ports, Montreal and Quebec, were also experiencing rapid growth in a new staple trade at this time. Because they were much smaller than the American ports, their trading structures perhaps appeared more open to entry. Certainly informed circles in Glasgow in the late 1820s were paying attention to the St Lawrence. Thus, in 1828, the year William Guild sent the first of a series of trial consignments of textiles to Montreal, Pollok, Gilmour and Company, Glasgow timber merchants who had been powers in the New Brunswick timber trade since 1812, opened branches in Montreal and Quebec; and the Allan Line, a Glasgow shipping firm, began its regular service to the St Lawrence.[28] When Guild's modest early shipments proved encouraging, he decided in 1830 to open his own dry goods house in Montreal, managed by his son, William Jr, and by Isaac Buchanan, who was not yet twenty years old.

In March 1830, the firm of William Guild Jr and Company of Montreal was formed. It was composed of William Guild and Company of Glasgow and of Isaac Buchanan, who would receive one-quarter of the new firm's profits. Peter Buchanan paid in £2500stg from the family estate as Isaac's initial capital. The new firm took over Guild's consignments in Montreal from the original consignees, Hart, Logan and Company; future purchases would be made by William Guild and Company, which would charge a commission of five per cent on all orders as well as five per cent interest on the balance owed it at year's end by the Canadian house. Isaac was to engage in no other trade and to withdraw only his personal expenses and the interest on his capital in any year, further profits being left to accumulate. Early in April, he left home for the first time, sailing from Liverpool to New York and moving on to Montreal in time for the spring trade.[29]

While important changes were occurring in the Canadian wheat economy in these years, as Lower Canadian wheat production declined in the face of crop failures and mounting Upper Canadian competition, the overall fortunes of the St Lawrence economy still depended more on the timber trade. Canada's forests had been little exploited until the Napoleonic Wars, when a preference on colonial timber made it competitive with Baltic supplies. British timber firms at once turned their attention to British North America and, spurred by British economic expansion, the timber trade developed rapidly on tributaries of the St Lawrence, above all on the Ottawa River, where the focus of exploitation by the later 1820s was upriver from the newly established community of Bytown. Timber of course required a much higher volume of shipping eastbound than had the fur trade; indeed, excess capacity westbound was created, and this encouraged immigration and imports of European goods. Quebec became the centre of the timber trade, where the lumber rafts were broken up, graded, sold, and shipped, while Montreal became the more vital financial centre and the importing and outfitting centre for the Ottawa and Upper Canada.[30]

Although based in Montreal, the new Guild firm found its opportunity in Upper Canada, where development was based for only a limited time on timber. Upper Canada's ability to pay for the rising volume of imports its citizens desired was at this time much enhanced by capital imported to pay for construction of the Rideau and Welland canals, but in the longer term Upper Canada would depend more for its success on growing and selling wheat. Before wheat could become a reliable staple export, reliable markets of adequate size were necessary, but such markets were unlikely to develop until Canada produced a reliable wheat surplus. This vicious circle was permanently broken only in the 1840s, but farmers in Upper Canada grew wheat from a much earlier time because it was the principal possible cash crop and domestic markets of growing significance were available. Foreign markets, necessary if wheat was to become a staple export, were found more slowly. Although after 1825 Canadian wheat had a preference in the British market when it was open, it was open only erratically. In 1830-1, Canadian wheat exports to Britain reached record levels, but for the next nine years the British market was largely closed while Upper Canadian production, despite fluctuations from year to year, tended to rise. This produced prices that touched ruinous lows: wheat sold for 32 to 38 cents (less than 2 shillings) per bushel in Toronto for a time during the winter of 1834-5. Even so, the expectation that adequate wheat markets would be found, spurred by the boom year of 1830-1, induced much immigration and investment into Upper Canada.[31]

This can be seen in the rapid rise of Upper Canada's population in the years around 1830. In 1814, Upper Canada had about 95,000 people; the population was said to be 150,000 in 1824, 213,000 in 1830, 347,000 in 1835, and 432,000 in 1840.[32] Most of the incoming migrants after 1830 settled west of Lake Ontario and north of Lake Erie, or immediately north of Toronto. To open a frontier area to agriculture took capital and time; perhaps eight to ten years were required to clear land, build essential buildings, open passable roads, and develop local communities. These areas were not, however, self-sufficient for that time. The settler required a variety of goods, many of them imported, and to secure them would sell his labour; lumber, if water transport was available; ashes; and, as soon as possible, any wheat or provisions he could produce.[33] Thus, trading opportunities existed from the time the settler arrived and could be expected to grow as he brought his land into production.

The characteristic Upper Canadian mercantile institution was the general store, which sold all forms of imported goods and handled much of the surplus produce of its area.[34] Such stores acquired a dominant role because they controlled local credit. In the few urban centres of consequence, a more specialized trading structure had begun to appear, but general stores were still numerous, and even in York, many storekeepers would in 1830 take produce in payment for goods. Most retailers in Upper Canada were supplied by Montreal wholesalers, and most of Upper Canada's produce leaving the colony was handled through Montreal. Montreal was thus the business capital of Upper Canada.[35]

Banking was developing rapidly in the 1820s and 1830s in both Upper and Lower Canada. This permitted greater trade differentiation and specialization than had been possible in the days when every merchant had to deal in imports and exports. The biggest of the banks, the Bank of Montreal, was said to confine its lending to a relatively limited number of leading Montreal firms; but in 1818, Quebec interests founded the Quebec Bank; Upper Canada's first chartered bank, the Bank of Upper Canada, was organized in 1822; and Kingston secured a bank of its own in 1832, when the Commercial Bank of the Midland District was chartered. The Upper Canadian banks had opened several branches and a number of agencies by the mid-1830s. The more substantial merchants at least could therefore rely on considerable banking assistance; this both reflected and facilitated the great expansion of Canadian trade in the 1820s and 1830s.[36]

William Guild Jr and Isaac Buchanan opened their store in Montreal in May 1830. Finding it difficult to break into the clientele of the older, larger importing firms of the Montreal business community, they sought out retail storekeepers arriving in the market for the first time. Most of these came from the rapidly expanding Upper Canadian frontier or from Upper Canadian lake ports thriving as the frontier developed. Because most such customers had little capital, they required long credit terms. In eighteen months, ending in December 1831, sales by William Guild Jr and Company exceeded £60,000cy,* but it would take, in Isaac's estimate, eighteen months to secure payment of these accounts.[37]

Isaac saw little danger in a long-credit business in Canada, where prospects for development seemed so great. Indeed, he proposed that they open a branch in York, where, he argued, accounts could be better managed and

---

* One pound Halifax currency (abbreviated cy), the British North American money of account, was equal to about sixteen shillings sterling (abbreviated stg) and to four American dollars. While there were fluctuations in the rate of exchange, these were not large enough to affect the relatively rough calculations that are all that are possible in this study. The business kept accounts in sterling in its Glasgow and (later) Liverpool offices; North American accounts, until about 1860, were kept in currency. Where there is a possibility of confusion as to which is meant, I have indicated in the text which is intended.

cash business could be secured from customers who preferred to avoid the journey to Montreal. Besides, Isaac was unhappy working with and under William Guild Jr, who, he said, was an incompetent businessman.[38] William Guild Sr did not share Isaac's liking for long credit business, for he feared that his capital might be completely locked up in Canada, but in view of Isaac's claim that cash business could be secured, he agreed to the York branch. To avoid undue commitment of capital, he stipulated that the Montreal store be closed. At the cost of most of the profits of two years of operations, it was liquidated during 1832 by William Guild Jr.[39]

York was a village of 1500 people in 1825 and 2900 in 1830, but in the next five years, aided by enlargement of its boundaries, it grew to almost 10,000. In 1834, it became Toronto, Upper Canada's first city. York's early growth was based on its role as capital of Upper Canada, but as settlers flooded into the north and west, it emerged also as a significant commercial centre. The 340 miles between York and Montreal constituted a relatively long distance. Wholesaling in Upper Canada thus became potentially a paying proposition, and York was well placed to dominate such wholesaling. In 1832, at least five local firms and four branches of Montreal firms announced wholesale trading operations in York. The suddenness of this resulted from competitive pressures, but underlying the emergence of wholesaling was the recent substantial growth of the local market.[40] To the citizens of York, including the newly arrived Isaac Buchanan, prospects for growth looked almost limitless.

In the spring of 1832, Isaac opened the York branch of William Guild Jr and Company, in a two-story warehouse on Front Street. Later he claimed that he was Upper Canada's first wholesaler,[41] but several other successful wholesalers in fact began operation at about the same time. During 1832, Isaac's sales at York amounted to £26,000cy, half goods consigned to the firm, the remainder goods on the firm's own account, and these yielded an estimated £1700 profit. But these sales too were on long credits, for Isaac found that the cash customers whose trade he had expected to capture all planned to import directly from England themselves or were already tied to Montreal houses. The elder Guild, alarmed, decided to visit Canada in 1833 to investigate the state of the business.[42]

By 1833, Isaac was feeling restless in Guild's business.[43] While he was by nature restless, he could identify several specific factors accounting for his feelings at this time. He was often lonely and dispirited in Canada, and frequently ill. He found supervision of the details of a dry goods business onerous, preferring to launch new promotions, such as the York store and a series of land speculations begun in 1833. He continued to quarrel with William Guild Jr. Even so, he often talked of making his career in Canada, for in view of his youth and his relatively limited capital, Upper Canada offered him scope that Britain never could. In the spring of 1833, he purchased at least eight parcels of land, or options on land, for £677cy. He confidently anticipated a return on his capital of twenty or thirty per cent per year with little risk, because he had inside information from the Crown Lands office. At the same time, he bought a share in a steamboat and launched a town speculation near Woodstock that he called 'Auchmar.'

Isaac failed to convince William Guild Sr of the virtues of a long-credit business. Still impressed by his protégé's abilities, however, Guild offered to turn over the York business to Isaac on favourable terms.[44] Enthusiastic at his land speculations and surer of his business judgment, Isaac was attracted by the idea. Peter Buchanan, who had serious reservations about the wisdom of land speculation, had nevertheless paid attention to some of Isaac's views.

After all is said & done this (York) market has hardly had justice hitherto.

I think I could do pretty well in York with proper Hands here and proper Home management. ... Altogether if things go on as they have been doing this Month I would be willing to continue a little Yet in the *U.C. trade...*[45]

Peter knew from Isaac and from mercantile gossip in Glasgow that the Guild business was acquiring a good reputation. And, belying his already growing reputation for caution, he had ambitions for responsibility and business growth that Laing's business could not satisfy.

Family obligations had also to be considered, however. Ignoring a variety of objections raised by Peter, his sister Jane had in October 1831 married Lieutenant George Douglas, one of whose faults, in Peter's eyes, was that he had no means of his own. Their mother and aunt had also to be supported. At one point, indeed, Isaac suggested that the family emigrate, and though his solution was not taken up, his analysis of the family's position was accurate.

We have means and are yet in a manner dependent. These means will not increase ... unless put into some dangerous Business or Speculation which as regards a Family would never answer. While if *brought to this country now* they are quite certain if laid out with common prudence to secure a large independancy [sic] for all of us for life.[46]

Guild's proposal to support Isaac offered a chance to satisfy family obligations and personal ambitions. Isaac returned home late in 1833 to discuss the question with his brother. He then agreed to take over the business of William Guild Jr and Company effective 31 March 1834, and left to open the spring trade. Peter Buchanan and Robert Laing signed an agreement in April to dissolve their partnership as from 31 January 1834,[47] and Peter followed Isaac, determined to see the territory for himself before agreeing to go into business there. He spent a month in Toronto observing the spring trade, meeting customers, and appraising Isaac's business establishment. Then he spent more than two months travelling through western Upper Canada, where Isaac had found most of his customers, and the American northwest, where much of the immense western development of the United States was to occur in the next twenty-five years. Impressed though he was by the possibilities of the American west, he returned convinced that the market in which his brother was established had sufficient potential fully to occupy their capital, which was small by the standards of Glasgow or even Montreal, but considerable in Upper Canadian terms. Moreover, unlike the western American trade, the Upper Canada trade, as it was beginning to develop, was directly linked to and controlled from Britain. General business conditions in Britain and North America were booming, despite low prices in the Canadian grain trade.[48]

Thus, on 22 October 1834, Peter and Isaac signed a 'Memorandum of Copartnership' which stated that Isaac's ownership of the Guild business was considered to have been shared by Peter from 31 March 1834; from 31 December 1834, the new business would be known as Peter Buchanan and Company, Glasgow, and Isaac Buchanan and Company, Toronto, and all profits and losses of the new business in both locations would be shared equally by the two brothers.[49] Peter then left for home, travelling the length of the Erie Canal, visiting the burgeoning New England textile centres, and meeting businessmen to whom he had been referred in Boston, New York, and Philadelphia.

The business was based directly on that of the Guilds. William Guild Sr offered Peter Buchanan access at any time to the invoices and patterns for goods that the Guilds had shipped to Canada and financial support for an indefinite period. He preferred such indirect participation in the Canadian trade to the more arduous tasks and higher risks involved in engaging in the trade on his own account. He could now withdraw from the Canadian trade without loss, while the Buchanans had been able to test the market they were entering. In key respects, the Buchanans were following directly in the venturesome tradition of Glasgow's Chesapeake traders: they were centring their business in a small, relatively remote community, far from the sea, almost on the frontier, and operating primarily on their own account and on a long-credit system. They were not following the Chesapeake pattern entirely, for they aimed to sell exclusively at wholesale in order to gain the greater volume of sales that wholesaling allowed, to avoid pricing difficulties that arose in combined wholesale-retail stores, and to secure a higher reputation with retailers. Unlike the Chesapeake traders too, the Buchanans were not primarily seeking supplies of a staple British import, though they would certainly watch for opportunities in the produce trades.

Peter Buchanan began to withdraw his funds from the business with Laing late in 1834, but transfer of his capital would take a year or more to complete. Meanwhile, he forced Isaac to begin to liquidate his other investments in Upper Canada so that all their capital could be brought into the business. Most of their funds came ultimately from their father's estate, because profits from their earlier businesses had done little more than support them. Peter Sr had left about £18,300, including £9000 netted from the Auchmar estate, sold by Peter Jr to the Duke of Montrose in 1830 to raise liquid capital. With the trustees' approval, Peter had bought only partial annuities for his mother and aunt; the remainder he had guaranteed to pay annually from business proceeds.[50] In May 1831, one sister, Margaret, died, and in 1834 the boys' mother died, leaving the three surviving children to share the family estate. In 1834, Jane Douglas drew on much of her share to purchase her husband's captaincy. Isaac Buchanan estimated in 1833 that he and Peter would have a capital of about £10,000stg to put into their business.[51] In view of these data on the family estate, this seems a reasonable figure, but a somewhat larger one is clearly possible. Figures for profits and capital in 1835 and 1836 imply an initial capitalization nearer £12,000stg, and that in fact seems the likeliest figure for the business's initial capital. By careful management, Peter and Isaac hoped to turn over this capital once every twelve months.

To support 1835 shipments of almost twice this sum (Table 2, p 164), the Buchanans required much credit. That supplied by Guild was indispensable; it consisted initially of the stock and accounts in Upper Canada, but some support, perhaps £2000, was guaranteed indefinitely. Peter and Isaac's aunt, Jean Buchanan of Roseneath, lent them £2000 on a relatively long-term basis, and Jane Douglas may have lent £1000.[52] Such family funds were significant in that they added perhaps 25 per cent to the Buchanans' initial disposable capital, but as profits and capital grew, such family money would soon come primarily to symbolize the family's confidence in the business, something Peter and Isaac valued highly. In March 1834, a line of credit was secured from T.W. Smith and Company, merchants and forwarders in Liverpool, who were expanding their role in the Atlantic trade.[53] In return for the right to forward all the Buchanans' purchases in Yorkshire, Lancashire, and the Midlands, Smith and Company would allow them to draw bills of exchange up to a ceiling of £7500, these bills to be covered by the Buchanans when they fell due. Peter and Isaac could draw upon this credit as credits extended by suppliers expired, to help carry the burden of their stock for the lengthy period from purchase to customers' payment. Because they handled all the Buchanans' Liverpool shipments, Smith and Company could estimate the scale of their business and control credit limits appropriately. Besides this support, Peter secured a cash credit of up to £5000 from the Glasgow Banking Company, 'undoubtedly Scotland's wealthiest private bank';[54] he thus began an association that would last as long as the business.

In Canada, the firm secured a substantial discount line from the Bank of Upper Canada, the province's leading bank. The long-credit system took the form of extending six to seven months' book credit, the costs of which were reflected in the sale price; thereafter, interest was charged, and customers were required to settle their accounts with six-month paper. It was this paper that the Canadian banks discounted, when it had three months to run. Customers in fact could not always meet all their paper when it fell due, except by providing another note, and this the business could again discount, for the credit-worthiness of such paper came from the Buchanans' endorsement on it. Thus, a wholesale business such as the Buchanans', operating on long credits, soon came to possess an ample supply of paper for discount, and Canadian bank discounts, though nominally short-term in operation, came to provide longer-term credit.

Although Peter Buchanan knew a good deal about the Scottish textile industry and about financial management and Isaac knew Upper Canada well, neither was a full-fledged specialist in the dry goods trade. The intricacies of textile fabrics, finishes, fashions, and pricing were, however, of great importance to their business success. Accordingly, they hired Robert W. Harris, the dry goods manager of William Guild Jr and Company, to fill the same position in Isaac Buchanan and Company. Coming from County Antrim in northern Ireland, Harris had trained in Dublin and was recruited by Guild, in Liverpool or Glasgow, in 1830. He was somewhat dour and unapproachable, but he earned the respect of others by his knowledge of his trade and his capacity for work. Isaac put his praise differently: 'I am very much pleased with Him altho' I have never known an Irishman here before whom I could put implicit faith in.'[55] During the next twenty years Harris would play almost as large a role as the Buchanans in the business's success. In November 1834, he travelled overseas with Peter Buchanan to buy goods for spring shipment in 1835.

25 Founding the business

In the *Glasgow Directory* for 1835-6, the firm of Peter Buchanan and Company, with offices at 39 North Hanover Street, appeared for the first time. It shared the title 'merchants' with over five hundred other Glasgow firms.[56]

3
Success in Toronto 1835-9

The inhabitants of Toronto, we believe, never before nor since it was a city, have experienced any thing like the depression ... which this spring has produced. There are, upon every hand, day after day failures, even of persons who were formerly considered in at least comfortable circumstances. (*Montreal Gazette*, 23 May 1835)[1]

In this gloomy climate, caused by low grain prices and, the *Gazette* said, by a want of circulating medium, Isaac Buchanan and Company began its first sales season. Because the British and American economies were booming, however, the Buchanans and other Upper Canadians assumed that local conditions would soon improve, especially as the Upper Canadian government had succeeded in entering the London capital market for the first time in 1834, borrowing £600,000 for transportation improvements. By summer 1835, hopes of an economic upturn proved justified. Poor wheat crops in many areas of the United States opened the American market to Upper Canadian wheat from 1835 to 1838, and wheat prices, declining since 1831, began to revive. The highest price of the decade at Dundas, 7/6 per bushel, was reached in the spring and summer of 1837. Further stimulus came from high British demand for Canadian timber, exports from the St Lawrence reaching record levels in 1835 and 1836.[2]

Hence uncertainty soon gave way to an atmosphere of boom, which, in conjunction with local political and commercial rivalries, led the Upper Canadian legislature in early 1837 to pass a series of measures that, had royal assent been given, would have authorized a ninefold increase in the province's banking capital.[3] Business groups began to speak enthusiastically of railroads, and the government and businessmen planned major new canal construction. Many Upper Canadians must have shared the belief of a retired army officer who commented in 1836 that 'any person possessing a little ready capital might lay it out to very great advantage at this time, such as would ensure thirty per cent of profit in less than six months.'[4]

Certainly the Buchanans and, evidently, their customers had such expectations. In August 1835, Peter Buchanan estimated, with fair accuracy, that profits for the year would be sixteen per cent clear on the cost of their goods delivered in Toronto; this was additional to the five per cent return on capital that was set aside before profits were calculated.[5] Such handsome earnings, equal to between thirty and forty per cent on Peter and Isaac's initial capital, inspired Isaac to urge expanding the business sharply in 1836. Peter preferred controlled growth, so he cut Isaac's dry goods orders and refused to agree to Isaac's plan to add groceries to their trade: thus, shipments for 1836 increased by only about seventeen per cent. It was another fine year in the Upper Canadian trade, and at its end the Buchanans calculated their net profit at thirteen per cent on sales. Peter and Isaac's Canadian capital, which they distinguished from their original investment in Glasgow, totalled £7707cy, an increase of their original investment by between fifty and sixty per cent in only two years (Tables 1, 2, 4, and 5; pp 162-70).

The Buchanans had reason to be well satisfied with their essential business strategy, yet a variety of changes in business plans and structures had already been required in the first two years of operation. They had, for example, found it impossible to attract significant commission business in British textile exports; in any case, high profits on their own-account trade soon made this an unattractive alternative. Shortly after opening they decided to offer a partnership to R.W. Harris. This would free Isaac to travel, relieve him of more of the detailed work of buying, selling, and accounting, and give the business more security in the event of the death of one of the Buchanans. Harris, anxious for advancement but lacking capital, agreed to a six-year partnership in which he would receive one-fifth of the profits of Isaac Buchanan and Company for three years and one-quarter thereafter. This agreement, signed on 31 October 1835, separated Isaac Buchanan and Company from Peter Buchanan and Company, the latter, composed of Peter and Isaac, holding a four-fifths share of the former. Because Peter Buchanan and Company supplied the capital for the business, it would charge Isaac Buchanan and Company a shipping charge of five per cent on all goods purchased in Britain, and a capital charge of five per cent on the balance owed to it at year's end by the Canadian house.* The new partnership structure was more complex, but it allowed the Buchanans to retain ultimate control of their business.[6]

---

* Some years later, the basis of the capital charge was altered; it was then applied to the average Canadian balance over the year.

In the winter of 1834-35, without consulting his brother, Isaac opened retail branches in Niagara, the original commercial centre of western Upper Canada and still an important shipping centre, and in Hamilton, the fast-growing town at the head of Lake Ontario. He planned to sell only for cash in the two towns, and he argued that this would allow the firm to occupy its market more thoroughly. Peter disagreed: neither branch, he thought, justified the risks, the diversion of capital from wholesaling, the managerial problems, and the sacrifice of their reputation as wholesalers only that Isaac's plan required. A two-year trial of the system confirmed his feelings. In 1836 the firm withdrew from the retail trade.

Similarly, other wholesalers who tried in these years to operate retail branch systems generally withdrew from them. Retailing seemed to function best where the retailer owned his business and had the greatest incentive to manage it well. The wholesaler's position was more flexible if he could retreat from unprofitable retailing operations simply by cutting off the customer's credit, and he had no need to intervene extensively in the management of successful accounts. Although the Buchanans always involved themselves in the affairs of their customers, they did not have to exercise as continuous a scrutiny as would have been required if they were themselves partners in the retail business. In any case, the Buchanans and, no doubt, many of their strongest competitors found themselves with ample trade without any necessity to deal with the complexities of retail branch management. In a climate of expansion, they had no incentive to challenge the developing Upper Canadian pattern of distinct wholesale and retail trades.

The Hamilton store was turned over to two employees, Price and Davidson. Their store and that of Walter Macfarlane, the Buchanans' chief customer in Toronto and the city's largest dry goods retailer, now became prototypes for the supply account system, which, Isaac considered, offered many of the advantages of the branch system. Under it, a retailer agreed to buy all his goods from the firm in return for concessions in price averaging five to ten per cent. He gave some of his orders to the Buchanans' buyer, who placed them in Britain in the Buchanans' name but arranged for the goods to be packed separately and consigned through the Buchanans to the customer. The Buchanans themselves furnished a sterling invoice, stating the cost of goods delivered on board ship in Britain, and charged the customer a standard advance on this invoice price.[7] Thus the customer appeared to the world as a direct importer, which advanced his reputation, while he in fact dealt only with the Buchanans. They in turn secured reliable outlets in the two main centres of their territory for concessions in price very little greater than they would in any case have had to accord to such major customers in such competitive retail markets.

Success helped Isaac quickly to gain a significant place in the small but stratified society of Toronto. He found himself very much at odds with Toronto's family compact élite, which was suspicious of those in trade; in turn, as an ardent member of the Church of Scotland, he deeply resented the compact group's efforts to establish the Church of England in Upper Canada, and in any event he found the local élite rather provincial. Because Isaac, unlike many of the new trading community in Toronto, was not only successful, but also a 'gentleman,' he was able to move to the head of Toronto's leading non-compact social group. Thus he was a principal organizer of the city's first men's club, the Toronto Club, of its St Andrew's Society, and of the Toronto Board of Trade, of which he was president for a number of years.[8] Peter Buchanan was clearly accurate when he remarked, a few years later, 'most people in Toronto have an immense idea ... of our Transactions & they seem to look upon us as complete nabobs.'[9] Having begun on a larger scale than other local businesses, the Buchanans had at once acquired the image of success; in their first two years of independent operations they had acquired the beginning of what they themselves regarded as success.

As 1837 began, the partners anticipated a third year of growth.[10] Harris was still hopeful early in May, but on 10 May mounting pressure on the banks in New York forced them to suspend specie payments. Banks throughout the United States soon followed, and Britain and Canada were immediately affected.[11] Among British firms associated with the American trade, there were many failures, and this crisis combined with a down-turn that had already begun in the domestic economy to create a major depression in Britain. Banks in Lower Canada suspended specie payments on 18 May, and Upper Canadian banks would have followed had their charters not forbidden suspension. As it was, their note circulation shrank by twenty-five per cent between 15 May and 15 June, and specie losses mounted alarmingly. In a special session, the Upper Canadian legislature authorized the banks to suspend, but the Lieutenant-Governor, Sir Francis Bond Head, considered suspension dishonourable and used his influence to keep the Bank of Upper Canada from suspending until March 1838. In September 1837, defying Head, the Commercial Bank suspended; as a result, it maintained its discounts at the level of the summer of 1837 while the Bank of Upper Canada curtailed its discounts by fifty per cent between June 1837 and January 1838.[12]

The Upper Canadian government found North American bonds unsaleable in London in 1837, and work was maintained on the canals only with great difficulty. The timber industry apparently escaped the 1837 crisis relatively unscathed because orders from Britain were well advanced before the full crisis hit, but 1838 brought the almost inevitable reaction, a very sharp depression to the industry. In spite of a good harvest in Upper Canada and available markets in Lower Canada and the United States, agriculture was depressed as a result of sharply falling prices. Immigration to Canada stopped completely. Declining imports and the consequent drop in revenue from customs duties brought the Upper Canadian government nearly to bankruptcy early in 1838.[13] Thus 1837 not only failed to fulfil Upper Canadians' expectations but actually reversed the expansion of the economy. This meant failure for many traders and reduced business, narrower profit margins, and more difficult collections for the remainder as all sought immediate liquidity.

The Buchanans' shipments were down slightly from 1836 to 1837, as a result of Peter Buchanan's curtailment of shipments for fall, made after the extent of the crisis became apparent. Sales were made at poor advances, and profits fell badly (Tables 1, 2, and 4; pp 162-8). As collections declined during the summer and fall, the Toronto house fell behind on payments to Glasgow. Peter Buchanan and Company's creditors sought reductions on their accounts when they fell due in the autumn, but Peter had had the summer to arrange his resources to cope with such reductions. By then too, discount rates were falling from panic levels, and bankers had begun to relax. To keep up remittances, Harris transferred the firm's account from the Bank of Upper Canada to the Commercial Bank, which agreed to keep his discount line at pre-crisis levels. In sum, the crisis posed substantial problems for the firm, but there was never a danger of failure.[14]

The partners' greatest worry as the year developed lay rather in the accumulating political tensions, exacerbated by economic depression, that led to rebellion in Lower Canada in November and an outbreak in Upper Canada early in December. Isaac Buchanan and R.W. Harris feared that a rebel victory would lead to annexation to the United States, and among the consequences of that would be the complete destruction of their business position. They readily accepted commissions in the hastily organized local militia; Isaac's company of Queen's Rangers served on the Niagara frontier while Harris commanded a company on city patrol and gaol guard duty in Toronto.

In 1838 fear of war with the United States remained and political factionalism returned swiftly to Upper Canada, but even so, business prospects seemed more encouraging. The British and American economies were already reviving, although 1838 would not quite bring either back to the peaks reached in 1836. In Upper Canada itself, Isaac Buchanan was impressed by the ease with which the rebellion had been defeated.

I dont think our prospects for Business is [sic] at all changed if there is any alteration, I think the future will be better for us than the past, you remember how jaundiced the feeling was in U.C. when you were out.[15]

Harris looked at different indicators.

Our stock is getting very low and there is [sic] no stock of consequence in the country so that I am of opinion your shipments, whatever they may be, will come to a good market and we will be able to dispose of them on much better terms than usual.[16]

As a result of crop failures in New England and Lower Canada and the opening of British ports, wheat prices turned upward in the spring and summer of 1838, reaching 6/10 per bushel at Dundas in October, then rising to 7/6 once more by the spring of 1839.[17] The Upper Canadian banks had all suspended by spring 1838, and Harris and Isaac, who had been writing to various newspapers to expound his currency theories, expected that this would produce more liberal note issue and discount policies, and easier collections for merchants.[18] The most vital factor in the Upper Canadian revival in 1838, however, was the Royal Army.[19] Forces had been much increased in Canada, and major defensive works were begun at several points along the frontier. The army's expenditures in hard currency greatly stimulated the local economy, and business began to revive.

Isaac Buchanan crossed to Britain to buy for 1838, and he and his brother settled their strategy in Glasgow. Anticipating that they would be in a particularly strong competitive position that year in Toronto because most smaller rivals had had their British credits cut off in the crisis, they considered alternatives to the long-credit system that they had been operating. Isaac thought they might force customers wanting goods to pay half in cash, half after twelve months; while Peter, a few months later, suggested giving only nine months' credit instead of twelve.[20] Because few of their customers had much capital, Isaac's plan required the firm to compete directly with the Montreal houses, something that had, in effect, not succeeded when tried in 1832-3, or it required a change in provincial banking practice to permit such modest merchants as their customers to secure direct bank accommodation. This could not be enforced by a private firm. Peter's scheme ignored the reality that they were already aware of: their customers depended on the harvest and farmers' sales of crops to secure funds to pay the Buchanans; the harvest ultimately dictated payment patterns, and it seldom paid the wholesaler to take drastic measures to enforce payment exactly on due dates. In the end, neither alternative seemed practical; the long-credit system would continue to be fundamental to the business.

Following Peter's cautious views, the partners decided to maintain shipments at about the level of previous years, to close weak accounts, and to use their competitive advantage to increase margins. In this way, their gains could be put on paper; vigilance in enforcing payments in twelve months was relied on to realize the gains. Peter Buchanan went to Canada to supervise the consolidation he desired, Isaac remaining in Glasgow to gain experience by managing shipments and finance alone. Arriving in Toronto for the fall sales, Peter met all customers, observed Harris in action, and visited many customers' stores. What he saw greatly encouraged him.

Harris more than lived up to his promise to 'sell very hard.'[21] He closed many accounts and demanded that those that were overdue pay before receiving goods. Because the economy was improving, customers were able to comply; payments recovered from the setback of 1837, remittances to Glasgow were ample, and borrowing in Britain was reduced as planned. Between February 1838 and February 1839, the firm reduced its Toronto discounts by one-third, from £15,000cy to £10,000, and Peter and Harris planned to reduce this figure still more. The annual Toronto balance, taken on 31 October 1838, proved even better than had been expected. Sales for the year totalled almost £49,000cy (Table 1, p 162); selling prices averaged 84 per cent above sterling first cost (this percentage including exchange) and 27 per cent above the cost of goods delivered in Toronto, well above the already handsome advances of 1835. With evident satisfaction, Peter remarked that 'I can assure you that we do not get the name of being cheap sellers.'[22] The partners added five per cent interest to their capital accounts, then calculated net profit at £8400 (Table 4, p 168). This was a return of at least twenty per cent on the combined capital of the Glasgow and Toronto firms. After four years of operations, the Buchanans had more than doubled their initial capital (Table 5, p 170). Yet they had reduced their borrowings and eliminated many marginal accounts. In the light of the year's results, Harris insisted on receiving a one-fourth share of the profits, one year before this was due him under the 1835 agreement. Peter readily agreed.

In 1838, in a sign of recognition in Glasgow of the firm's success, its bank, which had, by merger, become the Glasgow and Ship Bank, gave Peter Buchanan and Company the right to draw bills, up to a limit of £5000 at a time, on its account with the London bankers, Glyn, Mills, Hallifax and Company. Strictly speaking, this was not the firm's own account, for terms of access to it were controlled by the bank, which saw it essentially as an extension of the firm's Glasgow bank account; but the credit facilitated the firm's ability to make payments in England and to accept bills payable in London. As 60-day Glyns' bills could be used to pay suppliers' accounts, two further months' credit could be obtained. As with other drawing credits, the firm paid regular discount rates plus a commission and was expected to cover the bills when due. By 1840, Peter Buchanan would himself be known to George Carr Glyn, and the firm would be able to use the great London firm as a credit reference.[23] J.H. Clapham has written that in the 1850s

Scottish merchants seldom kept accounts in London or accepted bills payable in London, so far as is known. By 1873 the situation was reversed. It was 'quite an exception with large mercantile houses' in Scotland to 'accept a bill payable there.' They accepted those bills on London which the whole world wanted...[24]

Evidently the Buchanans, scarcely an exceptional Scottish firm, could draw and accept bills payable in London even in 1838, and this suggests that Clapham's source greatly exaggerated the transition about which he wrote.

While in Toronto, Peter took over much of Isaac's place in Toronto society. In later years he often criticized Isaac's public activities, but there were more pressures to act outside the business in Upper Canada than in Glasgow, and he yielded to these almost as easily as did Isaac, rationalizing that it was necessary for the good of the country and hence of the business. Soon after his arrival in Toronto, he helped to organize and spoke for the mercantile community at a large gathering to prepare an address to Lord Durham, who was returning to Britain. The Lieutenant-Governor, Sir George Arthur, regarded him as a leader of the mercantile community and several times summoned him for discussions. He joined Isaac's clubs and the local militia. Rather contemptuous of the local mercantile group, and like Isaac, hostile to the pretensions of the compact, he found most of his friends among the officers of the garrison. He was invited to fashionable balls, 'a favored exception of the class *called merchants* here!!'[25] Feeling more secure in his business position, he began to take pleasure in his role as a leader and in his more active social life.

Still in charge in Glasgow, Isaac looked forward to a year of expansion in 1839.[26] He considered that political conditions in Canada and Britain were favourable, war was no longer a serious possibility, and, provided the Canadian banks did not resume specie payments, there would be ample currency in circulation in Upper Canada to stimulate trade. High British output of manufactured cottons coupled with the United States Bank's successful support of raw cotton prices created a situation where cotton manufactures were priced very low relative to raw cotton prices.[27] Manufacturers had large stocks that they were anxious to sell, and cotton importers had withdrawn from the trade, thus creating surplus mercantile capital in the circles in which the Buchanans operated. To Isaac, this was the bottom of the market for cotton manufactures, and credit was amply available to take advantage of it. High British wheat prices early in 1839 suggested that it would be a good year for Upper Canadian agriculture. Despite the great success of the 1838 trade, he thought the Canadian market would not be overstocked in 1839, and he persisted in this view even after his brother and Harris, who at first agreed with him, changed their minds.

Isaac therefore decided to buy heavily, beginning in February by arranging a credit for £15,000 with the Liverpool cotton firm of Molyneux, Witherby and Company, in which Percival Witherby, a long-time acquaintance of the Buchanans, was a partner. This credit replaced that with T.W. Smith and Company, which was being closed by mutual agreement, Smiths feeling after their experience in 1837 that such drawing credits were too risky and the Buchanans feeling that Smiths set too many conditions on the account.[28] Ignoring repeated advice to ship only what was ordered, Isaac bought heavily for spring, then began at once to buy fall goods. By early July his shipments exceeded £45,000stg, twice what had been ordered from Canada. Then he resumed buying. The firm, he argued, could gain advantage over its rivals by shipping goods in the autumn for spring sale, so that its spring goods would be ready before the opening of navigation. By November, Isaac's shipments considerably exceeded £70,000stg, or approximately as much as the firm had shipped in the three previous years combined (Table 2, p 164). To finance this, Isaac drew on Witherby, the Glasgow and Ship Bank, William Guild and Company, and several major suppliers who were prepared to re-new paper. He made more active use of an account that Peter had opened with the Commercial Bank of Scotland as something of a standby in the event of difficulties with his main Glasgow bank. He persuaded H.S. Floud and Company, the London dry-salting firm in which his friend Seton Laing was a partner, to extend him a credit of £6000 as well. By reopening the account at the Bank of Upper Canada and discounting heavily, Peter Buchanan was able to remit £28,000 towards Isaac's 1839 payments before November.

Isaac had, however, greatly misjudged trends in 1839. Raw cotton prices collapsed; cotton manufacturers continued to increase output, but prices sagged further; and the industry entered perhaps its worst depression of the century, one that would continue until 1842. Meanwhile, discount rates rose sharply in 1839.[29] Isaac had launched his major expansion in a period of rising interest rates and falling prices. Canadian imports in 1839, moreover, proved enormous. The value of goods paying *ad valorem* duty and imported via the St Lawrence, a category dominated by British manufactures, rose in a single year by fifty per cent, from £1.2 million stg in 1838 to £1.8 million in 1839. Wheat prices at Dundas turned downward in the summer of 1839 and slid steadily towards a low of 3/7 reached finally at the end of 1840, yet at the same time the Upper Canadian harvest failed completely in 1839, and the province had to import wheat.[30] It has been argued that 1839 marked the beginning of better times in Upper Canada after the crisis of 1837-8, but the Buchanans, no objective witnesses to be sure, would have argued that this was only true politically.[31]

Faced with the flood of spring imports, Peter Buchanan and Harris pushed sales vigorously. Their sales in June were made at advances not too far below those of 1838, but Isaac's fall shipments were heavier still and competition intensified over the summer. Peter and Harris cut prices and sold to 'a much lower class of customers' than hitherto.[32] In the six months from 1 May to 31 October, a period including the peak of both spring and fall sales seasons, sales were £65,000cy, at an average advance on sterling cost prices of between 75 and 80 per cent, but Peter feared that advances would drop to 66 per cent in 1840. In November, Canadian discounts were at a record high, £24,000cy, up from £10,000 in June; Glasgow's debts were £49,000stg, 'double what we ever owed before at any one time...'[33] In February 1839, the inventory at Toronto was £5000stg first cost; on 1 February 1840 it was £35,000stg. Much of this was bad stock; even two years later much remained in the warehouse.

Partners' capital in Canada in November 1839 totalled £31,000cy (Table 5, p 170), or about £25,000stg, while British capital, growing only slowly in view of the firm's accounting arrangements, had reached at least £13,000.* In all, the firm's obligations exceeded its capital by almost two-thirds, despite the fact that the firm's capital was now more than three times the sum Peter and Isaac had invested in 1834. Assets, in the form of inventory and customers' accounts, had, of course, risen greatly in 1839, but the firm's unprecedentedly high level of debt could pose problems in the event of a sudden squeeze on credit, in Canada or Britain. Thus the business, as a result of Isaac's unilateral decision to expand, had chosen to follow a different path from the one evident in the history of many successful businesses.[34] Instead of moving to rely largely on internal sources of capital, as had been planned in 1838, the firm used its early success to borrow more and to expand more rapidly than would otherwise have been possible.

* The Glasgow firm's income came largely from its commissions on shipments and capital. Its outlay consisted of office expenses, banking costs in Britain, plus Peter and Isaac's annual expenditures, which, wherever incurred, were charged against the Glasgow accounts for all

Peter Buchanan, angry at their new level of dependence on outside support, blamed his brother entirely for the situation, but the Buchanans would certainly have had to lower prices in the competitive conditions of 1839 in any case. The high-quality customers that Peter wanted to concentrate exclusively upon were precisely the ones who could best exact lowest prices from their suppliers. Isaac contended also that if they did not grow with their market, they would lose their position in it. Yet the enormous expansion of 1839 involved considerable unnecessary costs and was entirely unplanned. Isaac returned to Canada in December 1839, having left the Glasgow and Ship Bank with power to act for them in case of emergency. The three partners now met to discuss the management of their suddenly much enlarged operation. They could at least be consoled by the record profit declared in 1839 (Table 4, p 168) and by the knowledge that if they could successfully operate on this larger scale, they would all be rich men in a few years. After working with him for fifteen months, Peter saw how essential Harris was to their business; he would be even more so if, as began to seem possible, Isaac entered politics. They therefore offered Harris better terms. On 13 February 1840, they signed an agreement to renew the partnership for six years from its date of expiry, 31 October 1841.[35] Harris would then receive one-third of the profits of Isaac Buchanan and Company, and restrictions on his movements that had been written into the earlier agreement were dropped. This signed, Peter left for home, pausing briefly in Kingston, which, it was thought, might well be the capital of the new Province of Canada, to assist a new customer to open his business. When he reached Liverpool, Peter began to buy further goods required for 1840, then returned to Glasgow. There he found the books and records in disarray, Isaac

or most of the history of the Toronto firm. Although Peter once calculated that the commission yielded 3 to 3½ per cent clear ('Calculations ... 22 Aug. 1835,' 13/11471), this was before living expenses were deducted and the regular 5 per cent interest was assigned to capital sums. Only occasional information survives on the annual Canadian balance (though in early years it should have been quite close to the annual value of shipments), but presumably a good deal of the capital charge on it went directly to pay interest on the firm's British borrowings. If my estimate of original capital is accurate not even the 5 per cent interest credited to capital accounts was retained at Glasgow in early years. Larger shipments, changes in the basis of Glasgow's charges, and accounting changes and transfers would later alter this, but Glasgow capital could never grow very rapidly. Model calculations based on various assumptions and on what is known about shipments, payments, market rates of discount, and borrowing suggest that the figure given in the text is entirely compatible with an initial capitalization of £12,000; if initial capitalization was nearer £10,000, then 5 per cent was paid on capital.

having been so busy with other things that he had completely ignored office routine.[36]

The business's first five years reveal several important long-term features of its operations. Thus, it is clear that the firm, in various ways, secured the credit that it wanted in Britain and Upper Canada. Suppliers were the first source of credit. Customarily, purchases for a season were charged to an open account that was closed by drawing on Peter Buchanan and Company in Glasgow, at four or six months, following completion of the order. Large suppliers spread their drafts over several months, while some with whom Peter Buchanan was on good terms, such as those in Leeds, would redraw to suit his convenience. Interest was usually charged after three months, but, Peter calculated, on average he would not have to pay for shipments until six months after delivery on board ship.[37] In Glasgow, the source of 25 to 30 per cent of dry goods purchases, it was not difficult to establish a reputation with suppliers and, where necessary, to work out special financial arrangements. Elsewhere, the firm bought from or through a small number of houses to secure the credit it required.

In Leeds, it bought largely through the two great firms of Gott and Lupton; in Huddersfield, it employed the services of an agent, David Midgley, for buying and financial purposes; and in London, it paid cash for goods except for those from its largest local suppliers, Leaf Sons and Company and, later, the Fore Street Warehouse Company, both large-scale wholesalers.[38] Manchester was the source of 35 to 40 per cent of the firm's annual shipments. There the firm's own buyer selected goods from various suppliers (Harris bought from 29 in January 1842),[39] but financing was done through a local agent, first William Crossley and later his successor, H.B. Jackson. For his commission, the agent offered advice on the market, oversaw finishing of goods, and filled orders sent by mail, but his basic service was financial: he took advantage of whatever credit suppliers offered, paid their accounts when due, and drew on Peter Buchanan and Company at appropriate dates to reimburse himself. This freed the buyer to select goods wherever he wished, guaranteed the firm the credit it desired, and gave it a valuable ally in the market. Peter Buchanan and H.B. Jackson became close friends over the years. When Isaac once proposed that the firm set up its own Manchester office, Peter objected strongly.

In Manchester our business is well done now (with the assistance of our own buyer) and cheaply also. Besides we are deriving considerable Banking facilities thro Jackson. ... We never can have less trouble than at present.[40]

In view of shipping time and other delays, the business was unlikely to be paid for its goods until fifteen months after taking delivery. Bridging the gap between British and Upper Canadian credit terms was, of course, a fundamental role of the wholesaler. To carry the burden of their purchases for this period, the Buchanans relied on their own capital and their various banking credits. They made their reputation in Glasgow, but from there it spread through personal and business links to other centres, as the Floud and Glyn credits indicate. Despite the use made of the Commercial Bank of Scotland, Peter soon reverted to using only a single Glasgow bank; it enhanced the bank's confidence to know that it had a reasonably complete overview of his transactions, and it was prepared to extend the credit Peter wanted.[41] The mutual confidence built up between Peter and his banker was a real asset to the business. With the exception of the bank overdraft and the relatively modest cash advances from relatives and the Guilds, the British credits were on bills of exchange. Such credits as those from Smiths, Witherby, Glyns, and Floud did not reflect actual flows of goods between the parties whose names were on the bills, but the names made it first-class paper even so. British business expansion in this era was heavily based on such paper handled through regular banking channels, and it was only later in the century that the system began to be superseded by the use of the cheque and the documentary bill.[42]

The experience of 1839 indicates that for a leading firm such as Isaac Buchanan and Company, sales were not the fundamental problem. There were many would-be customers in Upper Canada, and the problem was to choose from among them. Thus, as Peter later put it, 'it is easy enough to make large sales but the difficulty is to get paid.'[43] If the firm set its standard for customers too high, however, it would only attract them at very low prices; if standards were too low, the firm risked major losses through bad debts. It was possible, Isaac once claimed, to avoid both risks.

The wonderful success of my operations in Canada may be to a great extent attributed to my solemn determination not to trust Yankees and my exercising the most vigorous scrutiny before doing business with a man Canadian born – this drove me to a system of rearing up a new set of customers for myself who are generally two young Scotchmen associated as partners and every such concern that we supply in the Colony is now doing well.[44]

In fact, Isaac much exaggerated the extent to which the firm followed his system, not to mention its reliability, but unquestionably the firm strongly preferred that its customers and employees have British training,[45] for general standards of commercial practice were much higher there.

In selecting customers and managing their accounts, the partners relied on knowledge and judgment: they sought both to estimate the immediate trading future of the province and to know in some detail the business affairs and prospects of present or potential customers. It was possible to learn a good deal from the customer when he came to buy, but travel was the firm's main source of information. Every winter, once the roads had frozen and while the wholesale trade was least active, partners and, later, senior employees toured the hinterland.In summer, when weather permitted, shorter journeys were often made as well. On such trips, the partners met customers and inspected their businesses, investigated new retail opportunities, looked for new activities by competitors, sought information regarding local retail stocks and farmers' crops, and tried to spur payments on accounts. Equal attention could not be given to all, but larger customers were visited at least once each year, the partners also maintaining a considerable year-round correspondence with such customers. Few can have been unvisited for longer than two years.

The partners did not hesitate to demand to see the customer's books, aiming to judge his assets and liabilities, his sales, and his managerial abilities.[46] They inspected his stocks and assessed the strengths and weaknesses of his employees. Thus, they served as the equivalent of today's management consultant, offering advice on the whole range of business problems encountered by the retailer, including personnel, accounting, display, premises, business and political trends, and techniques of pricing, selling, and collecting. Yet even so there was much room for error and oversight. Accordingly, the partners sought above all to judge the man's character and integrity, and they looked especially for signs of weakness such as alcoholism and serious neglect of business details.[47]

With all such knowledge, it was still possible to lose money on accounts by underestimating the customer's total obligations. Gradually, as the development of the supply account system indicates, the firm concluded that both sales and security might be increased by monopolizing the customer's business. It would then be possible to assess whether his trading liabilities were reasonable in the light of his business opportunities. It was not always possible to secure such a monopoly, but the power of credit control could be used effectively with smaller customers and concessions on price with larger ones. Customers in turn found some advantages in having their obligations concentrated: this simplified their financial management and gave the Buchanans a greater interest in their success. Detailed analyses of eighteen bankrupt customers' estates survive, and in fifteen of these, the Buchanans were the only significant mercantile creditor. In effect, the business increasingly preferred to concentrate its risks rather than spread them.

If credit was relatively easily secured and customers offered themselves in some abundance, what prevented the firm from growing even faster? How did a business decide how much credit to seek and how large a volume of sales to push for? Most obviously, limits were set by the risk of failure, owing to short-term contractions of credit, and by competition from rivals, not only local ones but also those in other urban centres, in Canada and even in Britain. Once bound to a supplier by debt, the customer had difficulty in shifting wholesalers, unless he had the capital to pay his debts when due; accordingly, competition was more to secure good customers in the first place and to keep them successful and competitive in their local markets. Yet there was price competition. Stronger customers could, if the advantage was great enough, find enough cash to buy in Montreal or from local competitors, and it did little good to compel the wholly dependent customer to pay so high a rate that he could not compete in his local market.[48] Clearly the firm followed local price trends, but its strength and reputation were such that it did not have to go to the lowest prices on most items. As Peter later put the philosophy, 'a few per cents in most goods is [sic] not discernible and that advantage we can ... obtain and still be thought as cheap as our neighbours.'[49] The firm in fact tried to operate with three basic dry goods price levels, one for the large supply account customers, one charged generally to the trade, and one between these, charged to strong customers who were able to bargain effectively. The first and third of these tended to be quite close, as the same market forces worked on both. The second was regarded as the 'regular' one; in 1838 it was about six per cent above the other two.[50]

Ultimately, the partners' decisions on when to expand and how far to expand rested on their assumptions about the overall growth both of the economy as a whole and of particular regions within their hinterland, for this would determine the likelihood of debts contracted being met as they fell due. In essence, they assumed that growth would go on, despite year-to-year fluctuations, that ultimately farmers would be able to pay their debts to retailers who in turn would pay the wholesalers. In the first few years of operation, this confidence had been borne out. This was not, of course, an assumption that all would pay; the firm set aside sums each year to bad debt account and regularly closed delinquent accounts, charging losses on them to bad debts.

In the Buchanans' case, the chief pressure for growth and change came almost invariably from Isaac. Success confirmed his never modest belief in the essential soundness of his judgment and in the wisdom of always taking 'the bold course.'[51] He loved to promote new schemes, to innovate, to be known as the leader of new developments; he had little interest in the tedious routines of management, the meticulous processes that actually translated ideas into profit. In effect, it was Harris's job to manage and he did so very well; he was not without broader ideas on the business, but he had still not achieved fully equal status despite his recognition in the Toronto firm. Peter Buchanan's role was more complex and ambiguous. Though he pressed always for caution, for consolidation of gains, he was undoubtedly ambitious and alert to new opportunities. Some at least of the steps that Isaac took had first been canvassed by Peter, whose strategic insight was considerable; moreover, his vision, unlike Isaac's, was closely allied with a willingness to work long and hard at routines. Although Peter, unlike Harris, could deal with Isaac as an equal, perhaps even, in view of his stature as older brother, as a superior, it is doubtful that he could permanently and invariably have restrained his energetic, imaginative, and headstrong brother. But by accepting most of his brother's initiatives, he sanctioned them. Consciously or unconsciously, he accepted Isaac's role as the leader of the firm's new departures. As the early years reveal, the personalities of the new partners were of great importance to the development of the business, yet it should not be forgotten that Isaac had ideas underlying his initiatives, and these ideas tell us a good deal about the commercial world of the time. If few can have followed all the courses he proposed or pursued, some at least must have followed each.

4

General wholesalers at Hamilton 1840-5

The expansion begun in 1839 was resumed in 1840, as Isaac, with Harris's agreement, opened a new branch, a new agency, and two new trades; added a new partner and recruited another senior manager; and further increased the firm's volume of trade. By the time Peter learned of all this, he could not reverse Isaac's decisions without risking the destruction of the business.[1]

The focus of these actions was Hamilton, a town of about 3000 people, forty-five miles west of Toronto, on a fine harbour, and directly astride the main route into the western peninsula where Isaac had found so many of his customers. Peter himself had commented in 1839 that he would not rule out the possibility of a move to Hamilton, where local jobbers were doing good business, while Isaac had actually urged that they open a warehouse there.[2] By 1837 Hamilton had defeated its local urban rival, Dundas; opened a short canal to Lake Ontario; and secured its own chartered bank, the Gore Bank. Although the Gore took some years to raise its authorized capital and was often tarnished by rumours of unethical lending practices, it gave Hamilton a symbol of commercial independence; in 1840 it was beginning to establish agencies across the west in a bid to widen its connection and that of Hamilton.[3]

In 1840 Isaac and Harris heard that two or three of Montreal's strongest houses were considering opening Hamilton branches; these, they feared, could cut Toronto off from its western hinterland and endanger their business, with its heavy outstanding accounts in the west. Isaac went to Hamilton at the end of April to investigate the rumours, concluded that they were well founded, and at once rented a new warehouse nearing completion at the corner of King and Catherine streets. He and Harris stressed the defensive nature of this step to Peter Buchanan: Toronto would not be the capital of the united Canadas, and Isaac, who recalled how rapidly Toronto had outdistanced Kingston in the 1830s, considered that a Toronto shorn of its political power might in turn be unable to defeat a challenge from Hamilton. Besides, his 1831 move to a small, just developing centre had been so successful that another such jump did not seem unreasonable.

In any case, it seemed unwise to close the successful Toronto store; as he and Harris would have trouble managing two warehouses, Isaac asked John Young, Hamilton's leading merchant, to manage the new one. Young would have been a serious competitor, and he could bring proven ability, new trade, and capital to the new business. From Ayrshire originally, he had come to Canada in 1828, at the age of twenty, to work for William Ritchie and Company, the new Montreal branch of Pollok, Gilmour and Company. In 1832 he had been sent to Hamilton to open a branch, later known as John Young and Company; it sold dry goods, groceries, and hardware at retail and, increasingly, at wholesale, and shipped produce and staves to Allan Gilmour and Company at Quebec. Peter Buchanan, who had met Young in 1839, had been impressed by him and his business. Now, in 1840, Young's backers were feuding among themselves, and the future of Pollok, Gilmour and Company was uncertain.[4] Rather than try to compete with the Buchanans, Young had every reason to prefer an alliance with them. He readily agreed to join the new firm that Isaac would form, Buchanan, Harris and Company; Young would receive one-third of its profits and Isaac Buchanan and Company two-thirds.

Late in May, Isaac and Young signed their new partnership agreement in Montreal, where Young was meeting with his previous partners. Unable to find someone reliable to take over in Hamilton, the Gilmours finally agreed to let him wind up the firm. He closed his store in December 1840, handing over the retail business to his brother-in-law, James McIntyre, and James Osborne, a former employee. His good wholesale customers he sent to Buchanan, Harris and Company, which Isaac opened in September using stock from Toronto plus some goods ordered hastily from Britain. Young, obliged to pay his backers £6500, would need two years to realize his capital of £6000cy and to pay it into the firm.

Buchanan, Harris and Company was conceived on a large scale. Writing to an outsider, Peter Buchanan described the new enterprise with some pride:

My Brother you know is indefatigable to a degree and shortly after you left He & Harris found (or supposed) it to be necessary to open an establishment at Hamilton. ... And the result is judging by the description I have got of it that they have opened the largest establishment in British North America fairly eclipsing our head quarters at Toronto.[5]

Writing to his partners, he protested at the larger scale of the business, the new borrowing required, and the size of Young's share; and he threatened to withdraw from direct connection with the Canada trade. He vowed to return to Canada as soon as possible to consolidate the two branches; this the Canadian partners indicated they would agree to if the new business succeeded as they planned. For the moment, Peter could only fill the orders sent by Harris as the stock for the two stores was developed. Instead of a planned £15,000 to £25,000 stg, he was asked to place and find funds for orders of £55,000 to £65,000 (Table 2, p 164).

Peter and Isaac had felt Toronto's lack of a satisfactory grocery wholesale house: good customers, drawn to Montreal for groceries, would often buy dry goods there too. Isaac had actually produced several draft agreements with others to found a grocery firm, though none had materialized, but Peter had opposed any major diversion of their time and capital into the trade, preferring merely to encourage friends to take up the opportunity. If Toronto lacked a strong grocery business, Hamilton had none at all. Isaac, Young, and Harris all agreed that the new store to attract and hold good customers must have a grocery department. Because Young, who had experience of the trade, would not have enough time for it and dry goods, Isaac hired James Law, Toronto agent for the City Bank of Montreal since February 1840, to manage the new department. Law, then thirty, came originally from Glasgow; he had been employed by a Montreal grocery and produce house and had been non-resident partner in a Toronto grocery house that failed in 1839. Isaac, Peter, and Harris knew him well enough to act as his sureties when he became the bank's agent.[6] He was delighted to return to mercantile employment and agreed to manage the grocery department in return for one-quarter of its profits.

Isaac planned that Law, besides buying groceries in Montreal and New York, would return to Hamilton for peak sales seasons. His partners predicted, correctly, that this would not work: for their volume of business in Montreal, a part-time presence in the market was insufficient, especially given the difficulties of travel in Canada. Thus Law became the firm's resident agent in Montreal in 1841. His agency was treated in the accounts as part of the Hamilton grocery department, and he continued to receive one-quarter of its profits. But he could perform other services in Montreal, such as arranging forwarding and certain customs formalities.

Young had always handled Upper Canadian produce, and the Buchanans had done so occasionally. Molyneux, Witherby and Company, still looking to broaden their trade, were anxious to encourage consignments of wheat and flour, and ample Canadian bank credit was also available for the domestic portion of the trade. The grain trade facilitated collections from customers who wished, in effect, to pay in grain. With no need to tie up their own funds and Law, an experienced agent, to sell for them in Montreal, the Buchanans decided to expand their produce trade. In December 1840, Isaac arranged a joint account for up to 10,000 barrels of flour with Witherby, who had also discussed the matter with Peter. The Buchanans would draw on the Liverpool firm for funds to buy flour or wheat for flouring; Molyneux, Witherby and Company would sell the grain, charge a five per cent commission, then proceeds would be divided equally. John Young set up a joint account with Osborne and McIntyre, who would actually buy the grain, up to a limit of £10,000.[7]

Thus 1840 was another year of great expansion. Shipments, although far higher than Peter anticipated, did not reach the level of 1839, but dry goods sales, for the two locations, very much exceeded those for 1839; in addition, there were grocery sales of £16,000 (Tables 1 and 2; pp 162-4). Total sales for 1840 were two and one-half times those for 1838. Profit margins were shrinking, however, as over-production in the British textile trade and falling prices led to glutted world markets. Canadian imports rose somewhat from 1839 levels and Montreal importers were forced by overstocks to auction dry goods at low prices.[8] The Hamilton business did not balance its accounts until late 1841, but Toronto's 1840 profit, £5000cy, was the lowest since 1837 (Table 4, p 168). This was equal to seven per cent of the value of sales, less than half the return of two years earlier.

To finance continued heavy shipments, Peter Buchanan called heavily on his sources of credit. He complained in February 1841 that the Canadian houses still owed him for almost all 1840 shipments. Remittances were falling behind despite much-increased discounts: in October 1840, discounts in three Toronto banks, the third the recently opened Bank of British North America, totalled £56,000, about double the amount of a year earlier. Fortunately, the 1840 harvest was a good one, permitting the business to make progress on collections, and higher sales reduced swollen inventories.[9] On 1 May 1841, customers owed the firm £84,000cy; as this was considerably less than sales for the previous twelve months, payments evidently had been high during the winter. Yet it seemed to all partners that such a sum was a very large amount to collect from the economy of the west. Still, money could be made in Canada even in less than ideally prosperous times.

As 1841 began, and with Peter's agreement, in view of the importance of the Union to trade, Isaac concentrated on politics. Lord Sydenham, faced with opposition from French Canadians and Upper Canadian compact tories, had formed his own party to achieve the moderate, development-oriented politics that he had been sent to foster. Isaac, although he had once organized some Glasgow merchants to petition against Sydenham's appointment, on grounds of Sydenham's former connection with the Baltic trade, strongly supported the governor's aims of uniting Upper and Lower Canada, removing the entrenched élites from government, denying the full Baldwinite idea of responsible government, and settling the clergy reserves issue on a compromise basis that recognized the rights of other churches besides the Church of England. Isaac decided to run in the governor's interest in Toronto, citadel of the compact tories, and backed his decision with £1000 of his own funds. Because Toronto's business community was anxious that one of the city's two members should represent its views, Isaac attracted widespread mercantile support. Aided by resolute use of government patronage, and after a bitter campaign, which Isaac's rhetoric did little to calm, Isaac and J.H. Dunn, the Receiver-General, won a narrow victory in March.[10] In June, Isaac set out for Kingston and the first session of the legislature of the Province of Canada, leaving the business to his partners.

Despite his claim to 'have been very *instrumental* in all thats going on in the formation of parties, etc....' at Kingston, Isaac before long became disenchanted with politics.[11] With a large majority, Sydenham had no need to pay careful attention to each supporter, particularly one as idiosyncratically opinionated as Isaac. Isaac was compelled to confine his activities to membership on select committees of importance to businessmen, dealing with banking, currency, and trade, and to the unglamorous duties of the local member. He counted it a major victory when Sydenham's planned bank of issue was defeated, for he was convinced that this would have severely tightened credit in Upper Canada, and drawn the economy more fully within Montreal's orbit.[12] Yet his tasks did not often inspire him, and he had little taste for or ability at the manoeuvering that would be necessary to advance his position and power. Thus, when Peter Buchanan, anxious to come to Canada to examine the new business structures, asked Isaac to spend 1842 as manager in Glasgow, Isaac was quite ready to leave Kingston behind.

Peter arrived for the 1841 fall trade, having left his banker with authority to act for him until Isaac arrived. At the end of September came news that Molyneux, Witherby and Company had failed, after a disastrous cotton speculation. The Buchanans owed the Liverpool firm £11,000stg on acceptances to facilitate dry goods shipments, and their names were on Molyneux, Witherby and Company acceptances against produce shipments to a value of over £15,000stg. Both sums the business had to pay, and there could be further complications; to protect the firm, Isaac left for home at once.

To his astonishment, he found affairs in complete order. The Glasgow and Ship Bank, which was dominated by Glasgow's Dennistoun family, had arranged for A. Dennistoun and Company of Liverpool to pay all drafts for which the Buchanans were responsible and to collect produce accounts due (Witherby having generously declined to claim these). When some other charges were reckoned into the account, A. Dennistoun and Company had paid almost £30,000 on the Buchanans' behalf. The firm had escaped from the failure without loss, with much enhanced connections with one of Glasgow's most powerful commercial families, and with a clearer view of how high it now stood in the Glasgow business community.[13]

Isaac took advantage of this reputation to renew bills due several suppliers so that he could reduce his obligations to Dennistouns and the bank. He expected that Dennistouns would want to limit their connection with a single firm, but found that A. Dennistoun and Company were also looking for business beyond the cotton trade. They agreed to become the firm's Liverpool agent; to forward shipments; and to accept six-, nine-, or twelve-months bills totalling up to £10,000stg at a time that the Buchanans were to meet at maturity. At the same time, Isaac arranged to borrow up to £10,000 from Buchanan, Watson and Company, a Glasgow grocery house in the South American trade, lacking profitable business at the time, in which J.G. Watson, a business connection of Isaac's father, was a partner. Ostensibly this credit was to support the new grocery trade, but it could be used as the firm wished; Isaac kept it secret from Dennistouns lest they be alarmed at this increase in the firm's borrowings.

Meanwhile Peter Buchanan was altering the Canadian business. He and his brother-in-law, George Douglas, had been considering business opportunities for Douglas, to avoid further overseas postings to tropical or subtropical regions. Douglas had spent much time in Canada in 1840, chiefly looking into the Toronto and Montreal grocery trades, but in the end he and Peter decided he would join the Buchanans' own business.[14] He had no business experience, but at least had a modest capital, the proceeds of the sale of his commission, to invest. Harris agreed to his joining Isaac Buchanan and Company with a one-fifth share, but Douglas would actually be based in Hamilton and be trained by Young to manage the grocery department there. As part of this arrangement, Peter planned to force Young's share of the Hamilton profits down to one-quarter. Young resisted, for he saw no need for Douglas and Isaac's offer had been freely made; but in the end, having cut his ties with the Gilmours, he was compelled to accept. The reduction was to take effect 1 November 1842, and Peter agreed that the business would continue at least at its present scale thereafter. Douglas joined the firm in January 1842.

Young felt more able to accept the reduction in share because the business had a record profit to divide in 1841. After allowance is made for Hamilton profits counted again at Toronto, it is clear that total profits in Canada exceeded £16,000 (Table 4, p 168). As this figure included profits on sales in Hamilton in 1840, and was thus made on sales of about £250,000, the return on sales was less encouraging, amounting to about 6.5 per cent. During 1841, inventory was brought under control; on 1 December 1841, dry goods stocks at Toronto and Hamilton were valued at £21,000stg, just sixty per cent of the figure of twelve months earlier. Already the centre of growth in the firm's trade was Hamilton, which was attracting new customers who found its prices and stock competitive and its location convenient.

The partners were gratified by these results, in part no doubt because it was such a depressed year in many areas of the British economy, and also because of their recent alarm over Witherby's failure.[15] Canada did not fully share the British atmosphere, however. Relatively high grain prices persisted in Britain, wheat production increased in Upper Canada, and the volume of wheat exported from the St Lawrence in 1841, most of which came from Upper Canada, rose by 36 per cent over 1840. Prices, though quite low, were tending upward.[16] The atmosphere of expansion was enhanced by growing political stability and, perhaps even more, by Sydenham's announcement of an imperially guaranteed loan of £1.5 million, which suggested that large-scale public works would soon resume. Reflecting the optimism of the year, the legislature authorized six of the province's banks to increase their capitals by a total of £1.2 million cy.[17] The rise in the Buchanans' shipments and sales reflects this climate, as they and their customers anticipated a successful trade.

But at the end of the year, there were signs that retailers had overestimated their trade; on his winter tour, Peter found customers' stores overstocked, and he heard that the 1841 crop had already been marketed. Moreover, the British and American economies continued to slump.[18] Indicators reveal a serious downturn in the Canadian economy early in 1842, and this persisted until the summer of 1843. Wheat exports from the St Lawrence fell from 2.3 million bushels in 1841 to 1.7 million in 1842 and just 1.2 million in 1843, and wheat prices fell sharply in 1842. Depression is indicated in the decline in *ad valorem* imports to the St Lawrence, from £1,963,000stg in 1841 to £1,762,000 in 1842 and just £1,270,000 in 1843. Total note circulation of the Canadian banks dropped by twenty per cent between April and June 1842 and by almost forty per cent between April

1842 and January 1843. The circulation of the three main Upper Canadian banks fell especially; between April 1842 and April 1843 it dropped by almost fifty per cent.[19] The only encouraging feature was that work resumed on the canals as funds from the Sydenham loan became available.

By the time these trends became clear, the Buchanans had settled their course for 1842. Isaac had found ample credit, unprecedentedly low cotton prices in Manchester led Harris to want to buy heavily for stock, and the partners had in any case agreed to keep their business volume at 1841's high level. But the low prices in Britain tightened competition in textiles everywhere. Hamilton, Toronto, Montreal, and New York dry goods houses were all overstocked. In Montreal, importers again auctioned stock. Many British manufacturers experimented with direct consignments to Canada, while others sent travellers to seek orders. Such salesmen, lacking detailed knowledge of the local market, necessary if they were to sell on credit, were the least of the problems, but all these pressures together forced a new reduction in margins. In March, Peter hoped to hold advances at two-thirds on sterling costs to general customers and 60 to 62 per cent to the eleven supply accounts that the firm now had. By June, their biggest supply customer, Walter Macfarlane of Toronto, was getting goods at 55 per cent, a second was being offered 57 per cent, and a third was protesting at paying 58 per cent. Slightly over 60 per cent was all that could be got, on average, from general customers. With the average cost of getting goods to their stores, (including exchange, increased duties in Canada, all transport and insurance charges, and fifteen months' interest) now 49 per cent, the firm was selling in many cases at prices that would scarcely pay interest on its capital.

Sales for the year fell by fifteen per cent from 1841, the major drop being in dry goods sales at Hamilton; total profit on all Canadian sales was less than four per cent, just £6000cy (Tables 1 and 4, pp 162, 168). Almost no profit was made in the grocery department. Isaac, who continued to send forth a flow of new business ideas, again erred in buying goods in the fall for spring sale. Even the taciturn Harris denounced these.

I have to notice with great reluctance your spring shipments ... they are unfortunate in every sense of the word. ... The shipment now made contains many things which we would not have ordered under any circumstances and which, as overstock, will require to be run off in Montreal. ... The remuneration for importing goods is now so small that losses on bad stock must be avoided...[20]

These shipments left the firm heavily overstocked at the end of 1842. Toronto's dry goods inventory alone was almost £25,000stg, which was more than the combined Toronto and Hamilton stocks twelve months earlier. Year-end saw morale in the business at the lowest point in its history.

Peter decided to stay in Canada to see the overstock worked off and backward accounts collected. The firm imported no new goods for spring, and Harris bought only moderately for fall. Summer 1843 at last brought a revival of trade, stimulated by revival of the British and American economies, the vigorous construction now proceeding on the canals, and the Canada Corn Act, which completely opened the British market to Canadian wheat. The good Upper Canadian harvest in 1843 brought considerable cash into the economy despite low wheat prices.[21] Thus merchants had a chance to bring their businesses under control. While the Buchanans had a net profit of less than £8000, not much more than in 1842 (Table 4, p 168), they blamed this on bad stock and counted it a good year.

After almost two years in Canada, Peter Buchanan returned to Glasgow in the summer of 1843; there he spent a month in discussion with Isaac, who had professed more cautious views since his marriage in January to Agnes Jarvie, the seventeen-year-old daughter of a Glasgow merchant. Isaac had submitted his resignation from the Assembly at about the same time, after missing the 1842 session. He now proposed to concentrate on business in the most conservative way possible until he had acquired the capital to allow him and his wife to retire comfortably to Glasgow on the interest on his capital.[22] Though Isaac began further business alterations on his return to Canada, several of his changes had been fully accepted by all partners in 1843. The strategy was to consolidate in Upper Canada, then expand from a sound basis there.[23]

It had been agreed to close the Toronto store and to concentrate in Hamilton, to overcome the problem of divided stock and to simplify management. The partners felt that the Hamilton store was the better one and that it had superior accounts, although there was no clear superiority of one over the other in terms of rates of profit. Toronto's discount lines would be given up, but this was accepted by all as a desirable reduction in borrowing. Little business would be sacrificed because many of their Toronto customers were located west of Hamilton. Isaac calculated that the accounts north and east of Toronto that they would have to give up owed a total of £19,300, only 22 per cent of Toronto's outstanding debts, and not much more than ten per cent of the firm's total outstanding debts. The business would keep some customers between Toronto and Hamilton plus three Toronto accounts and one in Kingston, all four of which owed the firm too much money to find it easy to switch suppliers. The partners knew Hamilton was a less-developed centre than Toronto, but they considered their business strong enough to require fewer ancillary metropolitan services. Hamilton was in any case acquiring a fuller range of such services with every year.

Isaac Buchanan and Company was to be wound up. The Hamilton business would assist collections, for payments on accounts transferred there could be applied first to the older debts in Toronto. James Bickel, book-keeper and office manager in Toronto, took charge of collecting accounts that were to be closed. Stock was jobbed or transferred to Hamilton at the end of 1844. Capital sums calculated to have been earned by the Toronto partners from the Hamilton business since 1840 were transferred to the Hamilton books. Remaining capital sums, about £33,500stg at Peter and Isaac's credit and £6500 at Harris's, were transferred to the Glasgow books.[24] This represented the capital accumulated in the Toronto operation over nine years, with the exception of interest and profit accumulated at Glasgow. Peter and Isaac's capital there evidently totalled between £18,000 and £20,000 before the transfers were made. During nine years' operations at Toronto, they had more than quadrupled their initial capital (Table 5, p 170); this was a growth rate of over seventeen per cent per annum.

On 7 June 1844, the partners signed an agreement that a new business was created at Hamilton on 31 October 1843, and in Montreal on 31 March 1844, under the firm name of Buchanan, Harris and Company. Profits were divided 19 per cent each to Peter and Isaac Buchanan and R.W. Harris, 17 per cent to Young, 14 per cent to Douglas, and 12 per cent to Law.[25]

Law's admission to full partnership recognized his ability and the partners' intention to develop the Montreal business more vigorously, though in ways that did not tie up too much capital. First they looked to the burgeoning Anglo-Canadian produce trade. Their British connections would allow them to secure buying orders for Montreal, while their Upper Canadian knowledge and connections enabled them to secure grain consignments for sale in Montreal. As A. Dennistoun and Company and Canadian banks would readily advance money for the trade, the Buchanans could avoid great use of their own capital, yet when they chose, they could also speculate on their own or joint account. Law knew the trade, and Peter Buchanan wished to expand it; there were few barriers except competition to its swift development. As it was, competition was already forcing down commissions at Montreal, but the firm began to increase its trade quite rapidly. Most of Montreal's earnings from it still came from sales in Montreal, but some buying orders were obtained, and consignments were sent overseas when the market seemed favourable.

Late in 1844, Isaac Buchanan and James Law made a more controversial decision: they bought property on the Montreal waterfront and began to build a warehouse, which was opened early in 1845 under the name of Isaac Buchanan and Company. As many of their larger customers continued to buy groceries in Montreal, Isaac and Law proposed to develop a grocery stock there to enhance the firm's control over such customers. They ignored Young's objection that this might encourage more strong customers to go to Montreal and to buy dry goods there too, and Peter Buchanan's objection to commitment of capital to fixed property. Moreover, to make the trade pay, Law had to seek new customers, some of whom, Toronto grocery wholesalers, were, in effect, competitors of the Hamilton store. To reduce capital commitments, Isaac and Law hoped to secure consignments from Britain, but they soon found that there was a limit to the number of consigners, and the remainder of the stock would have to be supported entirely from the firm's own resources. Law quickly built a profitable business in Montreal, however, and partners' objections were thus overcome. William Guild Jr and Isaac Buchanan had been driven out of Montreal in the 1830s, but the Buchanans now possessed the capital resources and the connection among customers to be able to compete with established houses in Montreal.

Most Hamilton customers required iron and hardware, yet Hamilton also lacked an adequate outlet for these goods. Rather than see customers go to Toronto or Montreal for hardware, the Buchanans decided to open a second Hamilton warehouse, across the street, to supply such goods themselves, and thus to seek a full monopoly of all but independent customers' trade. As most of the elements in a hardware stock, unlike groceries, would come from Britain, Peter Buchanan and Company could charge a commission on them; overall, the trade would reinforce the trans-Atlantic axis on which the business was built. Peter Buchanan and Harris bought the first stock early in 1845, relying on orders sent by Law and Young, both of whom had some experience in the trade; hardware orders were largely placed through commission merchants in Birmingham, Sheffield, and Wolverhampton in order to get advice on stock and suppliers and to secure credit on the goods.[26] During 1845, shipments totalled £10,000stg, divided equally between hardware and various types of iron, much of which was available in the Glasgow area.

A key factor in Peter Buchanan's enthusiasm for the iron trade was the dramatic rise of the Scottish iron industry since the invention of the Neilson hot blast process in 1828. This development required and reflected a rapid expansion of markets, both domestic and overseas, and merchants played an important role in linking the industry to its new markets. During the 1840s, the focus of the British pig iron market shifted to Glasgow, and for a time in the late 1840s, nearly all Britain's iron exports came from Scotland.[27]

Peter first proposed to seek iron consignments in 1842. Over two years later, after a sharp upsurge in Scottish iron production and after the firm had a full Montreal agency and its own iron and hardware department planned at Hamilton, he succeeded beyond his greatest hopes. He secured the Canadian agency for Scotland's most famous ironmasters, the Baird family, whose sixteen furnaces accounted for over one-quarter of all Scotland's iron output.[28] As hardware was wanted mainly by regular customers while pig iron was required more by founders, some further broadening of the firm's clientele was now required; but Law was well able to manage this. Possession of the agency added immensely to the reputation of the Montreal business. Excited by this development, Isaac and Law overrode Young's renewed protests and decided that Montreal too should have a fuller stock of British iron and hardware. As a result, iron and hardware were added almost simultaneously to both branches.

Plainly Isaac Buchanan had modified his belief that business retrenchment and a retiring life were now his highest priority; in fact his restlessness drove him constantly into new business and political projects. In England in 1842 and 1843, he pursued his most common form of political activity, writing open letters, these in support of a strengthened imperial trading system. In 1844, in Toronto, he campaigned vigorously in support of Sir Charles Metcalfe, feeling that a reform electoral victory would lead to a separation of Canada and Britain. After settling in Hamilton, he organized a meeting of thirty-six businessmen at which it was agreed to form a Hamilton Board of Trade; he became its first president.[29]

Isaac had been in Glasgow as the Disruption in the Church of Scotland came to a head; his family connections and his deepest convictions placed him on the evangelical side. Back in Canada, he ardently espoused the Free Kirk cause and played a significant part in events as the Kirk split in Upper Canada. He offered £50 to up to ten Upper Canadian Free Kirk congregations, provided they named their churches Knox and met certain conditions protecting the congregation's power, especially over church property. Larger contributions were given to Knox churches in Toronto and Hamilton; by late 1845 he had given out £650 in this cause.[30]

In July 1845, Isaac set out to investigate business opportunities in New York. Britain had removed legal restrictions on trade in colonial produce with foreign countries in 1842. In 1845 and 1846, the United States passed Drawback acts permitting traders to recover duties on imported goods that were subsequently exported. New York, which dominated the American import trade and American finance and was pressing development of its trade in western grain, had larger and more varied stocks of goods, often at lower prices than Montreal, a year-round harbour with lower Atlantic freight and insurance rates, and trading links to all parts of the world.[31] By 1846, Upper Canadians could buy and sell in bond in New York, and legal obstacles other than customs duties to trade in goods produced in or shipped through the United States were removed.

Unlike Montreal's merchants, the Buchanans did not fear that these changes would damage the basis of their trade by allowing New York to take over the middleman's role in the Anglo-Canadian trade. Although they saw a long-term threat in the rapid growth of American manufacturing, Britain's lead remained very large in most lines of goods. For the moment, they felt that some adaptations to the changes would be sufficient to defend their position. Thus, while they had always made a few purchases in New York, the legal changes of 1842 greatly increased this possibility by opening the New York grocery trade to them. Prices for tea and some other items were so much lower in New York than Montreal that widespread smuggling had developed, and the Buchanans had lost much trade in a basic grocery staple. Now they could secure this trade. To pay for purchases, they drew bills on Peter Buchanan and Company, but as the firm lacked a reputation there, Peter, who explored the issue in 1842, was forced to secure a mercantile endorser for his bills for the first few years in order to buy from the largest importers.* This freed Law, who made most purchases, to buy, from the suppliers he preferred, an increasing range of items in New York, including leather, coffee, sugar, and tobacco as well as tea.

When the first Drawback Act was passed, Isaac Buchanan concluded that trade between Upper Canada and New York would further increase, and their larger customers would, as in Montreal, be drawn increasingly to New York for groceries. He judged it wise to establish the firm at once in a new trading channel of great potential. With the earlier Montreal agency as his model, he opened a New York office for Buchanan, Harris and Company in early September. It was to buy groceries for the firm and those supply accounts that otherwise could afford to buy in New York themselves, purchase any American manufactures that were required, principally hardware, and forward goods shipped through New York to or from the Canadian houses. Aware that this would not justify the costs, Isaac sketched plans to develop a general commission agency in New York, dealing in Upper Cana-

---

* Ie, rather than transfer money from Hamilton to New York, the firm drew on Glasgow from New York and remitted funds from Canada to Glasgow to cover such bills when they fell due. In part the intent of the practice was to justify a commission for Peter Buchanan and Company on American grocery purhcases, but evidently this was still the most convenient way to transfer funds.

dian produce and seeking buying and selling commissions from British firms.[32] By now the firm had some reputation in New York, but Isaac looked to older connections for the credit his office required. Through William Wood, resident partner in Dennistoun, Wood and Company, the Dennistouns' recently opened New York house, which was seeking new business, he arranged a drawing credit on J. and A. Dennistoun of Glasgow. Peter Buchanan and J. and A. Dennistoun considered that this latest connection might link their houses too closely, but they made no move to overrule their partners overseas, and indeed Peter arranged to employ the credit from Glasgow too.[33] Isaac suggested one or another name as manager of his new office, but as all brought objections from his partners, he remained in charge himself for the moment.

In opening the office, Isaac gave Peter Buchanan no time to comment and ignored the queries of Harris and Young. None opposed the step in principle, and Peter in fact had looked periodically at the New York trade since 1834, but all felt Isaac had acted precipitately. Current buying arrangements seemed to work well enough; war between Britain and the United States over the Oregon question was a real possibility; trans-Atlantic agency business of the sort Isaac hoped for was likely to be difficult to attract, except possibly in the newly developing Anglo-American grain trade; and, as Young pointed out, if Isaac developed trade in American manufactures he would undermine the very basis of the business, the Anglo-Canadian trade.

Moreover, Isaac's suggestions to move personnel continued the tensions that had built up among the partners. They had found adjustment to one another difficult and circumstances somewhat confining at Hamilton. Harris managed dry goods; Young, after recovering from a serious illness in 1844, returned to manage the grocery and hardware departments; when Isaac was there, his role, inadequately defined, was general management, especially financial, and produce business. Douglas really had no role at all; he had not developed much business ability, as Peter Buchanan, who even now defended Douglas in public, admitted privately to Isaac. Aware of his failings, Douglas planned to retire. Isaac and Young proposed to replace him by Young's brother-in-law, McIntyre, but Harris and Law saw no need for another partner. Harris indicated deeper resentment:

I might also repeat ... that I fancied every change in the business since 1839 has been to my prejudice altho benefitting you and him [Isaac and Peter].

If you ... have ... no further use for my services I am quite sure we will not have much difficulty in arranging a separation so that I may make the best use of my time elsewhere. You will be able to get your dry goods selected much cheaper than 19% of the business, and therefore if this is all the benefit I can be to the firm the sooner the members of it are rid of me the better it will be for them.[34]

Above all, Harris now sought a share in the Glasgow business. His threat to withdraw was a serious one, as Peter pointed out in seeking to silence his brother, for Harris was 'the only man in the concern capable of managing or conducting successfully the Dry Goods department,' the business's key department and the one where fashion and difficult choices in stock selection were most crucial.[35] If both Isaac and Peter were to reside outside Canada, Harris alone could be trusted to take full charge in Canada.

Besides, if several partners were to withdraw, taking their full shares, Peter and Isaac could be left with the worthless shell of a business should assets later prove overvalued. This danger explains Peter's growing insistence on setting aside large sums in reserve accounts. He considered their assets to be secure enough, but wished to minimize individual capital accounts so that a withdrawing partner would have to negotiate with others in the business to secure a share of the reserve accounts. Such accounts make it more difficult to work with subsequent figures for profit and capital.[36] The partners' debate raised the question of the business's future after 1848, when the current agreement was to expire. To allow Douglas to retire before then, Peter arranged for him to withdraw, effective in June 1845; his share of profits was allocated to a suspense account until the longer-term future was clear.

The many strategic changes of 1844-5 were conducted against a backdrop of economic boom in Britain and Canada.[37] Canadian statistics, oriented to the St Lawrence, no longer fully reflect the Canadian economy, in that American grain was attracted to the river under the Canada Corn Act of 1843 and Upper Canadians were making greater use of the Erie Canal. Yet the statistics may suggest trends. Wheat and flour exports from the St Lawrence rose from 1.2 million bushels in 1843 to 2.4 million in 1844 and 2.5 million in 1845, and it is clear that Upper Canada's exports increased sharply from 1843 to 1844 and at least held their own in 1845. Wheat prices averaged five shillings per bushel at Montreal through most of 1843 and 1844, and in 1845 they rose steadily to a peak of seven shillings in November. Imports via the St Lawrence paying *ad valorem* duties leapt from £1.3 million stg in 1843 to £2.0 million in 1844 and rose slightly higher in 1845, to £2.2 million. There was a 25 per cent increase in Canadian bank note issue between the autumn of 1843 and January 1844, and after a slow increase in the intervening period, there was a 33 per cent increase between June and October 1845.[38]

The Buchanans' sales increased markedly at Hamilton in 1844, while sales dropped, by how much is unclear, at Toronto; moreover, the firm changed its accounting year, yet it is evident that sales did increase from 1843 levels, perhaps by as much as 25 per cent. Profits increased much more, despite a fall in the figure at Toronto. The declared profit for Hamilton and Montreal, even after Peter's deduction of £7800 in allowances, exceeded £12,000, more than twice that of the previous year (Tables 1 and 4, pp 162, 168). Favourable harvests in 1843 and 1844 made for good collections and enabled Peter to reduce his dependence on borrowed capital.

The success of 1844 led the Buchanans to increase shipments in 1845, and their sales totalled £235,000cy, a record for a single year (Tables 1 and 2, pp 162-4). Sales in the new hardware department were quite modest; Hamilton's grocery sales fell, reflecting the impact of the new Montreal store; but there was a large increase in dry goods sales, though some of this simply reflected the closure of the Toronto store and transfer of its accounts. Continued heavy Canadian imports, however, contributed to greater competition. The advance on sterling costs required to deliver goods in the store at Hamilton had fallen to just over 43 per cent, but mark-ups had also shrunk. One valued customer was offered goods at just fifty per cent. After setting aside large allowances when it balanced its accounts for 1845, the firm declared a net profit of only £8000cy, just three per cent on sales; the hardware department actually showed a loss of £400 (Table 4, p 168).[39] At the same time the business had fallen behind on payments to Glasgow. On 1 January 1845, Buchanan, Harris and Company owed Peter Buchanan and Company £111,500stg; on 1 December 1845, the comparable figure was £141,000.[40] Instead of being further reduced, borrowing in Canada and Britain had to be increased. When a financial panic hit London late in 1845, Peter Buchanan was relieved that his relations with creditors were good, for the business was more vulnerable than it had been for several years.

An estimate can be made of the firm's overall financial position at this time, by drawing on Peter's calculations and other surviving figures (Table 6, p 172). Thus, the firm's 1845 sales were equal to about twice the value of partners' capital. It is possible that outstanding accounts were up to fifteen per cent higher than the table shows, but if so, Canadian obligations must have been similarly higher, in view of the known figures in the table. Even the highest likely figure indicates that customers were, on average, paying within the normal twelve- to thirteen-month period, for outstanding debts did not exceed 1845 sales. Capital borrowed from British sources accounted for about two-thirds of the firm's obligations, with Canadian banks the chief source of credit in North America. Total borrowings were over one-third higher than the total of partners' capital and suspense accounts; hence, if the firm's assets were worth less than about sixty per cent of their nominal value, partners' capital would disappear. Clearly this was not a 'nice snug business,'[41] but neither was it especially exposed. Indeed, not to have borrowed extensively in the climate of expansion of the time in Upper Canada would have been the more remarkable course. The firm had capital enough to see it through all but a total commercial calamity in Upper Canada and Britain; the partners' decisions in the 1840s show that they did not anticipate such a calamity.

The figures reveal the extent of the firm's growth; although there is a marked drop in the rate of growth of capital in 1844-5, this reflects in part Peter's new emphasis on building up suspense accounts (Table 5, p 170). Even so, the partners were becoming wealthy men. Harris had now accumulated over £15,000cy. Law, who also had started with no capital, had built up over £4000 in five years. Young's account had not grown very rapidly, indeed had lately been shrinking as, with his partners' agreement, he built his large house, 'Undermount,' on Hamilton's mountainside. He continued to be an important figure in Hamilton's business world. Peter and Isaac Buchanan now had a capital of almost £87,000cy, about £69,000stg, equal to an almost sixfold increase in their original capital. Peter's was much the larger share, for Isaac's pattern of expenditure had always been more lavish. Thus, between November 1843 and March 1845, his outlay exceeded any other partner's; it totalled £3160, or approximately £500 more than his Canadian profit and interest in this period.*[42] Isaac never took much pleasure in accumulation for its own sake; wealth was to be enjoyed and used, particularly in the promotion of important public causes.

As he succeeded in the Canadian trade, Peter Buchanan's ambitions led him to look with interest at greater business projects. Thus, in the fall of 1845, news of the Irish potato blight and rising grain prices in Britain led Peter to expand his firm's role in the grain trade and to seek a footing in it at New York. There was no time to buy Upper Canadian wheat and grind it, so he urged Isaac to buy American flour in New York and, if possible, 30,000 bushels of Ohio wheat to be laid in Britain in bond. He expected that, despite the flood of orders going out, prices by Christmas would be high enough to permit this grain to be landed almost duty-free. Isaac bought a good deal of

---

* Isaac's annual expenditures exceeded the total salaries paid at Hamilton (eg, in 1846). The 21 employees at that time (8 in dry goods, 6 in hardware, 5 in groceries, and 2 in the office) were paid a total of £2240; several also were housed by the firm. Senior clerks in each department and the office currently earned about £200 per year; a number of them later became retail customers of the firm.

grain, apparently on joint account with A. Dennistoun and Company, and although prices turned sharply downward in November, some profit was made from the speculation.[43]

In the fall of 1845, the Hamilton group promoting the Great Western Railroad of Canada, which was to run from Niagara Falls to Windsor, via Hamilton, asked Peter, who was the most eminent businessman in Britain with ties to Hamilton, to assist in securing English capital for the project.[44] He readily agreed to join Sir Allan MacNab and two others in London, for the railway seemed clearly to be in the interest of Hamilton, the west, and his business. With the English railway boom rushing to its greatest heights, they soon had subscriptions for all 55,000 shares from an eleven-man syndicate including the great George Hudson himself. The scrip taken and at a high premium in London, Peter enthusiastically joined his fellow negotiators in seeking a speculative profit from Great Western shares. But when the inevitable collapse came, Peter began to reveal his priorities. He accepted a Canadian request that he act for the company in negotiations to attempt to get the scripholders to pay on their subscriptions. Thus began a period of ten years in which Peter acted as agent in England for the company or one of its subsidiaries. Clearly he was interested in the profits that such involvement might bring, but his own business would yield him surer and ampler returns for the time he spent: he was far more concerned that the line actually be built.[45] He was also interested in developing some of the connections he had begun to form in the rapidly emerging British railway community.

By the end of 1845, the business had successfully if not entirely harmoniously completed its five-year transition from dry goods wholesaler in a single location to a much larger and more complex general wholesaling business. In expanding, the firm did not change its focus on the western peninsula, as the move to Hamilton clearly reflected. Its basic strategy was to seek as large a profit as possible from that region, by trading in almost all the possible areas of opportunity, three importing lines and produce exports. The New York office found one or two Toronto customers, the Montreal house had developed some trade in Lower Canada and in eastern Upper Canada, and the Hamilton store had a few customers, taken over from the Toronto branch, to the eastward; but more than three-quarters of the firm's total business was done with the area west and northwest of Hamilton (see Figure 2, p 111), the focus of so much of the rapid agricultural settlement of the period. The partners had good customers there and excellent knowledge of the region; these, with Peter Buchanan's sources of credit in Britain, were essential to the strength of the firm's middleman position.

Although there were two or three general wholesale houses in Toronto,[46] the Buchanan firm was almost certainly larger and more complex. Few in Upper Canada commanded the capital and credit to operate several branches and multiple departments. The typical wholesaler was more specialized, dealing in only one of the three main lines of imports – or even, in some cases, in only specialized lines of dry goods. As the economy grew, most such firms could readily continue to employ their profits without broadening product lines or find opportunities outside trade into which capital might be diverted. The Buchanans had largely chosen to keep their capital in the business; they chose also to compete in trades that were normally separated into specialized lines. This posed some managerial problems, but despite the first-year loss in hardware, the business system that had been created was well able in an expanding economy to earn profits in all branches and all trades.

5

Independence 1846-51

During the 1840s and 1850s, Glasgow continued to enhance its dominance of Scottish industry and the Scottish domestic trade.[1] Yet although it remained Britain's fourth-ranked port, behind London, Liverpool, and Hull, it was failing to keep pace with Liverpool's growth and increasing command of the Atlantic trade. Large numbers of ships still sailed from the Clyde for world markets, carrying the cottons, linens, and iron that Scotland produced, but Liverpool by the 1840s was coming to dominate completely all the great Atlantic import trades, first cotton, then timber, then grain. Most of the Atlantic passenger traffic as well now flowed through Liverpool.[2] In some respects, Glasgow was becoming an outport of Liverpool.

The Scottish cotton industry was seriously affected by the deep depression that ended in 1842; efficient producers survived, particularly in higher quality trades, but the depression confirmed Lancashire's dominance of the industry as a whole. It now supplied the machinery, most of the techniques, and many semi-manufactured materials to the Scottish industry. There would be no more talk of Scotland's some day rivalling Lancashire, and the industry would not be a major contributor to further growth in Glasgow.[3] Liverpool's better developed hinterland gave it a growing lead over Glasgow, and Glasgow traders had reason to fear that, once clearly established, this lead would concentrate trade increasingly at Liverpool. Traders who remained in Glasgow found their position, if not actually weaker than it had been, at least potentially so. Accordingly, many Glasgow merchants, including Pollok, Gilmour and Company and the Dennistoun interests, had opened Liverpool branches. The Cunard Line, founded in Glasgow in 1839, based its operations mainly in Liverpool.[4] By 1850, a process of consolidation and amalgamation was beginning in Scottish banking, as the heroic age of Glasgow's banking enterprise began to give way to Edinburgh's more conservative banking philosophy.[5]

Yet it would be wrong to see the business atmosphere of Glasgow as at all gloomy. Banking consolidation, for example, may not have harmed Glasgow's growth, for extensions to the branch system must have enhanced the city's ability to draw on the resources of all Scotland – smaller centres may have been the real sufferers, if there were any. Moreover, the rapid rise of iron exports, notably to North America, had added a dynamic new trade to the city. Just as in the past, as one old trade levelled off or even declined, Glasgow enterprise had found new opportunities. The city, local strategists thought, grew by avoiding undue specialization. Continuing growth confirmed local optimism, as one 1850 pamphleteer suggests:

In the rapidity of its progress, perhaps no City has rivalled, far less surpassed, GLASGOW, the Commercial Metropolis of Scotland. This has chiefly arisen from this City being, if I may use the expression, *cosmopolitan* in its commerce and manufactures...

Glasgow also, in its commercial relations, trades with every quarter of the globe, and its merchants deal in the various products of every country. It hence appears that one branch of manufacture or trade may be dull while another may be prosperous; and, accordingly, Glasgow does not feel any of those universal depressions which so frequently occur in places limited to one or two branches of manufacture or commerce.[6]

Certainly, as the Buchanans' experience illustrates, a Glasgow firm with capital and initiative could continue to compete most successfully with English firms in overseas trades.

At Hamilton, the other key centre to the Buchanans, the business outlook of the 1840s and 1850s was, if anything, more positive than in Glasgow despite an undercurrent of competitive insecurity and urban rivalry. Hamilton's population doubled from 1841 to 1846 and again by 1851, when it passed 14,000. By 1858, Hamiltonians reckoned, it had doubled again, although the next official census, in 1861, would show only a 34 per cent increase since 1851.[7] In 1847, Hamilton was incorporated as Upper Canada's third city. There seemed, and not only to the editor of a directory writing in 1856, no reason not to extrapolate current developments into the indefinite future.

Hamilton, from its geographical position, its peculiar natural advantages, and through the indomitable energy and enterprise of its citizens, has, within the past few years, made rapid advances toward becoming the chief Commercial City in Canada...

Although, comparatively, the youngest of Canadian towns, it has outstripped many of the older and more favored places, and is now only second in importance to the capital of Canada [at the time, Toronto]. It is the principal wholesale mart of the Western Province; and if it progresses in the same ratio as in the past five years, it will soon leave in the distance even Toronto, and become what Nature has intended it to be, and what its enterprising citizens are determined to make it, the first of Canadian cities.[8]

By the 1850s, the western settlement on which the city's growth depended was pushing northward into Huron and Grey counties, while land clearing went on rapidly in already settled areas. Mixed farming was already developing in eastern areas of Upper Canada, and a variety of other products were produced for the market even in the west, but wheat continued very much the staple crop for most of the province. Upper Canadian farmers produced 3.2 million bushels of wheat in 1842, 12.7 million in 1851, and 24.6 million in 1861. While an increasing proportion of this wheat was sold in the United States, the ultimate source of demand and price was in fact the British market.[9] Upper Canadian prosperity was further stimulated by the rapid rise of sawn lumber exports to the United States in this period and, in the 1850s, by further major imports of British capital. A total of over $100,000,000 was imported, largely to build 2100 miles of railroad in a colony that previously had almost no railroads; close to two-thirds of this construction was in Upper Canada, much of it in the west.[10]

Hamilton and Toronto were battling with one another and with Montreal for control of the western trade. By the mid-1840s, Hamilton had secured a nearby hinterland and relatively good road connections to the west and northwest. It then placed its hope for continued competitiveness and/or wider dominance in the Great Western Railroad, nominally begun in 1847, actually begun in 1850, and completed early in 1854 from Niagara Falls to Hamilton to London to Windsor. The Great Western was the first major Upper Canadian line to be completed, and its links to the New York Central-Michigan Central systems guaranteed it much through traffic, especially passengers. The city of Hamilton subscribed for $200,000 in Great Western stock in 1850 and by 1860 had borrowed $900,000 to promote railroad development.[11] Down to at least the mid-1850s, the strategy appeared to be working. Thus, the value of imports entered at the city's customs house increased from $941,000 in 1848 to $2,026,000 in 1851, $5,106,000 in 1854, and $5,400,000 in 1856 (Table 10, p 177).

The Buchanans had introduced large-scale wholesaling to Hamilton in 1840. In 1845, the town had only ten businesses that claimed to import dry goods and/or groceries at wholesale and five that imported hardware; there were about 63 retail stores; and the professions were represented by nine doctors and sixteen lawyers.[12] By 1856, the city's business community had grown considerably: Hamilton had 8 general wholesale firms, 6 specifically dry goods wholesalers, 4 specifically hardware wholesalers, at least 17 commission merchants, and 31 retailers in dry goods alone.[13] None of these firms rivalled the Buchanans' in scale, and few can have paralleled their business structure. The Gore Bank was Upper Canada's smallest chartered bank, but Hamilton was also served by branches of four other major banks.

Toronto at this time had more merchants in most of these categories and continued to handle more trade.[14] But the gap did not seem unbridgeable, now that the Great Western was open, especially as Hamilton's rate of population growth appeared still to be exceeding Toronto's. Montreal of course remained Canada's trading capital, with a much larger and more specialized trading community,[15] and it hoped that the completion of the Grand Trunk Railway to Toronto in 1856 would permit it to begin to gain or regain some of the trade that Toronto and Hamilton had gathered in the 1850s.

These developments were important in creating the setting in which the Buchanans operated in the next decade. By 1851, the business would reach the position of financial independence that Peter Buchanan had always desired and would itself open a Liverpool branch. Yet this was far from foreseeable early in 1846, when the announcement of repeal of the Corn Laws put the whole future of Anglo-Canadian trade in doubt.[16]

Peter Buchanan's immediate response to the news of repeal was to seek meetings with various influential business and political figures in London to press the case for some continued preferential treatment for Canada. On receipt of the news, Isaac, still in New York, departed for England, leaving James McIntyre as manager of the New York office.[17] He loosed a furious barrage of letters and newspaper extras defending protection and a colonial preference, arguing his case for paper currency, praising Lord George Bentinck, and denouncing all who disagreed. He predicted that repeal would lead, after a 'fiery ordeal,' to annexation of Canada to the United States. He therefore proposed to liquidate the business and gave notice of intent to dissolve the partnership.

I have now however after mature deliberation to give you and my other partners notice that if the Imperial parliament departs from *the principle* of *protection* (or of an import duty on corn for Revenue which shall have the effect of a protection to Colonial Industry) our Establishments at Montreal and Hamilton c.w. shall be broken up as far at least as my Interest is concerned at the termination of our present partnership on 31st March 1848, and that I shall use my influence to have as little business done in the interval as possible.[18]

Isaac's emotional response brought him swiftly into argument with his brother. Peter shared, in part, Isaac's fears and his conservative outlook on questions of empire, but he saw no value at all in Isaac's kind of lobby and protested especially at Isaac's frequent references to their own business; this could only create an impression among their creditors that the business was in serious difficulty. He wrote often and bluntly, if with little evident effect, to his brother.

Your violent & offensive language has already injured our cause and has led almost everyone to treat your opinions with little or no weight...

You are too blinded by prejudice to take a cool and dispassionate view of matters...

For gods sake keep cool & quiet...

Do not let it be said that your inconsiderate conduct has been the ruin of yourself & partners.[19]

In London throughout the spring on Great Western business, Peter sought to counteract the impressions Isaac left; it did not take long either for him to realize that repeal could not be defeated and that the business would have to adjust to the new circumstances. His thinking was much influenced by the bankers and financiers with whom he was now in contact and by news from his partners in Canada; he began to see new opportunities opening up.

Whatever the tariff arrangements might be, trends in the British economy remained major determinants in Canadian prosperity. Many British indicators in 1846 pointed to declines from 1845 levels, as an industrial depression began to develop: the textile industry was in difficulty, the iron industry was moving into a position of over-production and falling prices, and the end of the railway share boom of 1845 left many uncertain of general economic prospects. Yet the factor that most contributed to the sense of insecurity in British business circles by the summer of 1846 was the news of deepening famine in Ireland and a poor crop at home. This developing tragedy in fact compensated for any sense of depression in wheat-growing areas of the world. By early autumn, British wheat prices, which had fallen earlier in the year from late 1845's high levels, were rising steeply, and at the beginning of 1847 they stood at double the average for 1846; British wheat imports in 1846 were triple those of 1845.[20] Wheat was 4/6 per bushel at Montreal at the end of August 1846; by June 1847 it would be 8/6.[21]

Thus, while 1846 has been seen as a depressed year in Canada, this view is probably incorrect as far as Upper Canada was concerned.[22] Those who had long sought to develop the St Lawrence as a protected channel for American produce bound for the British market found their dreams shattered in 1846, but not all Canadians shared these dreams. Certainly the timber trade, suffering from over-production in 1845 and the beginning of the abandonment of the British timber preference, was depressed, and this would have had its effects throughout the Canadian economy, but the buoyant grain trade outweighed these in western Upper Canada at least.

The Buchanans, sharing the widespread insecurity, cut back their dry goods shipments and sales in 1846 (Tables 1 and 2, pp 162-4), but they continued to expand their grain trade. As the volume of grain handled through Montreal rose, excellent profits could be made there by those able to engage in the trade on a commission basis. The sum carried from 'commission account' to profit and loss at Montreal more than doubled from 1845 to 1846, largely as the result of increased grain commissions.[23] The Montreal firm increased its profits in the twelve months ending 31 March 1847 by eighty per cent over the previous year, and as a result the firm declared a profit of £11,500cy, the highest figure yet at Montreal and Hamilton in a twelve-month period (Table 4, p 168). This represented a ten per cent return on partners' capital.

Early in 1847, Peter Buchanan, J. and A. Dennistoun, and another Glasgow firm, D. and A. Denny and Company, set up two joint accounts to facilitate major produce speculations they were planning. William Baird of the Denny firm was one of the Gartsherrie family and a personal friend of Peter Buchanan; he had sent frequent grain orders to Isaac Buchanan and Company in the past two or three years. Peter Buchanan and Company had previously operated smaller joint accounts with the Denny firm and, of course, with A. Dennistoun and Company of Liverpool. Now the three Glasgow firms combined in the 'DBD Account,' while the Denny and Buchanan firms set up the 'DB Account.' Further confusing the matter in the Buchanans' books, the Denny firm continued to send some ordinary buying commissions to Montreal.

These accounts and several much smaller ones that Peter engaged in were to buy wheat, flour, and Indian corn in New York and Montreal for shipment in spring and summer to Britain. Purchases were financed partly by drawing bills on the British firms involved, but substantial sums were also sent in gold and pig iron. For example, in early April 1847, £40,000 in gold sovereigns were despatched to New York. In New York, Buchanan, Harris and Company bought the grain and arranged shipping. Dennistoun, Wood and Company handled banking and insurance for DBD transactions, the two firms dividing a buying commission of 2½ per cent. In Montreal, Isaac Buchanan and Company performed all services and collected the full commission. Sales in Glasgow were primarily the responsibility of D. and A. Denny, while sales elsewhere in Britain were made by the Dennistouns. No selling commission was charged and profits and losses were divided equally between the participating firms. Involvement in these accounts carried Peter Buchanan and his firms into an entirely different scale of grain operations.

The extraordinary rise in grain prices and imports severely strained the British financial system. Gold drained from the country at an alarming rate. Interest rates soared. In May and June 1847, grain prices reached their highest levels since 1817. But world wheat supplies proved surprisingly abundant, a rush to sell began, and prices collapsed. In August, a number of grain importers failed. Among them was D. and A. Denny and Company.[24]

Rumour in Glasgow put the loss of Peter Buchanan and the Dennistouns from the Denny failure at £100,000 each. Peter contradicted this, downplaying his losses and claiming that he was quite secure despite the amount of grain he still had at sea; this, he said, had been purchased so cheaply that no losses would be incurred, but in fact, he now faced serious financial problems. As bills that D. and A. Denny were to have paid fell due, he or in some cases Dennistouns had to pay them, then claim reimbursement from the Denny estate. He anticipated having to meet £36,000stg of such paper, and this disrupted his financial planning, especially when redrawing against consignments became impossible as all firms sought safety in a time of mounting credit stringency. All bills and charges had to be paid before those who held his grain would release it. This imposed further immediate costs, and every delay was expensive in a time of falling prices. Delay also increased the risk of spoilage, especially as McIntyre had bought some bad flour.

At times Peter Buchanan had to turn for extra support to his bank, now part of the Union Bank of Scotland but still dominated by the Dennistouns. He could scarcely bargain on an equal footing with J. and A. Dennistoun over payments on their joint Denny liabilities or commissions to be charged on certain transactions. Peter finally estimated his losses from his major grain speculations at about £10,000. This was a very substantial, but not ruinous, figure.

By October, however, the British financial crisis that had begun in August had become acute, as all firms rushed for liquidity. Even without the grain trade complications, Peter's payments were, as always, heaviest in the fall, when suppliers' bills against shipments fell due; in November 1847, his total obligations were £20,0000 and in December, £38,000. If he could survive these months, his total obligations in January and February were only £5700. But all his creditors were pressing him to reduce his obligations to them or on paper endorsed by them. Anxious to preserve his reputation, he agreed to all such requests and asked no one to renew bills that were falling due. To his longer-term backers, including J.G. Watson and Seton Laing, whose firm was now known as Laing and Bruxner, he pleaded the Denny problems as a reason to delay requested reductions by some months; Laing agreed only after checking with Glyns for a credit reference and being given the deed to the firm's Hamilton property as further security.

As he looked ahead to November, Peter realized that his situation was perilous. Accordingly, Isaac Buchanan hastily left Glasgow for New York early in October. From there he pressed the Montreal and Hamilton houses to discount all available paper, to postpone all possible local payments, and to buy all possible exchange for remittances. In New York, relying on the firm's reputation as a major grain dealer, he drew bills of exchange on Peter Buchanan and Company up to a total of £10,000 to £15,000, sold these for cash, and bought sterling exchange for remittances. This was pure accommodation paper; issued in relatively modest amounts, it was a normal business device, but its use on such a scale reflects the seriousness of the firm's situation. The Canadian partners complained that Isaac was disrupting their financial plans, but they did not know the tightness of Peter's position.

As a result of Isaac's exertions, ample cash reached Glasgow in November and December, and the pressure at last began to ease in the money market. Now the Canadian houses came under pressure as their heavy discounts and local payments fell due and many customers failed to meet their obligations. The partners pushed collections hard, but as other houses were also doing so, collections proved difficult. In fact it had been a year of substantial Canadian grain exports, despite the fall in prices after June, but as so often in the last phases of a boom, customers had been caught themselves speculating in grain or land and could not now meet normal obligations. Peter Buchanan complained in March that he had received no remittances since January, while the exchange Isaac had drawn now had to be met. Only in April did the pressure finally ease on both sides of the Atlantic. It would take until 1849 before the firm freed itself entirely from dependence on accommodation paper drawn from New York.

The firm's Hamilton sales in 1847 had declined slightly from the level of 1846, Hamilton's grocery department recording its lowest sales since the first year of its operation (Table 1, p 162). The Canadian partners, who had had almost no say in planning the great produce deals of the year, adamantly refused to share any of the loss, despite Peter's argument that the New York office, in which all were partners, had been a party to the contract. As a result, Peter Buchanan and Company declared an overall loss for the year of

£11,450stg (Table 4, p 168). By contrast, Montreal showed a record profit of £17,000cy, even after losing £4000 on its own-account grain dealings in 1847. It had been an excellent year for any Montreal business that chose and was able to engage in the produce trade on a commission basis, for volume had been high, as had average prices. Although results for the Hamilton business, including the commissions earned in the New York grain trade, do not survive, it is clear that the business as a whole survived a very difficult year with some profit at least. If profits were not finally very large in terms of volume of grain handled and risks run, the firm had at least become an important one in the trans-Atlantic grain trade. Had the Denny failure not cost Peter Buchanan quite so dearly, he might well have moved permanently into the trade on a large scale and in the process added an important Anglo-American trade to the business's operations. After his narrow escape, however, he would once more give highest priority to reducing dependence on outside sources of credit and running fewer risks.

As 1848 began, the future of the business was made more uncertain by the continuing failure of partners to agree on arrangements to replace the present partnership, which expired in March.[25] It had always been assumed that eventually Peter Buchanan would retire, handing over control in Glasgow to Isaac, but now it was Isaac who wanted to withdraw, as he had said he would in 1846. He still had not decided whether to retire from trade altogether or to try to take over the New York office of the business together with the account of the firm's largest customer, Hope, Birrell and Company of London, and put his theories of Canada's trading future to the test. Despite frequent arguments between Peter and Isaac and the awkwardness of not knowing the overall business future until Isaac's was settled, Peter proved very solicitous of his brother and would not force a decision on him until 1848.

Peter increasingly sensed that it would never be easy to wind up the business. In the straitened financial circumstances of early 1848, however, a wind-up would cost the business especially dearly in lost collections. Thus, when he and Harris finally met to discuss the new partnership in February, they were agreed on the importance of continuing the business. On the assumption that he would retire, Isaac was offered the firm's Montreal property at a value of £7750cy, the firm agreeing to lease it from him for £800 per year. The remainder of his capital would be transferred to Glasgow's books so that Peter and Isaac could settle the mode of its payment privately. Peter and Harris agreed to continue the business in Canada; they would each take twenty-four per cent of its profits, Young and Law would each have nineteen per cent, and Robert Leckie, Law's assistant in Montreal, would have eight per cent. Law's rise reflected his outstanding success in managing the Montreal business; Leckie, who had clerked in the Glasgow office before going to Montreal, was the son of a friend of Peter and Isaac's father and was a protégé of Peter Buchanan.[26] Peter, who had come to realize the growing necessity to bring younger men along, hoped someday to see Leckie become manager at Glasgow. He wanted to advance Leckie's interest at once, despite Leckie's inexperience, because his own power in the business was unlikely ever to be greater. To facilitate his admission, Peter would lend Leckie £3000 to give his account some weight. Six per cent of profits were assigned to a suspense account in Peter and Harris's names, apparently still somehow on Douglas's account. James McIntyre, who had been promised a partnership by Young and Isaac, was instead guaranteed employment in the firm at £500 per year. Harris would transfer capital from Glasgow's books to Hamilton's to make his account there up to £15,000cy, to compensate for the loss of Isaac's capital.

The contentious clauses in the new agreement were those designed to protect Peter Buchanan's capital. He insisted that suspense accounts be built up to a total of £40,000, and the entire balance owed by the Canadian houses to Peter Buchanan and Company was to be paid before any capital was divided from the Canadian business. Peter proposed to limit the obligations at any one time of the Canadian houses to Glasgow, and this ceiling was to diminish over the four years of the agreement. Instead of charging five per cent commission on shipments and five per cent interest on the annual balances due, Peter proposed to charge ten per cent on all due balances, as a spur to prompt payment by the Canadian houses. Thus, he was determined to reverse the build-up of the Canadian houses' obligations to his firm and the firm's overall reliance on borrowed capital in Britain.

Peter now sought Isaac's assent to the terms while Harris sought that of Young and Law. Isaac at once protested, though on no specific grounds, contending that Peter had ignored, misunderstood, and mistreated him. As the younger brother, he had always been subject to his brother's authority to some degree, and Peter had certainly not become less authoritarian as he grew older. Isaac's resentments overflowed in a series of vituperative letters expressing his intention to make his way in the world independently. Peter simply refused to discuss the matter and finally forced Isaac to accept the agreement. Only the disposition of Isaac's capital, which Peter had secured payment of in full, was left open.

Young and Law protested with but little less vehemence. The ten per cent charge, they said, would work much like the existing arrangement in good times, but could wipe out Canadian partners' capital in one bad year. They saw no need for another partner, and Young was especially bitter at Leckie's rise and McIntyre's exclusion. When it became clear that the two were adamant, Peter decided to go to Canada to negotiate in person. There, to avoid a wind-up, he was forced to agree to restore the old commission system on shipments, though the firm's standard interest charge on capital sums, overdue debts, and the like was now to be six per cent, and to postpone Leckie's admission as a partner by a year. The new four-year partnership agreement was at last signed in July 1848.

In view of his treatment, McIntyre quit the business. To manage the New York operation, the partners selected Frederick Lane, a clerk in the office there. Lane, the son of a London friend of Peter Buchanan, had begun work in Glasgow, then been posted to Montreal, and finally been moved to New York by Isaac. Although he was not thought entirely qualified, there seemed no one else available, and it was hoped that he would grow into the job. This proved, however, to be the end of expansion in New York, for Lane was no James Law and New York, of course, was not Montreal. Lane lacked the drive, willingness to take responsibilities, and '*edge*' that had led Law to build Montreal from a subordinate office into a major contributor to the business's strength.[27]

Isaac returned to Glasgow early in May. His house in Hamilton was sold to Harris in June. He finally agreed to take the Montreal property and to leave his remaining capital in the firm at five per cent interest until he had found a use for it. At the moment his plans were to live relatively quietly, though he would continue his campaign against free trade. After fourteen years of joint business association, the alliance of the two brothers had been formally broken. Yet their interests remained closely linked; Isaac's capital was in the business, and as he would reside near Glasgow, first in Edinburgh and then in Greenock, Peter would at times ask him to deputize in the office.

These partnership negotiations were conducted against the backdrop of gloomy business conditions in Canada and Britain. Though the British financial crisis passed away relatively quickly in 1848, the industrial depression that had preceded it was slower to lift. It was not until 1849 that all British indicators pointed to a revival; the expansion begun then continued, apart from a moderate downswing in 1851, until late 1853.[28]

The Canadian business outlook continued very uncertain. There were first of all the long-term commercial and political uncertainties that preoccupied the Montreal and Quebec business élites, and Isaac Buchanan, and that would lead in 1849 to the Annexation Manifesto. Economic indicators likewise pointed downward. Imports to the St Lawrence fell from £3.1 million cy in 1846 to £2.9 million in 1847 and just £2.1 million in 1848 (comparable figures for imports paying *ad valorem* duties were £2.2 million stg, £1.8 million, and £1.2 million); levels in 1849 were about the same as in 1848. Grain exports from the St Lawrence reached a peak in 1847 of 3.9 million bushels (flour converted to its equivalent in wheat), fell by almost 45 per cent to 2.2 million in 1848, then recovered to reach 3.6 million in 1849. Prices, however, tended steadily downward over the period; the average price of a bushel of wheat in Montreal in 1847 was 6/6, in 1848, 5/7, and in 1849, 4/6, and prices in early summer of 1847 had been as high as 8/6. Note circulation of the Canadian banks reached a peak in October 1847 but then fell in the next eight months to the lowest level since August 1844. Thus, 1848 was a year of real depression in Canada.[29]

Yet having survived the financial crisis, the partners had some reason to anticipate that they could profit in such circumstances.[30] Many of their smaller competitors had had their British credits cut off, and competition for such trade as there was should therefore be substantially reduced. After the unsatisfactory outcome of his daring produce ventures of 1847, Peter Buchanan again stressed consolidation, and he no longer had to contend with his brother's differing views. When his strategy began to work, as it had in 1838, he made converts of his partners. The business would borrow less, place stronger emphasis on collections than on sales, set a higher standard for customers, and set prices as high as could safely be managed in terms of the customers chosen for continued support. It would reduce the supply account system, so as to secure the best price on each type of goods, though strong customers would continue to secure the most favourable terms. There was no point in running excessive risks or seeking excessive sales.

It is totally impossible that any one house importer or manufacturer can monopolize beyond a certain share of the Canada trade. The old established houses will not permit it and they have advantages wh [sic] do far more than counterbalance a few per cents of difference in price.[31]

Produce business was now, where possible, to be done on commission.[32]

Throughout 1848, the partners complained at the dullness of trade. Sales at Hamilton in a nine-month period that included the peak sales months of May, June, September, and October were just £88,000, less than half the volume of the peak year of 1845. Profits on this were about £8000, or slightly less than ten per cent (Tables 1 and 4, pp 162, 168). The Montreal house earned £7000 net, and Peter Buchanan expressed particular delight at its success in the commission grain trade, from which at least half this profit was realized. It handled over 66,000 barrels of Upper Canadian flour itself, and another 12,000 on Montreal advance were delivered to Oswego late in the year. As total flour exports by sea from the St Lawrence were 384,000 barrels in 1848, it is clear that Law had been able to retain a significant place in the market, if a smaller one than in 1847. Thus the partners had every reason to be satisfied with their year's results and to plan to continue their strategy in 1849.

In Upper Canada, recovery from the depression was well under way by mid-1849, and 1850 was a very prosperous year; 1851, if anything, brought a setback, as Upper Canadian grain prices reached their lowest levels in over fifteen years. The basis for Upper Canadian prosperity was ultimately the British wheat market; and Britain now drew at least one-quarter of her annual needs from imports. Although prices declined steadily from 1848 to 1851, it was probably more important to the Upper Canadian farmer that he had a guaranteed wheat market at prices that evidently left him normally with some margin of profit over basic costs of production. Upper Canada produced a record wheat crop in 1849 and abundant crops in 1850 and 1851. By 1850, moreover, the Canadian timber industry was reviving as American demand mounted for Canadian lumber and British demand was renewed at a relatively high level despite diminishing tariff preferences.[33]

The trends outlined here are reflected in the figures for imports handled by Canadian ports. From 1849 to 1850 there was a great increase at Hamilton, Toronto, and Montreal; there was a further large increase at Montreal and Hamilton in 1851; and, reflecting overstocks, there was a decline or a pause in the rate of increase at all ports in 1852 (Table 10, p 177). Hamilton and Toronto in these years began to narrow the gap between themselves and Montreal (Table 12, p 179). In part this was the result of rising Canadian-American trade, but for manufactured goods this was in fact still largely a transit trade in British products. The Buchanans were well placed to use whichever trade route between Britain and Upper Canada was most economic at any moment, though such evidence as survives suggests that they continued to rely mainly on the St Lawrence.

The business continued its cautious policy in 1849, sales at Hamilton in groceries and dry goods amounting to just half of what they had been in 1845. In 1850 and 1851, sales were higher, but not strikingly so (Table 1, p 162). Law handled over 58,000 barrels of flour at Montreal in 1849, shipping most of the grain he received to Britain to avoid further depressing the local market; the partners were elated at Montreal's 1849 results, though no actual figure survives. They realized that their connections in Britain and

Upper Canada protected them from some of the business pressures that had made it so gloomy a year in the Montreal commercial world. Law's volume of produce and his profits declined further in 1850 and 1851, in part as a result of rising competition from the American market, but also because the business was unwilling to pursue consignments actively as rates of commission dropped back from 1848 levels, four to five per cent, to a level like 1845's 1½ per cent without an advance and 2½ per cent with one. At such rates, it was not worth seeking consignments more actively.

This was all the more the case in that Hamilton's profits and collections were proving very satisfactory. Margins of 10⅔ per cent on dry goods, 8 per cent on hardware, and 6½ per cent on groceries yielded net profits there in 1849 of almost ten per cent on sales; profits in 1850 were higher still, over eleven per cent (Table 4, p 168). Early in 1851, Peter Buchanan described his best dry goods selling price as sterling cost plus 75 per cent; six years earlier the comparable mark-up was under 55 per cent.[34] Lower prices in Britain in relation to other costs and higher duties in Canada help to account for this shift, but not all the increase in mark-ups was accounted for by these factors. In 1849, for example, Peter calculated that a mark-up of about 50 per cent covered the costs of dry goods laid down in Hamilton. Rates of profit had risen markedly for importers since 1845.

The success of the years 1848 to 1850 can be indicated by the growth in partners' capital (Table 5, p 170). In March 1848, the four remaining partners' Canadian accounts had totalled £42,700 and a further £35,800 was at the credit of bad debt and suspense accounts; at 31 December 1850, the five partners' Canadian accounts totalled £94,300, and £35,000 remained at the credit of bad debt and suspense accounts. The sum at Harris's credit had almost doubled, Peter Buchanan's and Young's accounts had more than doubled, and Law's had almost trebled. Leckie now had some capital of his own. In three years of operations in what has often been seen in Canada as an era of depression, the partners had gained over £50,000.*

Indeed Peter Buchanan had achieved a position of almost embarrassing liquidity by late 1850. Collections had considerably exceeded sales in Canada (Table 3, p 166), and this had enabled the balances owed to Peter Buchanan and Company to be much reduced. Remittances by late 1850 were being

---

* Capital in Britain probably was lower at the end of 1850 than it had been in 1846, however, most of the loss having come in 1847. Harris's capital transferred to Canada in 1848 matched or outweighed Isaac's transferred to Britain, and Isaac was drawing on his Glasgow capital after 1848. Capital in the Glasgow books at the end of 1850 was likely in the order of £57,000 to £62,000stg, or £71,000 to £78,000cy. If so, the profits in 1850 were about 12 per cent on partners' capital, plus 6 per cent interest.

applied entirely to that year's shipments, something that had not been the case since 1839.[35] Peter Buchanan planned to pay cash for all spring purchases in 1851, and he even spoke of investing £20,000 in a sleeping partnership in Seton Laing's London business. Isaac's predictions had proven entirely wrong, as Peter did not hesitate to point out. The business had never been in a better position than late in 1850. As Harris described it:

All the features of the business improved slow and unsatisfactory accounts wound or winding up, heavy slow balances in most cases reduced and a sufficiency of new active business created to keep up the profits ...[36]

In these conditions, Peter Buchanan began to consider the future of the business, feeling able to make new strategic changes. Like Harris, who had been elected president of the Great Western Railroad in 1849, he was now more deeply involved than ever in the railroad, as he sought to raise funds for it in Britain.[37] Peter was becoming a figure of at least some consequence in the Glasgow business community. In 1849 he was elected to directorships of the Buchanan Society and of the Merchants House, which no longer had much political importance but was, in 1851, 'still regarded by the best class of our citizens as one in which it is an honourable duty to enrol themselves.'[38] He had bought a house for £2500 in a comfortably fashionable section of Glasgow's west end in 1847 and begun to collect paintings. Relying on his confidential clerk, William Leitch, and on Isaac, to manage the office, he began to take regular holidays, in the country and on the continent. Increasingly plagued by arthritis, he now wished to withdraw and enjoy some of his capital. He knew that the Canadian partners hoped to secure a share in the Glasgow business, not only for reasons of profit but also for the recognition of equality with him that this would imply. In view of his much larger capital, however, he had no intention of surrendering control of Peter Buchanan and Company.[39]

Instead he proposed to found a branch in Liverpool, in which all could be partners. He and Isaac had regretted the business opportunities they could not pursue without such a branch, but they had until recently required the financial backing of their Liverpool agents and Peter had not wanted to divide authority in Britain. A Liverpool branch could buy the firm's goods in England, handle shipping and insurance on these, sell produce consigned from North America, and seek a larger place in the booming Liverpool-New York trade. Peter Buchanan and Company, which would lose many of its roles, would initially lend capital to the Liverpool branch. If all went well, the loan would gradually be repaid and Peter could withdraw from the business, leaving it strongly based in Liverpool.

It was a good plan, but it began to be complicated by its interconnection with another issue, that of Isaac Buchanan's future. Isaac had been energetically, if futilely, campaigning against free trade since 1848; he had, for example, sponsored an essay contest, with prizes totalling £200, for working men on 'their own interests,' particularly the evils of free trade.[40] His activities had been costly, his expenditures averaging about £3000stg per year. Thus, although he still possessed the Montreal property, and earned £800cy per year from it, his other capital, which had amounted in 1848 to £16,880stg, had by the end of 1850 been reduced to £12,200.[41] Rather than reduce expenses accordingly, he planned to return to business. Undoubtedly he resented the almost paternal interest that Peter took in his welfare, and he therefore spoke of establishing his own firm. But his prospects would be surer if he returned to his old business.

Peter disclosed Isaac's interest to Harris in the summer of 1850. Harris agreed that this might be done by setting up an office headed by Isaac in Liverpool, but Young and Law, on hearing the idea a few weeks later, refused absolutely to accept any subordination, real or apparent, to Isaac. Isaac decided to go to North America to meet Young and Law and to investigate other business possibilities that he might take up instead. By the time he returned, in November, he had decided to found his own Liverpool grain and cotton firm while awaiting the outcome of his and his ex-partners' deliberations. Peter Buchanan, to avoid a split, now hastened to Liverpool and opened an office. He installed a young clerk, William Muir, in nominal charge, but Isaac, who was given a room for his independent operations, would in practice be the manager. In this hurried fashion, though with a clear plan in mind, the business joined those Glasgow firms that considered a Liverpool branch essential to their business future.

Peter and his partners agreed that their business relationship had never been more harmonious than since Isaac had withdrawn. Nevertheless, Peter was persuaded that Isaac had changed or would change as a result of his errors and financial reverses since 1846; Isaac, he said, now saw the necessity to confine his activity to business and his expenditures to a minimum. Indeed, Isaac's capital now did not equal Harris's or Young's, an embarrassing circumstance that Peter offered to ease quietly by lending Isaac enough to make his account up to £25,000cy. Did Peter really believe his arguments? It is hard to know, but in any case he felt responsible for the well-being of Isaac and his family. Certainly he doubted Isaac's capacity to manage a business alone. Seeking a basis for continuance of the business, Peter wrote often to his Canadian partners and argued, at times heatedly, with Isaac. He stipulated only that the new business include a Liverpool office and a place for Isaac; when negotiations proved difficult, he armed himself with power to act for Isaac and hurried to Canada in March 1851.

There he found Young and Law still firmly allied. Harris, although no blind supporter of Isaac, would remain loyal to the Buchanans in the event of a split; he sought to mediate between the two camps, and after a week's hard bargaining a new partnership agreement was reached.[42] Isaac would rejoin the business, but in Hamilton, while Harris took over in Liverpool. All five senior partners would receive 18.8 per cent of profits, the other 6 per cent going to Leckie. David Law, James's brother and now the firm's main dry goods buyer, would receive 10 per cent of the profits of the dry goods department, and a similar arrangement was to be made for Lane in New York. The new firm's capital would be £120,000cy in Canada and £40,000stg in Liverpool, the latter provided initially by Peter Buchanan and Company as a loan. Peter Buchanan would be the only partner in the Glasgow firm, though Harris could take an interest in it. Isaac was specifically refused this option. Two other clauses were aimed at Isaac; a partner was required to obtain leave in writing from other partners before 'undertaking any public business,' and a partner infringing the contract could be expelled by any three partners. Any two partners could dissolve the firm on twelve months notice. The firm was renamed in all locations:

Liverpool: Buchanan, Harris and Company;
Hamilton: Buchanan, Young and Company;
Montreal: Harris, Law and Company;
New York: Isaac Buchanan and Company.

This was a harsh agreement for Isaac, but, Peter argued, it offered him the chance to earn his way back into others' confidence. Although legally bound by the agreement, Isaac threatened to break it up; he was most deeply humiliated and angered by his exclusion from the firm name at Montreal and from Peter Buchanan and Company. His honour and reputation as a businessman were, he felt, at stake. He was being treated as a junior partner. Finally, however, he yielded to Peter's insistent pressure and suggestion that he try himself to renegotiate the more offensive clauses of the agreement. In July 1851, Isaac and his family returned to Canada.

There he persuaded Young and Law to agree that he too might be a partner in Glasgow, if Peter agreed, but he was forced to concede, in a separate letter, that if Glasgow remained the real centre of the business in four years, all partners would have a share there. Peter Buchanan, on learning of this guarantee, repudiated it absolutely, but he accepted the revised contract in other respects; with this, the contract that would carry on the business for four years from January 1852 was finally completed.[43]

While in Canada in 1851, Peter Buchanan had laid the basis for another major strategic departure. He and Adam Hope agreed to establish a wholesale dry goods, grocery, and hardware business in London, Upper Canada, to be known as Adam Hope and Company. Hope had come to Canada in 1834, at the age of 21. He had worked for John Young, then, with Young's backing, had with Thomas Hodge opened his own retail general store in St Thomas, a thriving village half-way between London and Lake Erie. There he prospered moderately and earned the Buchanans' respect in turn.[44] In 1845, when Angus and Birrell of London, the Buchanans' largest customer outside Toronto and Hamilton, had broken up, the Buchanans had been involved in the arrangement to have it continued by John Birrell and Adam Hope.[45] Hope, Birrell and Company planned to build a modest wholesale trade, but were held largely to retail business by the Buchanans. Even so, their account on several occasions exceeded £20,000 and became the largest on the business's books. It was London's largest business, and Hope and Birrell became leading figures in the small local business community. Settlement was proceeding rapidly to the west and north of London, and by 1851 it was Upper Canada's fifth largest urban centre and gaining rapidly on Bytown and Kingston. The town looked forward to even greater growth once the Great Western Railroad was completed.[46]

Several factors were probably involved in the proposal to back Hope in a wholesale business. Just as the Buchanans had moved into Toronto and Hamilton, they were moving into a centre that was beginning to develop a wholesale trade and occupying the market strongly before rivals did so. As in Hamilton, they were allying their interests to the strongest and most reliable of the local merchants. Moreover, Hope's account was so large that a partnership was perhaps the most secure way to protect and profit from the Buchanans' real stake in the business. Peter Buchanan commented that the new business would prove valuable besides in training young men whom the Buchanans wished to bring along. Hope had a capital of £4000 to invest in the new business, and the Hamilton firm, in the name of R.W. Harris, contributed £16,000, or approximately what was owed the business by Hope, Birrell and Company. Hope was to receive 30 per cent of the profits and R.W. Harris, on behalf of Buchanan, Harris and Company of Liverpool, would receive 70 per cent. Goods from Britain would be supplied for a commission of 5 per cent; goods from New York and Montreal by the Buchanans' houses there for 2½ per cent. Hope's retail hardware business would be retained, both wholesale and retail departments to be managed by Hope's brother Charles. Retail groceries would be taken over as a separate but closely connected business by Walter Simson, Hope's grocery manager. John Birrell was to carry on the retail dry goods business on special terms from the Buchanans. Although the Buchanans' interest in the business was not made public until 1854, it took effect in January 1852.[47]

Thus at the end of 1851, the business was using its financial strength and independence to develop two new branches. The year brought some increase in sales at Hamilton, but market overstocks brought pressure on advances and a reduced rate of profit. James Law called it 'a middling year' in Montreal,[48] and the partners were satisfied that they had done well in a poor year. The year ended, however, with tension still high in the business, as a result of the bitterness surrounding Isaac's readmission. The two Buchanans on the one hand and Young and Law on the other were already preparing for a possible complete split of their business interests.

6
The firm splits 1852-6

During the next five years, from 1852 to 1856, unprecedentedly favourable circumstances produced Canada's greatest boom of the nineteenth century.[1] The business's trade, profits, and capital grew enormously; by the end of 1856, partners' capital accounts totalled £369,000cy, Peter Buchanan's alone amounting to £194,000 (Table 5, p 170). It was a time of extraordinary business opportunity, if also a time of increasing competition, as existing firms grew rapidly and new firms rushed to enter both existing lines of trade and new, or more specialized, ones that began to open up. As in the past, however, an era of great expansion had its perils for the Buchanans, as was apparent by the end of 1856.

The British economy, after a slackening in late 1851, resumed its full-scale expansion by summer of 1852, and this trend continued through 1853.[2] Poor harvests in 1852 and 1853 pushed British wheat imports and prices sharply upward. British demand for Canadian timber remained strong, while Canadian lumber exports to the United States mounted rapidly. Canada's provincial and municipal governments needed little encouragement to seek to borrow to encourage development; when Canadian governments and railway companies at last succeeded in selling bonds and shares in London in 1852, this inaugurated five years of immense capital importation, as Canadian railroads moved from projections to realities. Land values, prices, and wages all rose remarkably; for example, Michell's index of the wholesale prices of fifteen foodstuffs at Toronto virtually doubled in the four years from 1851 to 1855.[3]

Many indicators in the British economy reached peaks in 1853 or early 1854. The Crimean War affected trends variously in the next two years, but for most indicators upward trends resumed by 1855 to continue into 1856 or 1857. Such trends alone can, of course, be misleading from the point of view of individual firms; indeed, many in Britain's cotton industry considered the entire period from 1854 to 1857 one of depression, at least in profits.[4] For Upper Canada, the most important new factor in Britain in these years was that the war cut off wheat supplies from Russia. The result was still higher wheat prices in Britain and North America in 1854 and 1855. Wheat was 6/2 per bushel at Toronto in January 1854 and reached 8/8 in May; it held steady for almost a year, then rose sharply to a nineteenth-century peak of 11/3 ($2.25) per bushel in April, May, and June 1855; by early 1856, it had fallen to five shillings, but a strong recovery followed, and wheat remained around seven shillings throughout 1856. Although wheat crops failed in many areas east of Toronto, agriculture was in these years extremely prosperous in the west.[5]

These overall trends are also indicated by import figures for Canadian ports. Reflecting overstocks in 1851, imports did not rise greatly in 1852, but 1853 brought large increases: 50 per cent at Hamilton and Montreal and 82 per cent at Toronto. British textile imports to Toronto were up by 150 per cent and to Hamilton by 67 per cent. Even so, imports were higher still in 1854 as the boom continued to gather momentum. There was a pause or decline in 1855, as a result of excessive imports in 1854, but a new upward leap followed in 1856, when Montreal, Hamilton, and Toronto all had record high levels of imports. Montreal's 1856 imports were almost twice those of 1851, while Toronto's and Hamilton's were over two and a half times higher (Tables 10, 11, and 12; pp 177-9).

The Buchanans' sales in general paralleled these trends (Table 1, p 162). In 1852, the business held imports to 1851 levels. Although it handled much produce, on commission and on its own account, it chose to take small profits as these became possible, rather than gaining the full benefit of the year's price rise.[6] Yet profits virtually doubled from 1851, and increased cash collections reflected the prosperity of the country and continuing attention to account management. For 1853, the firm took a bolder line, increasing imports by as much as two-thirds, financing this from Peter Buchanan's increased capital, by making greater use of remaining outside sources of credit, and by securing a credit of up to £6000 from the Liverpool firm's bank, the Liverpool Borough Bank, another Dennistoun-dominated enterprise.[7] Sales were easily made, evidently at very satisfactory advances. London's sales and profits almost doubled in a single year, and it is clear that profits at all locations increased substantially (Tables 1 and 4, pp 162, 168).[8] This can be seen by the rise in Young and Law's capital; their accounts totalled about £42,000cy in December 1851, but almost £70,000 in December 1853. Significant accounting adjustments had been made in the interim, but it is clear that their 37.6 per cent share of profits, together with 6 per cent interest on their capital, had produced a net gain after living expenses were deducted of about £20,000cy. This represented a rate of increase in their capital for the two years of at least 20 per cent per annum.

Whether despite or because of the success of 1852 and 1853, the schism between Young and Law and their partners did not diminish. By the autumn of 1852, Peter Buchanan had concluded that a break-up of the business was inevitable. 'You should leave no stone unturned to prepare against a day of dissolution. Come it must...'[9] He now argued that 'our Business need be nothing more nor less than a pasttime [sic] and pleasure if managed as it ought to be but there must exist a perfect understanding...'[10] This he found unobtainable with Law and Young. Confident of their business's strength, and suspecting that Young and Law were only awaiting a favourable moment to break up the business, Peter and Harris notified their partners on 13 May 1853 that they intended to dissolve the partnership in twelve months unless a negotiated end to the firm came first.[11]

In August, Young came to Glasgow to meet Harris and Peter. It was soon agreed that Young and Law would retire on 31 December, the other partners taking all assets and liabilities of the business. Half the bad debt account was transferred to profit and loss, adjustments were made to cover stock and property taken over by the remaining partners, and it was agreed to pay Young and Law jointly £56,000stg in seven equal instalments, every six months from six to forty-two months after dissolution.[12] Thus, the two men secured payment in full of their capital, secured by a strong, ongoing business. This was precisely what Peter Buchanan had himself long desired, and his willingness to agree to such liberal terms reveals how confident he now was of his business position.

Two businesses were now to be created out of one. Young and Law, with William Leitch, Peter's office manager since 1840, planned to establish a business paralleling the Buchanans' in Glasgow, Montreal, and Hamilton. The new firm would pose a real challenge to the Buchanans, for its partners could claim with some accuracy to have been the Buchanans' key operating personnel in recent years.

Leitch secured financial backing from three long-time supporters of Peter Buchanan and Company and one longstanding consigner to the Montreal firm: the Union Bank of Scotland; Glyn, Mills and Company; A. Dennistoun and Company; and George Sandeman, one of the Glasgow family of wine merchants, who would discount some of the bills given Young and Law by the Buchanans. Although Peter Buchanan tried to block these lines of credit, he failed. Nor could he prevent his traditional suppliers from dealing with and extending the usual credit to the new firm. Such British reaction indicated in part the competitive climate in the British business world at the time, but it also reflected the high standing of the entire Buchanan operation: the withdrawing partners began with a high reputation, yet that of the original business was in no way diminished.

The Montreal firm had a number of consigners' accounts, with which Law had corresponded directly. Confidence was a vital feature of such business, however, and Peter knew the consigners personally and had opened most of the accounts himself. By 1 November he had secured all but two of their old consigners for 1854, including the Canadian agencies for Hennessy's cognac and William and John Graham's ports and sherries. He could not keep the Sandeman agency, but the Graham line, though of lower quality, was a partially satisfactory substitute. Ironically, Peter had first been linked to Hennessy's in about 1844 through the Sandemans, but he had come to correspond directly with Augustus Hennessy as the firm's cognac sales had mounted. By 1850, the firm was annually importing an entire shipload of cognac direct from the Charente, taking a good deal of this to its own account rather than selling it on commission. The Bairds waited until they had seen Law, who came to Glasgow in January 1854, but they then decided to leave their agency undisturbed. Thus, Peter successfully held all but one of the firm's old accounts. To consolidate his victory, he brought Robert Leckie to Britain and France to meet all the consigners.

Such agencies were not hugely profitable in themselves – Hennessy paid a commission of 4 per cent, while Bairds paid 5 – but the returns were sure. Although consignments made up only about one-fifth of Montreal's sales in most years, cognac, wines, and iron were very important staples in the business's Montreal operation: because they came from overseas, not from New York or the local market like many other grocery and some hardware items, they served to draw customers to the Montreal firm. It secured these supplies on liberal terms, without having to lock up its own capital in them.* Even in a world where commercial branding had scarcely begun to develop, the Baird and Hennessy names and products were well known and brought prestige to the business that handled them.[13]

---

* The persistence of commission trade in what was largely an own-account business stemmed from the initial effort to develop the Montreal firm on a basis that would not tie up as much capital as the Upper Canadian ones and, it would seem, from the preference of such major suppliers as Bairds and Hennessy to bear more of the risk and seek more of the profit on their products; in any event, no one now saw much reason to disturb successful and largely harmonious business relationships. Payment of Hennessy's invoices was due in London three

Another battle was fought between the new and old firms for personnel. The business had a large, experienced staff, and Young and Law could offer more responsible and better paid positions to those they wanted. The Buchanans responded by offering higher salaries and new engagements to all key personnel. In the end, they lost only Leitch and David Law. As Canadian wage rates were rising in any case, the cost of this victory may not have been very great. It was, however, a serious problem to find a successor to David Law. The buyer, as one described it, had 'to secure the best assortment with at the same time as good a stock of the Staples of the Trade as would make the whole *attractive* not only to our regular but transient customers.'[14] Staples, such as inexpensive cottons and, in the fall, heavy woollens, were always in good demand, but tended to carry the lowest advances. Higher priced and higher styled goods, properly selected, would raise profits and attract new customers. Indeed, in 1854 the firm sent its buyers to France and Germany for the first time in search of such goods, which sold especially well in prosperous times. The buyer had also to avoid bad stock that would have to be sold at a loss through local jobbers, or in Montreal, New York, or even Britain. Thus, he very significantly affected the firm's competitiveness.

Because Adam Hope wanted to send his own buyer to Britain and because increased volume had made the job more complex, there were now two buying positions open in the firm. At Hamilton, H.S. Carlton, an ambitious salesman, and A. Fair, until now a clerk for Peter Buchanan, would alternate as buyers for the present. Alexander Kirkland, formerly a customer at Brantford, was picked for the London job, but Isaac then chose to reward his brother-in-law, James Jarvie, with a share of the post. Jarvie, who had good training but a weakness for alcohol, had progressed well under Hope's eye. Now the strains of travel and buying led him to start drinking heavily again.[15]

months after date, but Hennessy would delay payment by three or even six months, on payment of interest of course. On Bairds' consignments, payment was due at the end of the shipping season, by which time the Montreal firm had paper for discount from its iron customers. In some years, however, Bairds did not want to consign. To meet the problem of keeping regular customers supplied, the Buchanans arranged to take orders in Canada and fill them in Glasgow for a commission of 7½ per cent. On these, payment was ostensibly due, as was usual in Glasgow, in fourteen days, but Peter Buchanan arranged to have Bairds draw on him at six months date instead. This, he said, was a highly unusual arrangement, to be kept confidential; it may well have been so, for he was by then a good friend of at least one of the Bairds. In 1854, the peak year of the Scottish-Canadian iron trade, the Buchanans ordered almost £18,000stg from Bairds on the latter system and sold about an equal amount of iron consigned in the normal way. The Baird agency was not entirely exclusive, for Bairds would sell to others who could meet the terms of the Glasgow market, but it brought a substantial, if fluctuating, volume of trade to the Montreal firm.

By the summer of 1854, the business had four inexperienced buyers in place of the one skilled predecessor.

The final battle was for customers, especially the much-desired 'independent' customers. The business had extended its connection considerably in expanding sales in 1853, and the Buchanans were especially anxious to hold this new clientele. During the winter, Isaac Buchanan, Harris, and Leckie travelled throughout the province explaining the break-up, taking orders, and extending produce advances. After the spring sales season, they were satisfied that they had held their connection well. To do so, they had had to lower their mark-ups, but growing competition, of which Young and Law's new business was only one example, was in any case putting downward pressure on mark-ups.

It was also necessary to restructure the partnership and to replace Young and Law. Harris had found Liverpool lonely and uncongenial; he continued to suffer from serious lameness, the result of a fall from a horse several years earlier; and his presidency of the Great Western had compelled him to travel across the Atlantic more than he would have liked.[16] Accordingly, he preferred to return to Hamilton, where Isaac also wished to remain. Signalling this decision, Isaac had, soon after his return to Canada, purchased an 86-acre estate and farm that he called 'Clairmont Park' on the mountain outside Hamilton. Between 1852 and 1854 he built an attractive cottage-style house, called 'Auchmar,' there. It was, Harris tartly commented, a very fine house, if inconveniently distant in the winter; 'the cost, however, must be very large' – as indeed it was, amounting to at least £5000 for construction alone.[17]

The Liverpool office would now be managed by George Borthwick, Harris's office manager and either a former employee or the son of an employee of the Bairds. As he was relatively inexperienced, Peter Buchanan would have to supervise him closely. Soon it developed that Peter, although he often praised Borthwick, would not give full confidence to him, and this proved to be the end of the planned refocusing of the business in Liverpool. The office became an agency for the placing of orders and handling of shipping, produce, insurance, and financial routines; it would not be an independent centre of power in the business. In Glasgow, Peter now began to give more responsibility to one of his clerks, Robert Wemyss, formerly a Union Bank employee, with a view to developing a successor to Leitch.

Peter had fuller confidence in Robert Leckie now, but he had been impressed by Harris and Law's criticisms of his protégé over the years.[18] Hence it was decided to have two relatively equal partners in Montreal: Leckie would be responsible for the goods departments, and the second partner would handle correspondence and finance. For this post, Peter suggested Alexander Campbell.[19] The Campbell family, like the Leckies, lived in Roseneath, the country village where Peter and Isaac's parents had had their summer home. Alexander Campbell had emigrated to Canada in 1832 at the age of nineteen, and by the early 1850s was manager of the Hamilton branch of the Bank of British North America. Peter and Isaac did not know him intimately, being much closer friends with his older brother George, a very successful doctor in Montreal, but they felt they knew him well enough to offer him a partnership despite his lack of capital. Campbell seized the opportunity to escape from salaried employment.

Neither Leckie, who had now accumulated £6000, nor Campbell had the experience or the capital to secure the power that Harris, Young, and Law had each won in turn. Thus, the Montreal firm was made a separate partnership, known as I. Buchanan, Harris and Company. Buchanan, Harris and Company, again the firm's name in Hamilton, would contribute £10,000 in capital and receive half of Montreal's profits, while Campbell and Leckie would each receive one-quarter of the profits. The Glasgow and Liverpool houses would charge Montreal 2½ per cent on gross outlay on Montreal's behalf; Montreal in turn would charge the Hamilton and London houses a total of £300 per annum plus actual outlay for services rendered in Montreal.[20]

Buchanan, Harris and Company, in Hamilton and Liverpool, and Peter Buchanan and Company were reconstituted under a partnership agreement between Isaac, Peter and Harris, signed early in November 1853. Each firm consisted of the three men, sharing equally in all profits. Harris had at last secured a full partnership at Glasgow, and with it recognition as an equal of the Buchanans.

The final stage in the restructuring was to conclude an agreement with Frederick Lane that gave him one-quarter of the profits at New York, the remainder going to the Hamilton firm. On 2 January 1854, the Buchanans announced the end of their thirteen-year association with Young and Law and the continuation of the business by themselves.[21] They had taken on a large task, for Young and Law had been major contributors to the growth of those years. It was now imperative to bring new people forward to replace them,[22] but of the junior partners and senior employees, it would turn out that only Adam Hope had the kind of strength and took or was given the kind of authority that John Young and both Laws possessed.

As they planned for 1854, the partners were determined above all to maintain their position in competition with Young and Law.[23] They anticipated that Canadian imports would rise sharply, but even so expected a fine trade.

While Peter Buchanan proposed simply to eliminate shipments of goods on which profits were low, notably pig iron ordered for customers, his Canadian partners argued that this year especially they required full stocks in all departments to maintain their connection. As retailers bought heavily in the spring, the Canadian houses flooded Glasgow and Liverpool with further orders. Much preoccupied by his work for the Great Western, and especially the politics of its subsidiary, the Hamilton and Toronto, Peter Buchanan gave only partial supervision to the Glasgow office. In Liverpool, Borthwick, who had no financial information, simply filled orders as they arrived. Only in midsummer did Peter realize that British shipments for the year would be almost double those of 1853, and over £100,000cy in purchases in North America had also to be paid for by the houses there.[24] He had yielded to pressure for increases from every sector of the business. Evidently, the North American partners and employees considered that they could sell any stock they could get. Only Harris and Isaac knew of the financial limitations under which Peter operated, but they too were active in politics and the railroad.

In planning for 1854, Peter had calculated that shipments of much over £100,000 would pose financial difficulties.[25] Now he had to find twice that sum (Table 2, p 164). His bankers in Liverpool and Glasgow readily gave permission to run higher overdrafts on occasion; he reopened his recently closed credit with Seton Laing's firm, now known as Laing and Campbell; he turned again to A. Dennistoun and Company and arranged a drawing credit for £15,000; and he pressed the Canadian houses urgently for remittances. In the autumn, even a brief interruption in remittances could keep him from meeting his payments. He therefore had Adam Hope and Company and T.H. McKenzie of Dundas, the firm's largest account, send him a number of acceptances at various dates; these he planned to discount with other banks or to use as collateral for extraordinary bank advances if any emergency arose. As a precaution, he opened an account with the London Joint Stock Bank, with which he had dealt closely on railroad matters. He even had the deed for their Hamilton property sent forward for possible use as collateral. In a single year, the firm's independence of outside sources of credit vanished.

Sales in 1854 increased by about one-quarter over 1853 at Hamilton and by about one-third at London (Table 1, p 162), but they were at lower mark-ups, and London at least sold to customers of a lower class than would previously have been considered. Moreover, sales did not keep up with shipments, and the business had to carry extremely heavy inventories, totalling £185,000 in value in the three locations, into 1855. At Hamilton the stock totalled £116,000 and was said to include much bad stock. For this Peter Buchanan blamed inexperienced buyers and inadequate supervision; he complained that 'this is a greater evil than at first it may appear & its baneful effects will be an incubus on the business for years rendering what ought to be a profitable business an indifferent one...'[26] Although 1854 produced a record profit in absolute terms, the increase at London and Hamilton was disappointingly small, and Montreal's profits actually dropped (Table 4, p 168), as a result of stiff competition, notably in the iron trade, and of the virtually complete shift of Upper Canadian wheat exports to American channels.

Peter Buchanan, determined to reverse the trend to greater indebtedness, set a limit of only £40,000 on spring shipments for 1855. Grudgingly he acceded to additional orders that eventually brought the final total to £73,000, but by cutting fall orders more resolutely he was able to reduce 1855 shipments by 39 per cent from 1854's level (Table 2, p 164). Yet his financial position remained precarious: during the year he had to meet heavy debts from 1854, to pay another £16,000 to Young and Law, and to repay £6000 to Seton Laing, who had lost substantially by a customer's bankruptcy. Late in the year, James Watson, the Glasgow banker who had invested in the business, died, and Peter had to pay £5000 to his heirs. He knew too that the Dennistoun interests were under considerable pressure. Cash collections and improved remittances were the keys to his survival, but these were slow to come in 1855. The Canadian houses had to make heavy local payments, postponed in 1854, and could not remit freely until summer. Late in the summer, with the prospect of a good harvest, collections and remittances at last increased, and this enabled Peter to finish the year in much improved financial circumstances.

Sales for the year held steady or fell off slightly at London and Montreal, but Hamilton's increased by 28 per cent as a result of working off the 1854 overstock and of increased grocery purchases in North America that made for a huge increase in grocery sales. Hamilton's 1855 sales were a record for the entire history of the business (Table 1, p 162). These produced satisfactory profits, but at Montreal profits again declined, causing the senior partners to complain of bad management there. Cash collections were satisfactory, but borrowings in Canada remained high in order that Peter could lower his indebtedness in Britain.

For 1856, Peter planned further reductions in borrowing, although he authorized a modest increase in shipments over the level of 1855. 'The feeling among prudent and cool thinking men is that we shall have a violent crisis 12 or 18 mos. hence.'[27] Sales in Canada in 1856 fell somewhat, however, and despite Hamilton's much higher sales in 1855 by comparison with 1854, cash collections failed to increase in 1856 (Tables 1 and 3, pp 162, 166). Grain prices had remained encouraging, but in 1856 the wheat midge destroyed or damaged crops in a number of longer settled areas in the west. When the Canadian banks reduced the firm's discount lines, as part of their own reaction to circumstances that paralleled the Buchanans' in some respects, this forced a cut in remittances. Peter was under severe financial pressure on several occasions in the spring and fall of 1856, and on 1 January 1857, he owed £26,500 more than he had a year eariler. His gains from 1855 had been wiped out. To maintain shipments in 1857 he could see no choice but to keep his borrowings at such levels for another twelve months at least. Montreal's profits in 1856 were better than in 1855 (Table 4, p 168), though still disappointing, and Montreal had kept up remittances. London's account was significantly reduced from its level of twelve months earlier, as Hope had at last begun the slow process of collecting overdue accounts. The source of the problem was Hamilton.

Peter Buchanan and Harris considered the problem there to be managerial. The post of buyer still was not resolved certainly, although Isaac had just promoted to it R.K. Masterton, a salesman and traveller hired earlier from a Hamilton competitor, and he would come to be accepted as a reliable if not outstanding manager and buyer. Harris took much time away from work in 1855 as a result of illness – he now had difficulty hearing and, at times, speaking and writing – and his condition deteriorated in 1856 to the point that he left for a long spell in Europe. When business pressures brought him back to Hamilton in the autumn, he fell ill again early in 1857 and left for Florida to recuperate. Thus, Isaac Buchanan was in sole charge at Hamilton for most of 1855 and 1856.

Isaac, Peter knew, was no bookkeeper. To help him with office and financial management and to give Borthwick more experience, Peter sent Borthwick to Canada for the summer and fall of 1854, 1855, and 1856. But this could not solve the year-round problem at Hamilton, Accordingly, in October 1856, Harris hired an office manager, Plummer Dewar, who came from Glasgow and was a member of the Merchants House there. Dewar had come to Canada as accountant of the Great Western Railroad in 1855, but he was anxious to leave this post because the company was undergoing a managerial revolution, in which Isaac Buchanan was a principal factor. Dewar was a great admirer of Isaac, and this led Harris and Peter to hire him initially for only one year. If he brought order to the office, he would be well worth his high wage, approximately three times that of any other salaried employee, £750 per annum.

Political interests, Peter had long thought, were at the root of Isaac's failings as a businessman, and both the 1851 and 1853 partnership agreements had placed limits on partners' political activity. Yet if it is doubtful that Isaac tried very hard to avoid public affairs, it is also true that a man of his wealth, energy, and interests could scarcely avoid public life in a city as small as Hamilton. In any case, never openly doubting his rightness or his abilities, Isaac was always ready to join in a battle to advance his views, however appropriate his tactics and whoever his opponents might be. If his chosen weapon was, all too often, the press, this was in part because he was convinced that his own sincerity and disinterestedness would be plain to all. Peter Buchanan could never understand this characteristic of his brother, and he wondered why Isaac would not learn both his limitations and more subtle strategies for achieving his aims. Peter considered, and frequently reminded Isaac, that his chief reason for remaining in business was to advance the welfare of Isaac and his growing family, and this made Isaac's transgressions seem only the more galling. But to Isaac, business power, money, and social position, though he actively sought them and valued them highly, were of little significance in themselves; they must be employed to good ends. As one contemporary described him, 'he was a kind of commercial knight errant, to whom trade had slender attractions, if severed from daring.'[28] Thus, despite his pledges to eschew active politics, Isaac challenged Hamilton's long-time member, Sir Allan MacNab, in the 1854 election, arguing the need to secularize the clergy reserves and expressing the fear that MacNab in moving towards the Grand Trunk was betraying Hamilton's railway interests. The aim, he told his partners, was not to win but rather to force MacNab to change his position on the issues. MacNab, however, sidestepped them and handily won re-election.[29] An incensed Peter Buchanan, on learning that Isaac had issued an address to the electors, broke off all communications with Isaac, except through Harris, for eight months.

By 1856, Isaac's political interests largely focused on the Great Western. Although he had no official position in the company, he had long taken a close interest in its affairs and had acted in it on his brother's behalf. Now his concern was a challenge posed to the railroad and to Hamilton by Samuel Zimmerman, Upper Canada's leading railroad contractor, who was rumoured to be acting with the Grand Trunk.[30] The Great Western's valuable through trade was vulnerable to any competing line built along what was known as the Southern route from Buffalo to the Detroit River; the distance was shorter and the grades were much easier.[31] Charters had been granted to two companies, the Woodstock and Lake Erie, on which some work had actually begun, and the Amherstburg and St Thomas, which together covered the Southern route. In the summer of 1856, Zimmerman was moving to acquire full control of both. In view of his great influence – and even greater reputation for influence – it seemed that he might well succeed in building the line, despite the unfavourable state of capital markets. As for the Grand Trunk, it was in financial difficulties, but there seemed no obvious reason why it could not draw once more on the public purse to buy the completed lines from Zimmerman. If so, the Great Western could be outflanked, and, Isaac feared, Hamilton would lose an important bulwark of its commercial independence. Gloomily, Peter Buchanan agreed that Isaac was probably right, but he was unprepared to try to stop Zimmerman; that, he now felt, was up to the Canadian public. He continued to sell his Great Western shares in London as rapidly as he could.

Railway and personal rumours, arguments, and accusations mounted rapidly in Hamilton in 1856; in this frenzied atmosphere, Isaac set out to save the railroad and the city.

[I] had to leave town hurriedly as [this was] the only chance of saving the Great Western Railway from a fearful conspiracy in which we fear Mr Brydges is connected. But for my presence all would have been lost.

[I] may say confidently that I have outgeneralled Mr Zimmerman & the Grand Trunk. I think you may take for granted that the western half of the Southern Road will be securely in our hands...[32]

Isaac and J.S. Radcliff, vice-president of the Great Western, had subscribed for shares in the Amherstburg and St Thomas to a value of £500,000, using Isaac's personal cheque for £50,000 as a deposit while Radcliff drew on the London office of the Great Western to reimburse Isaac. While this went forward, Isaac in early August purchased control of the Woodstock and Lake Erie by paying £25,000 to one of its directors. To gain possession of its assets, he gave Buchanan, Harris and Company's bond, endorsed by Adam Hope and Company, to the Bank of Montreal, guaranteeing to pay the company's debts up to a limit of £30,000.

Some in Hamilton and the Great Western had disagreed with Isaac's fears, most notably C.J. Brydges, the company's very capable young managing director. Early in 1856, Isaac had accused Brydges of betraying Hamilton interests and Brydges had accused Isaac of meddling in company affairs and undermining his authority. Prompted in part by Peter Buchanan's intervention on Brydges' side, the two had made up their feud, but tensions remained. Now Brydges pointed out that it was not at all in the interests of the Grand Trunk to encourage through trade across the south, given its basic strategy of trying to draw through trade from the western United States down the whole length of its main line; and he argued that much of the Amherstburg and St Thomas route was of no value to the Great Western. Therefore, he wrote, 'my clear duty to the shareholders of the Great Western Co. is to give every possible opposition to the great scheme you [Isaac] have propounded'[33] – which was, in essence, that the Great Western use the funds already raised for the purpose of doubling the track to build a separate line for through traffic along the entire Southern route.

Peter Buchanan and Harris (when he was in England) no longer routinely attended the now weekly meetings of the Great Western's small but increasingly important London board. In July and August 1856, they were taking the waters at an English spa and, indeed, were discussing the timing of their complete withdrawal from company affairs; with its line in full operation and its shares carrying a handsome premium on the London Stock Exchange, their task as they had seen it in the 1840s was completed. When they heard from Isaac of his activities to secure control of the Amherstburg and St Thomas charter, they were incredulous, and wrote back to urge him to plan a way out for himself in case it should be necessary; Peter then wrote a letter, which Harris reluctantly signed, urging the board to back Isaac and Radcliff. It is evident that they thought the board would accept Radcliff's actions and that they did not expect Isaac actually to have to pay on his £50,000 cheque. They did not yet know that Isaac had gone into the Woodstock and Lake Erie, in this case using the firm's name and money.

Thus, they were not present when Radcliff's bills came forward. Two members of the English board, weary of new branches that never seemed to pay, agreed with Brydges and opposed accepting the bills; only J.B. Smith, MP, of late the most active London board member, who was a supporter of Radcliff, voted to accept. By a vote of two to one, the bills were sent back. Smith then resigned in protest. Only now did Harris and Peter learn that their money was involved; they tried and failed to reverse the board's decision, but without Smith's vote they could not do so. Peter at once launched a campaign for proxies, but with little real hope of winning. The two directors who voted 'no' had accurately reflected shareholders' views.

When news of the London decision reached him, Isaac rushed to England to argue his case in person with the British directors and public. When he arrived, Peter told him he was already too late, then bluntly demanded his resignation from the business. 'The idea of having a partner involved to the extent of a million of money is monstrous and has already caused great talk.'[34] Harris, his health and spirits visibly deteriorated by recent weeks' events, turned back from a trip to Baden and left for Canada, to demonstrate that the business there was not solely in Isaac's hands. Isaac, who had so recently considered himself a hero, protested that he was, quite unjustly, being made a scapegoat. He had, he said, acted in all their interests, just as Peter had in his decade as London agent for the Great Western.

Isaac, however, neglected vitally important differences between his actions and his brother's. Peter's most daring step had been to join a small group of leading London railway financiers in seizing control of the Hamilton and Toronto Railroad Company late in 1852. As they had planned it, they would earn a good profit themselves and still turn over the completed line to the Great Western at a saving to it: as the money had already been raised, construction could go ahead rapidly, before costs rose too much higher. Yet controversy and complications had arisen in Canada and Britain that threatened to damage Peter's reputation with some of his more cautious creditors. He had greatly regretted his action and, as Isaac well knew, had become heartily sick of the tangled politics of Canadian railways. Even with his excellent connections and the capital for the Hamilton and Toronto in the syndicate's hands, it had taken him over three years to escape entirely from the venture. He had worked very hard for the company, but had earned nothing from it because delays in starting construction had sharply raised costs. By 1856, moreover, the English shareholders and Canadian public had much more experience of Canadian railroads, their underestimated costs, their usually overestimated revenues (the Great Western having been a conspicuous exception here), and their complicated and unsavoury politics. As Peter wrote to Isaac in August 1856:

The people here will not believe but that you and I hold the most of the ground on the Southern Line. They say it is monstrous to suppose that any one would have acted as you have done without a very great & paramount private self Interest. They say to believe this they must think you a fool and that they do not!!![35]

Thus, Isaac was left in uncertain control of two charters of uncertain value. He had spent over £25,000 in bribes and expenses; his cheque for £50,000 could still be presented for payment, though he now controlled one of the two competing boards of the Amherstburg and St Thomas and could probably prevent this; and he might have to pay up to £30,000 to the Bank of Montreal. For the first time in his career, his impetuous method of attacking a problem had put him in a position from which he could not extricate himself. He returned to Canada, leaving his brother to attempt to form a company to relieve Isaac of his charters and obligations. The English shareholders now demanded Harris's resignation as president of the Great Western; and as a result of Isaac's actions, Harris left in disgrace a company he had served for seven years and from which he had never taken a penny.[36] The new president was English, but Harris's successor as head of the company's now subsidiary Canadian board was, ironically, John Young.

Isaac returned to Hamilton where, because Harris was soon too ill to do so, he would continue in practice to head the business. When his loss was finally added up, it totalled over £50,000, an enormous sum of liquid capital to lose in a time of mounting credit stringency.[37] At least half this sum was paid in 1856, and it was one important factor in the deterioration of the business's financial position. Yet it is clear that the firm's reputation in financial circles remained high, as the ready acceptance of Isaac's cheque and bond suggests, and there is little evidence that the charges of corruption that were aimed at Isaac by various politicians and newspapers had any effect on this. Indeed, it was probably better that the charges were of corruption, not incompetence. Moreover, had the business not earned so much in recent years, it is doubtful if even Isaac would have acted as he did.

Thus, 1856 ended with the business in some disarray. Heavy payments on railway account still loomed, at a time when the business's overall financial situation was as difficult as it had been for many years. Even so, Peter Buchanan urged his brother to forget his financial loss and the slurs on his character that had arisen in 1856.[38] They were, after all, still very rich men, and the money, Peter was sure, could be made up. He was far more afraid of the consequences for the business of continuing inattention to it by its most active and important Canadian principal.

Clearly the managerial problems at Hamilton were real, but they were just one cause of the difficulties in 1856 – though they may have been the only cause that the partners themselves could deal with. In fact, the expansion of the 1850s, indeed of the last twenty years, was drawing to a close. In all, far more debts had been incurred by Upper Canadians in the boom climate of the 1850s than could possibly be met from the resources of the country. Creditors pressed increasingly for payment of their accounts as a drive for greater liquidity began. What the Hamilton house lacked in 1855 and 1856 was a firm hand guiding this process; and the result was that accounts were inadequately supervised, credit was extended too liberally, and Buchanan, Harris and Company almost certainly failed to get its full share of such funds as there were in the west.

7

Depression and reorganization 1857-60

As 1857 began, the Buchanans, still anticipating a commercial crisis, were intent on reducing overdue accounts and swollen inventories.[1] An industrial depression was already developing in Britain, and many indicators of a downturn in the Canadian and American economies had also appeared. In the fall, tightening conditions suddenly became an acute financial crisis, as the failure of the Ohio Life Insurance and Trust Company triggered a heavy run on eastern banks. Businesses relying on short-term credit were increasingly refused renewals, and this led to many failures. By mid-October, most American banks had suspended specie payments.[2]

The American crisis at once affected Britain as American merchants, many of whom operated on open accounts or unsecured British accommodation paper, found it difficult to meet obligations. On 27 October, the Liverpool Borough Bank failed, with obligations of over one million pounds, and its largest shareholders, the Dennistoun interests, suspended payments on 8 November, with liabilities exceeding two million pounds. Within days the Western Bank of Scotland and a number of Glasgow merchants, all much involved in the American trade, had failed, and the City of Glasgow Bank had suspended. On 12 November, the government suspended the Bank Act as failures continued throughout Britain.[3]

Canadian banks, already reducing discounts and note circulation, now pressed reduction more vigorously. Failures soon followed. In Toronto, for example, by 31 December 1857, 25 of 389 businesses listed by the Mercantile Agency had failed, with total liabilities of $2.7 million.[4] These included two important local private bankers who had formerly been general wholesalers, R.H. Brett and E.F. Whittemore, and Ross, Mitchell and Company, a large Glasgow-based general wholesaler that had always, in the Buchanans' eyes, been under-capitalized.[5] In Canada as in the United States, the crisis affected frontier areas more than longer settled ones. Montreal, with its more established business structure, recorded only 15 failures out of 909 businesses, with liabilities of $500,000.*

Although severe, the crisis soon passed, once those most vulnerable to a sudden tightening of credit had failed. Early in 1858, discount rates fell sharply and specie flowed back into the banks. It took considerably longer, however, for most sectors of the Canadian, American, and British economies to recover from the depression associated with the financial crisis.[6] The Canadian lumber industry was severely depressed through 1858, while falling wheat prices and poor harvests greatly depressed Upper Canadian agriculture. Wheat was $1.92 (9/7) per bushel in Toronto in June 1857; by January 1858 it was only $.85 (4/3) per bushel.[7] Reflecting the depression, Canadian imports fell from 1856 levels in 1857, and fell still further in 1858, the Upper Canadian ports being most severely hit (Table 13, p 179). At Hamilton the greatest reductions were in the leading lines of British manufactured goods, 1858 figures being from 70 to 90 per cent below those of 1856 (Table 11, p 178). The runaway Upper Canadian boom of the 1850s had ended in a devastating crash.

All branches of the Buchanans' business found money unprecedentedly tight in the spring of 1857. Sales were difficult to make at any profit. Peter Buchanan, still trying to complete payments for 1856 shipments, anxiously pressed for remittances, but collections were slow. At Hamilton, they were lower in every month than in the same month a year earlier. Even in the summer the Canadian houses found it necessary to sell some accommodation bills drawn on the Glasgow and Liverpool firms in order to meet Peter's minimum monthly requirements; this, of course, simply postponed the problem. When the crisis struck in October, collections in Canada fell sharply. Even first-class Montreal customers who had never before missed a payment could not meet their paper as it fell due. For the first nine months of 1857, Hamilton's cash receipts were about 90 per cent of 1856 levels; for the last three, however, they were only 52 per cent of those for the last three of 1856. In December 1856, Hamilton took in £27,000; in December 1857, £11,000. Thus, Peter Buchanan came under increased pressure from Canada at the same time as two of his sources of credit, the Dennistouns and the Liverpool Borough Bank, failed. He would have to pay not only for ship-

---

* Canada officially converted its currency to the dollar system in 1858, £1cy equalling $4.00. The Buchanans gradually adjusted their North American accounts accordingly. Where series overlap or confusion is possible, figures in the text are given in both; for simplicity, figures in statistical tables are given consistently in either one or the other form.

ments but also, as bills came due, for at least £18,000stg in bank credit on which he normally relied heavily in late autumn. The remittances that carried him through November came entirely from the sale of ninety-day drafts on Britain in New York, Hamilton, and Montreal. At the beginning of 1858, the firm had an average of £15,000 per month in such paper on the circle.

To junior partners, Peter, though insisting on full remittances, made light of his position, but he knew that his own business was in extreme danger.

Two absolutely necessary things we want. The first is a raise by some legitimate means to keep us going now and the second is breathing time to recruit our resources after such a crisis and struggle. The first is the chief difficulty to overcome...[8]

For short-term help, he turned mainly to the Union Bank, seeking an extraordinary increase in his line of credit there. In April 1857, his overdraft was £18,100, almost certainly as high as it had ever been, yet by early November he had been able to raise it to £27,000; two months later he had somehow increased it to £48,000. As well, he had in the fall discounted at the bank £20,500 in acceptances from Hope and McKenzie. The Union, itself badly squeezed in November, must have found it difficult to extend such extra credit to many of its accounts. It perhaps felt more secure by January, but even so its confidence in Peter Buchanan is evident. Other relief in late 1857 came from Hennessy's, who agreed to renew paper; from H.B. Jackson, the firm's Manchester agent, who endorsed bills for him; and from the London Joint Stock Bank, which lent him funds on the security of composition paper received from the Dennistouns' estate and of some of Hope's acceptances. Later in 1858, George Wythes, an English railway contractor with whom he had dealt closely, endorsed £5500 in paper for him with a London bank; and Peter opened a credit with the Liverpool firm of John Gladstone and Company to replace his credit at Dennistouns as he retired his paper with the latter. The severity of the Upper Canada depression was well known and gave Peter some excuse for his difficulties, but to maintain the firm's image of solvency, he sent a buyer into the markets early in 1858. He then sent Robert Wemyss to Canada to look into accounts and followed in May 1858 himself to see how the business stood.

This was to be the first of two inspections given the Canadian business by Peter Buchanan in the wake of the crisis, and it revealed several features of the business at its peak in the mid-1850s, besides pointing up areas of difficulty. The total assets of the business now exceeded £800,000cy (Table 7, p 173). Three-quarters of these were represented by customers' accounts at the three main North American locations,* and most of the remaining assets consisted of inventory valued at its cost in the store. Both the firm and, in fact, its individual partners on their own accounts had largely avoided the dangerous territory of land and share speculation despite the temptations these had perhaps offered. Not even Isaac's railroad venture had been entered with a view to making a profit. Such restraint reflected the strength of the main business in its partners' eyes; they saw no reason to speculate dangerously outside the business. On the liability side, the firm owed somewhat over £400,000, divided about equally between Canadian and British sources, while partners' capital exceeded £360,000 even after the payment of Isaac's railroad debts. Despite its large obligations, then, the firm had hardly been running extreme risks; if its assets yielded even half their nominal value, it was solvent. Why then was it so vulnerable in 1857?

In essence, Peter's problem was lack of remittances, especially from Hamilton. London and Montreal, despite difficulties in securing payments from customers, had maintained theirs fully except in November.[9] They had been fortunate in keeping up their discount lines and in securing exchange from their bankers, though they had had to take up much discounted paper themselves late in the year. Hamilton's net remittances for 1857, however, after deducting the amount required to meet accommodation paper drawn from Hamilton and New York, were only £10,000. Cash receipts at Hamilton, though they were only equal to 80 per cent of the previous year's sales, one of the poorest records in the firm's history there, had exceeded sales for the year, and they did exceed £200,000 (Table 3, p 166). Moreover, Isaac Buchanan had somehow raised Hamilton's discounts from £48,400 in September 1857 to £86,000 by early 1858. Yet almost all this money had gone to meet North American payments.†

At the end of 1857, Hamilton's outstanding debts totalled £365,000, owed by 400 accounts, while London's and Montreal's together amounted to £242,000. Peter's enquiries did not neglect the latter, but in view of the problems of recent years, he naturally concentrated on Hamilton. How much were these accounts really worth? How best could they be managed to yield maximum returns? It was possible to sue customers into receivership or to

---

* Sales to branches were the largest part of New York's business. Other sales were made mainly to Hamilton customers, and as a result New York accounts were often merged with Hamilton's in the firm's general memos. See quarterly statements of accounts, New York, 1 May and 1 Aug. 1846, 84/59886, 8; F. Lane to Isaac Buchanan, 13 Jan. 1859, 37/30511-12.

† Such payments were for purchases (particularly of groceries), customs duties, local taxes, routine operating expenses, partners' drawings, inland freights, any net outlay on produce, interest charges, and Isaac's railway and political expenses.

seize and sell assets assigned in earlier years to the Buchanans as collateral and thus to secure ready cash by rapid liquidation. But what were customers' assets? In large part, they consisted of outstanding debts, mostly owed by farmers, and property, notably lots and buildings in the towns, villages, and hamlets of the west. The managerial problems of running a customer's business and collecting his accounts were so great that the partners preferred almost any other course to a direct take-over. That indeed was one reason that accounts could get behind, for it seldom paid to force a customer out of business for modest overdue payments. Collecting farmers' accounts would not be easy, because many – perhaps most – farmers had gone far into debt during the boom, borrowing to buy land, equipment, buildings, and store goods. When, after the mid-1850s, grain prices fell and wheat crops failed in many areas, most farmers were tightly squeezed.

It made more sense to take over property, but the partners were merchants, not land dealers. In 1858 this solution was particularly unattractive, for land values had plummeted. This was true of farm land but was still more the case with town lots, many of them in small places that had in fact reached their maximum size; such lots were nearly worthless, whatever they might recently have been valued at by their owners. Land sales did not usually yield cash at the best of times, and now almost no one had ready money. As one hard-pressed customer put it early in 1858, 'a Baillifs [sic] sale yields but enough to cover costs.'[10]

The partners preferred another course: to supply customers with strictly limited quantities of goods to enable them to carry on trade and to attempt to realize their own assets by a similar gradual process. This approach required good judgment on the part of those in charge of credit granting, good advice to and relatively close supervision of the customers who were supplied with goods, and ultimately a general economic revival that would put more money in the hands of farmers. It was the method that had worked so well after 1847. A third possible strategy, to regard most of the old assets as valueless and to concentrate on making enough from new business to work out of difficulty, was not even considered by the partners.

To adjust the business to reduced circumstances, the partners planned to reduce outlay by cutting salaries and partners' drawings and by dismissing excess staff.* As Glasgow was essential to their finances, they closed the

---

* Relatively comprehensive information on the size of the work force as of the end of 1857 survives as a result. Hamilton had 34 employees (13 in dry goods, 7 in hardware, 8 in groceries, and 6 in the office); London had 20, and an annual wage bill of £2440; Montreal had 10, and a wage bill of £1600. It is not clear how many were let go; five years later, Hamilton had 11 employees in dry goods, 7 of whom were not on the earlier list.

Liverpool branch to save costs, turning it over to George Borthwick to run as an independent agency. He was guaranteed their forwarding business for several years, but, lacking capital, he would not find it easy to add new sources of income to strengthen his chances of business success. In New York, they closed their store, leaving Lane in charge of an office, which was necessary if they were to continue to buy and sell bills on the New York exchange market.[11]

Customers' accounts of each Canadian branch were divided into three groups. First and smallest was a group of first-class accounts that would pay in full. Such customers, well able to change suppliers, were in an excellent position to extract better terms from the business. A second group consisted of accounts that would no longer be supplied with goods, and these were not expected to yield much of what they owed. The largest group of accounts, at least at London and Hamilton, consisted of those that were overdue but from which the firm hoped to extricate itself with little loss by careful rationing of goods. To keep such customers from escaping their obligations, the firm would take all possible securities from them. At least one, T.H. McKenzie, was also required to insure his life, naming the firm as beneficiary.[12]

The business planned to hold its shipments and other costs to a figure below collections each year and to apply the surplus cash and as much as possible of its profits to reduce its debts. This could of course lead to a downward spiral, as lower sales led in the following year to lower collections and hence to still lower shipments and sales; clearly there was a point below which reductions could not be carried if the business was to continue with its existing branch and departmental structure and its current capitalization. Depressed economic conditions had an important role to play, but this policy of 'working off' also contributed to the decline of sales after 1857. Thus, sales at Hamilton in 1859 were less than 40 per cent of those of 1856, while Montreal's were about 70 per cent and London's 60 per cent (Table 1, p 162).

At the end of 1858, Peter Buchanan owed £113,000, less than two-thirds the amount of a year earlier, and the policy of reduction appeared to be succeeding. His bank overdraft was only £9000, and though the business continued to rely on over £10,000 per month in accommodation paper drawn from New York, its overall credit position was much better. During the year, London and Montreal greatly reduced their balances in Glasgow, although Hamilton increased its debt by £9000.

Collections, however, fell almost as sharply as sales, particularly at Hamilton; there 1859 collections were only 47 per cent of 1856's (Table 3, p 166). In 1856, 1857, and 1858, collections equalled only 80 per cent of sales of the previous year, while 1859's collections only just equalled sales of 1858. In

1859, Hamilton's outstandings were only 12 per cent below their level of 1857, while annual sales had fallen by 42 per cent in the same period. Sales in 1857 were equal to 51 per cent of outstanding debts while those in 1859 were equal to only 33 per cent of debts.* London's outstandings actually increased by six per cent over the same period, though sales each year did equal fifty per cent of outstandings. By 1859, it was clear that reduction was not yielding major sums from backward accounts. At the end of 1859, Peter Buchanan owed £12,000 more than a year earlier, probably as a result of increased shipments, and the firm continued to rely on accommodation bills from New York.† London had again fallen behind on remittances, and Hamilton had remitted only for shipments, paying nothing on its enormous arrears.

The partners in Canada, and Peter Buchanan, when he discussed the issue with creditors, blamed poor harvests and low grain prices for the difficulties, but even a better harvest in 1859 had not yielded all the improvements that might have been expected. Profits had shrunk even more sharply than sales, as surviving firms fought for a share of the trade that remained. Yet junior partners still considered the business to be fundamentally prosperous and far better off than its Upper Canadian competitors; and the ease with which the business found the credit it required reflects its continuing high standing in the world. Recognition of this was made the more evident in 1860, when Peter Buchanan was elected to the board of the Union Bank in Glasgow.[13] To Peter, however, it was now clear that the business was 'sailing under false colours' with its current capitalization.[14] He had begun to consider reorganizing the business to improve its competitiveness and above all to present its position more accurately in its accounts.

During these years, Isaac Buchanan found himself drawn ever deeper into politics as he sought with increasing desperation to escape from further possible liabilities in connection with the Southern railroad; to secure his money from it, if possible; and, if necessary to achieve these aims, to have the

---

* Sales in 1853, the business's last 'normal' year, had equalled 104 per cent of outstanding debts at year end; Memo, Peter Buchanan, 1853, 91/63754.

† During the year, Peter tentatively inaugurated a new system of long-term borrowing when he sold through various channels up to £14,000 in mortgages, mainly in Scotland, on property that had come into the firm's hands outright or as collateral. Peter Buchanan and Company guaranteed principal and interest payments on these. It was an unorthodox method of commercial fund-raising, and Peter stopped it when rumours of the transactions reached the Union Bank. See Peter Buchanan to David Smith, 17 Dec. 1859, and to George Borthwick, 29 Dec. 1859, 5 and 10 Jan. 1860 (copies), 68/54187-8, 194-5, 205, 209.

railroad actually built.[15] After Isaac had left England in September 1856, Peter had concluded an agreement with Samuel Zimmerman and George Wythes, who were to form a joint company, build the line, sell it (probably to the Great Western) when done, and repay at least some of Isaac's expenses during the course of this. Inevitably, business and political complications arose, but still it seemed possible that the money would be found and the project would go forward. Then on 12 March 1857, Samuel Zimmerman was killed, one of sixty to die in the Desjardins Canal railway disaster. For some time it was rumoured that Isaac had been with him on the late afternoon Toronto to Hamilton train and had also been killed.[16]

Zimmerman's death, Isaac's political style, fierce local railroad politics in the west, and the proposal of Arthur Rankin, member of the Assembly for Essex, to charter another company to build along the Southern route all created intense controversy about the Southern. In the spring of 1857, two legislative inquiries into it went forward simultaneously.[17] A select committee, chaired by M.H. Foley, investigated the entire history of the Woodstock and Lake Erie, while the Standing Committee on Railroads, on which Rankin himself served, explored affairs surrounding the Amherstburg and St Thomas and Rankin's bid for his own charter.

Isaac crossed to Britain early in 1857 on railway business and to buy for the firm, but he can have had time for little else but Southern affairs for months thereafter. All through May 1857, he and his legal advisers were attending one or other committee, at both of which he was a prominent witness. The Foley committee clearly believed Isaac's story, 'given with great candour and commendable simplicity,' but it had no doubt that, whatever Isaac's motives, he had been wrong in bribing Henry de Blaquière and some other directors to resign from the Woodstock and Lake Erie. This was only the last episode in what had been throughout an unsavoury story.

That gross wrong has been practised by parties officially and otherwise in connexion with the said Company, is fully established, and that those concerned in the perpetration of such wrong are individuals who have hitherto occupied high and honourable positions in society and in public stations, is a circumstance of peculiarly humiliating and painful character.[18]

Although the report recommended no action save investigation by the Attorney General, John A. Macdonald, who must have had little desire to launch any railroad inquiries, it undoubtedly wounded Isaac at his most vulnerable point, his honour.[19]

Meanwhile, the Railway Committee learned that Rankin had been offered a 'sub-contract' with a guaranteed profit of £25,000 for assisting Zimmerman to secure the charter of the Amherstburg and St Thomas; and it explored the murky area surrounding Rankin's seeking a £50,000 guarantee on a sub-contract from Isaac – presumably in return for abandoning the charter now sought – had Isaac offered a bribe, or did Rankin demand it? As the charter made its way through the committee, it became plain that Rankin, despite being a member of the four-man subcommittee that was assigned to gather evidence, could not get his charter through unamended. He thereupon agreed to insert clauses protecting claims of the municipalities along the route and promising to pay many of Isaac's and Zimmerman's expenses in regard to the Southern. As the *Globe* saw the result, 'all the old rascalities practised by both parties ... appear to be recognized and indemnified by the bill...'[20] In the end, it was too much even for the Assembly, and the charter did not complete its passage before the end of the session.

To Isaac it seemed plain that his chances of protecting his interests and his honour would be enhanced if he too were a member of the Assembly. More than any other issue this explains his decision to run in the 1857 election for Hamilton. Apart from the Southern, which Isaac said he wanted to keep in Hamilton's control, Isaac stressed that he was an independent, of liberal leanings, who opposed George Brown and his allies because of their belief in 'political economy.'[21] This time MacNab was not a candidate, though it was said he was backing Isaac's opponent, Hugh C. Baker, president of Hamilton's Canada Life Assurance Company. After a costly and rather bitter campaign, Isaac triumphed, by a margin of 1408 to 1104.[22]

At the same time, Isaac was one of the principal organizers of the Association for the Promotion of Canadian Industry, a protectionist body that attracted considerable manufacturing following in Toronto and Hamilton in the depressed circumstances of 1858. He sent lengthy letters to newspapers and the recently founded *Canadian Merchants' Magazine* advocating protection, monetary reform, and, within a year or two, a Canadian-American Zollverein, all in the interests of full employment and the betterment of the lot of farmers and working men.[23] It did not trouble Isaac that Canadian, unlike imperial, protection was scarcely in the interests of his importing business, and he ignored Alexander Campbell's complaints that such views were impractical and were not helping the firm's relations with the banks.[24] Evidently he considered his business was above such narrow considerations – or that its only hope of revival was in a complete transformation of the Upper Canadian economy. In 1859, he was a leading opponent of the government's higher tariffs on grocery items that had necessarily to be imported and were essential to the diets of all.[25] If he attracted few who could support him consistently in all his crusades and if the practical results of his campaigns were slight at best, this does not seem to have been a major concern to him.

As a member of the legislature, however, Isaac was at least able to help secure passage in 1858 and revision in 1859 of the charter for a company known as the Niagara and Detroit Rivers Railroad Company. Included were clauses protecting his rights in the Southern route. He could not look for a return until the line was actually built, and he continued to pursue his efforts to have work begun, but he had at last removed all danger of further liabilities on account of the railroad.[26]

It is difficult to know how effective was his role in the business in these years, but he again became a partner in the fall of 1858. He then refused to accept the year's accounts unless his railway losses were accepted as a business expense. Arguing that the loss was incurred for the firm as a whole, and knowing that he was Peter's principal heir, Isaac portrayed the issue as one between his children and Harris's heirs:

The cause was a thoroughly good one and only failed through the scandalous mismanagement and heartless indifference and petty jealousy of PB & RWH.[27]

I suppose my children attempted to be robbed ... and I take the means to protect them, to save them in fact from starvation...[28]

Isaac threatened to call in arbitrators if his demand was not met. Although this would fully expose the business's difficulties, Peter knew that Isaac was quite capable of doing so in the name of honour. In any case, he saw no special reason to protect Harris's heirs, and, he rationalized, a compromise might restore Isaac's attention to business.

Thus, he proposed to divide the loss into four equal parts, of which he and Harris would each take one. Harris refused, but Peter pressed him steadily until at last, in tears, he acceded.[29] Peter argued that the £26,000 credited to Isaac was a gift, that neither he nor Harris took any responsibility for the loss, and that they would never have acted as Isaac had. At the same time, Peter finally persuaded Harris to make a will, a most important step in that Harris planned to divide his money among more than twenty heirs.

By 1859, Harris's health had greatly deteriorated, and he no longer took much part in business decisions. If he died, the business would either have to pay the sum of over $300,000 at his credit or, Peter knew, to reveal its difficulties by showing how far its assets and capital had depreciated. For this depreciation, Isaac blamed general economic conditions and almost incessantly proposed new stratagems to work the business out of trouble. Peter found Isaac's analyses, even if they might be true at some points, to be quite irrelevant to their situation:

The state of the Hamn Business demands great attention & consideration. I.B. will never change it.[30]

I despise the mawkish sentimentalism in which you seem to deal. ... It is a long course of disaster and bad management which has produced this distrust...[31]

Throughout the fall, therefore, Peter worked alone on his plan for a general reorganization, frequently consulting his lawyer, Adam Paterson, to insure that his actions could withstand a challenge in court. In February 1860 he gave notice to all partners that he intended to dissolve the business in six months and take it over himself, as the partnership agreements empowered him to do. By setting such a time limit, he would facilitate the negotiated settlement on which he was intent. When Isaac at once began negotiations, Peter rebuked him. He would control the entire process himself. Following completion of spring shipments, he embarked in May for Canada.

Peter aimed to concentrate his own and, especially, Harris's interests at Hamilton, ostensibly to facilitate their retirements.[32] Harris, very weak of mind, now lived with his niece in London, and it is difficult to know how real was his assent to the changes; certainly he could do little to prevent them. Peter first made himself sole partner at Glasgow. In January 1860 he transferred the £41,000 at Harris's credit, the £24,000 at Isaac's, and £51,000 of his own capital to the Hamilton books. Hamilton's debt to Glasgow was reduced to £112,000stg, more than net annual remittances in any of the three previous years, but not perhaps an unreasonable total obligation. Peter's own capital in the Glasgow books was now £61,000 (Table 8, p 174). Because the first charge on the Canadian houses, before capital sums were paid out, was Peter Buchanan and Company's balance, this ensured that in any dissolution he would withdraw some of his capital before others could do so.

In Canada, Peter rewrote accounts to make them accord with reality. Junior partners who saw capital written away tended to see 'reality' differently, and to conciliate them, Peter wrote the reorganization back to 31 December 1859, to give them more of 1860's profits. The conclusions that he reached were embodied in a series of partnership agreements signed in August 1860.

Montreal was the healthiest branch, in terms of security of assets. Still, Peter estimated, overdue and doubtful debts there would yield a loss of

$29,000, and this sum he wrote away in proportion to partners' shares. This reduced Buchanan, Harris and Company's share to $84,000. One-third of this would remain in the business as Isaac's share, while from their shares, Peter and Harris paid an allowance of 5 per cent on Montreal's accounts and stocks. This increased Montreal's contingency accounts to almost $59,000 and reduced the sums to be paid out to $34,000.[33] Thus, Peter and Harris withdrew only about 50 per cent of the nominal value of their shares, while the Montreal firm was left with its books showing a working capital of $58,000, less than half the pre-reorganization figure and just 13 per cent of the gross value of 1859 sales (Tables 1 and 8, pp 162, 174).

The business would be carried on by Isaac, with 36 per cent of profits, and Leckie and Campbell, each with 32 per cent. Leckie's health was precarious, illness having just paralyzed permanently his right arm. Campbell was seen by his partners as insufficiently energetic; moreover, his average annual outlay of about $6000 was double the sum agreed upon in 1854. It had since 1856 much exceeded his share of profits and made for a growing debit balance in his stock account. But although Peter questioned the abilities of both men, he saw no possibility of making immediate changes.

The business in London, while still burdened by overdue accounts, was by 1860 looking much better, as Hope made good progress in reducing his overdue balance at Glasgow. Further bad debts were written off in 1860, then to existing contingency accounts Peter added the entire profit from 1859, $29,000, plus an allowance by him and Harris of 5 per cent on outstanding accounts. Suspense accounts were thus increased to about $88,000, an amount almost equal to the total value of the accounts Hope had put into liquidation. Isaac would leave $40,000 in the business, to remain its largest shareholder, and withdraw his remaining capital, $24,000; after deducting allowances, Peter and Harris would withdraw just over $52,000 each, about 80 per cent of the nominal value of their shares. This left the London business with a working capital of $120,000, an amount equal to 50 per cent of 1859 sales, and with a commitment to pay out an equal sum to retiring partners in the next five years (Tables 1 and 8, pp 162, 174).[34]

The London business would be carried on by Isaac Buchanan, with 34 per cent of its profits, Adam Hope, with 30 per cent, and William Muir and C.J. Hope, each with 18 per cent. Charles Hope, Adam's younger brother, was manager of London's very successful hardware department. Muir, the thirty-year-old manager of the grocery department, was the son of an old Buchanan family friend at Rothesay and, initially, a protégé of Peter Buchanan and George Douglas.[35] His fortunes had been enhanced when he married Harris's favourite niece and travelling companion, Eliza, for Harris then advanced him $20,000 to secure a partnership. No one was entirely convinced of Muir's fitness for the job, but he had in the past performed competently enough and Hope could still supervise him quite closely.

These two settlements were preliminary to the reorganization at Hamilton that was Peter Buchanan's main concern. He had decided to have all accounts valued, to write off capital, and then to offer Harris a compromise that would secure the business from having to deal with Harris's heirs. Early in 1860, Isaac had valued Hamilton's accounts and written off $171,000, fourteen per cent of total outstanding debts. Peter thought Isaac too optimistic, so he asked R.K. Masterton and James Watson to conduct independent valuations. Averaging their figures, he reduced the estimated real value of Hamilton's accounts to $880,000.[36]

The firm's inventory at the end of fall sales in 1860 was $170,000. If it was the same at the end of spring sales, then Hamilton's two chief assets in the summer of 1860 totalled just over $1,000,000. Hamilton currently owed Peter Buchanan and Company £122,000stg, about $600,000; its bank discounts in 1860 averaged about $280,000; and it certainly had local obligations and debts to Montreal and New York.[37] At best, the real net worth of the business was less than $100,000. By comparison, partners' stock accounts at Hamilton alone totalled about $400,000 (£100,000) at the end of 1856, and since then there had been the large transfer of accounts from Glasgow.

As a result, Peter decided not to offer a compromise to Harris, but instead to wind up the old business and found a new one without Harris. Harris must have felt that he was being robbed of the fruits of his life's work; whereas the value of his account on 31 December 1856 had been $367,000 (Table 5, p 170), it was now perhaps no more than the $69,000 he would receive from Montreal and London. Indeed, if Hamilton's assets failed to equal its liabilities, he was probably legally obliged not to draw the sums realized from London and Montreal.*

Peter transferred the old firm's obligations to the new, for they had to be met, then transferred some accounts of undoubted value. This left the old business owing the new a large sum, $1,167,000, that would be reduced by the new firm's crediting all sums collected, over and above obligations to the new firm, to the old business. He hoped these collections would in time

---

* This issue would have been clarified had a later legal dispute between Harris's heirs and trustees been tried. The payments made under these settlements apparently went to Buchanan, Harris and Company, and might simply have helped to meet its capital needs. Harris's estate in fact received some funds, but the legal position is unclear.

permit the debit balance against the old to be wiped out; its books could then be closed by distributing any assets to Harris or his heirs and to the Buchanans. Reorganization could not in itself make assets yield more or diminish liabilities, but Peter hoped to enable the new business to operate rationally. The new inherited from the old a still strong reputation and a connection, for which it does not appear to have paid; the old would benefit by having an ongoing business to collect its accounts. Isaac, whose expenditures each year on his growing family (Figure 1, p 12), his country estate, and his political activities befitted the nabob status that Hamilton accorded him, was to restrict his expenditures in line with the much reduced valuation now put upon his assets.

To enforce these changes, Peter proposed to make Robert Wemyss, in whom the Union Bank had great confidence,[38] a partner at Hamilton, where he would take charge of accounts and finance. Isaac and Peter would each receive 40 per cent of Hamilton profits and Wemyss 20 per cent. Because the old business transferred no capital to the new, Peter juggled accounts to put $80,000 at the credit of his account and $40,000 at credit of a 'reserve capital account' to avoid arousing the curiosity of bookkeepers.[39] Isaac accepted all these changes only because he had to. He bitterly resented the vanishing of his capital, the ceiling on his outlay, his exclusion from the Glasgow business, and Wemyss's transfer, which he saw, correctly, as a rebuke to himself.

While preparing for the reorganization, Isaac had inspected the books at New York and discovered that Frederick Lane and his bookkeeper, John Forrest, had each been speculating in land and houses on the firm's funds. Since 1852, Lane had been withdrawing small sums through the use of fictitious bills payable, but the collapse of the land market in 1857 left him unable to repay the sums taken. Isaac thought of suing Lane, but Peter warned him not to do so; 'we are very much in [Lane's] power as long as we require to operate in Exchange in New York.'[40] Under pressure from Isaac, Lane agreed to turn over his property and retire quietly to his wife's family home in Virginia, where he died soon after. Alexander Campbell, who investigated in detail, calculated Lane's withdrawals at $16,000 and his other obligations to the firm, in the form of an overdraft and interest charges, at $11,000; his property, when sold, yielded enough to cover at least half his debt to the firm. Forrest had advanced funds or made the firm security for an advance of $55,000 to his sons, who were bankers and land dealers in Chicago, and had himself overdrawn $26,000. In this case, much land was available as security, and the firm's final losses were small.[41]

Yet the partners' inattention to detail had enabled Lane to go undetected for eight years, and the business was indeed vulnerable if a junior partner in New York could, by divulging the extent of their use of accommodation paper, threaten the entire business. Peter Buchanan was determined to close the New York office as soon as possible. To manage it in the meantime, he and Isaac despatched Hamilton's very competent bookkeeper, David McGee.

Peter at last left for Glasgow early in October. He planned to manage alone there for about five years, by which time Wemyss might have the experience to succeed him. This was the first thorough examination of the business since 1853, and the deterioration of its position since then was immense. As late as the end of 1857, total capital had been shown in the books as $1,448,000 (£362,000) (Table 7, p 173). Following the reorganization, the books showed the various partners with a capital of, at most, $484,000, at Montreal, London, and Glasgow, although a further sum was still in the business until paid out by Montreal and London. It was, Peter said, an 'unprecedented sacrifice of fortune.'[42] Borrowed capital in the business as a whole in the latter part of 1860 was averaging about $1,000,000 at any time, at rates between 7 and 8.75 per cent.[43] Thus, the total capital being employed in the business was, if Peter's capital figures were right, between $1.6 and $1.7 million. Sales in 1859 totalled $1.1 million or about 70 per cent of total capital employed. Capital was being turned over so slowly that in the tight competitive conditions of the time the business may well have had trouble paying interest charges let alone earning any profits.

How had this situation arisen? Why had the business been unable so far to work itself out of trouble as it had after previous crises? Clearly managerial factors do not alone explain the firm's difficulties. Fundamental changes were under way in the Buchanan's commercial environment: above all, the era of extensive growth in southern Upper Canada had ended with the collapse of 1857.[44] If few can have expected the boom, or southern Upper Canadian agricultural frontier expansion, to have continued forever, few seem to have anticipated that the crash would be so hard. In its wake, almost everyone in Upper Canada had to try to meet fixed obligations from assets whose value had suddenly fallen and incomes that were shrinking, not growing. Those who had been most cautious in the previous three years had the easiest time, but few can have escaped the pressure entirely. Significantly, all three leading Upper Canadian banks failed between 1866 and 1869, principally because they could not cope with the problems they met following the collapse of 1857.[45]

This problem of liquidating what now proved to be overvalued assets was the Buchanans' major one, but certain broader underlying trends were also in motion. Thus, by 1860, the urban pattern of southern Upper Canada was largely determined; it was relatively clear which would be the significant centres, provincially, regionally, and locally, and which the marginal ones.[46] Towns not yet on a railroad and even many small ones that were had few prospects for major growth. Similarly, it was increasingly evident which were the more and which the less fertile and prosperous agricultural areas. No longer would it be one of the wholesaler's roles to judge future prospects of whole areas when he extended credit. Moreover, to the extent that a wholesaler's existing connection did not reflect the patterns that were crystallizing, his assets were probably exceptionally overvalued. In the Buchanans' case, Hamilton had large accounts, totalling over £3000 in each place, in 13 centres that had not yet reached a population of 1000 and in 14, ten overlapping with the previous group, that were not yet on any railroad; hence, fully half of its largest accounts were in communities with limited prospects at best (Figure 2, p 111). Even in 1856, George Borthwick had questioned the ability of most Upper Canadian merchants to do much over £2000 in good business in a year, because their market areas were not large enough.[47]

Besides judging areas, the wholesaler had to assess the credit-worthiness of individuals. That there was always a substantial element of risk in this is indicated by the turnover of the Buchanans' customers. Thus, of 140 customers at Toronto and Hamilton in 1842, only between 11 and 18 have descendants on Hamilton's list of 172 active accounts in 1857.[48] This is little more than ten per cent of the names on either list. Most of the remainder had had their credit cut off by the firm, probably in one of its three major prunings of accounts, in 1844, after 1847, and in 1856-7, or, for various reasons, had gone out of business. Some few had earned enough to become independent of any one wholesaler. At London, even in 1854, two years after opening, 63 of 227 accounts were being denied further credit. Of the fifteen largest London accounts at that time, nine remained on London's books in 1861, but five of these were being liquidated, leaving only four that were still considered sound, active, and reliable after just seven years had passed.[49]

The fundamental problems for the wholesaler were to avoid excessive losses on such customers' accounts and/or to have only a limited number of such losses at any one time. But it was equally vital to find new accounts to replace them, and this would now be much more difficult. Southern Upper Canada was largely settled, the growth rate of the province's rural population now slowed very markedly, and indeed net emigration from the province

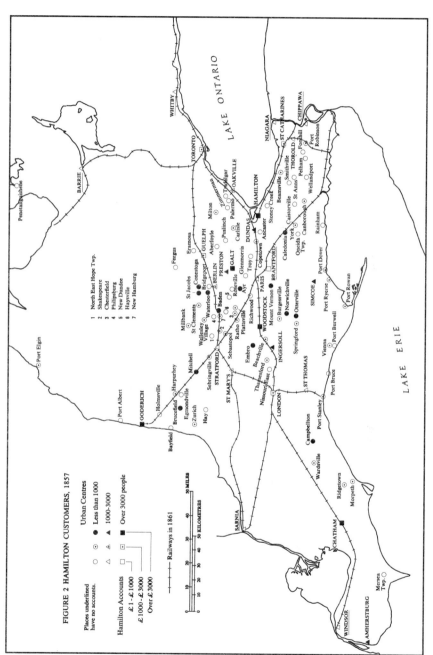

FIGURE 2 HAMILTON CUSTOMERS, 1857

Places underlined
have no accounts.

Urban Centres

○   Less than 1000
⊙
△   1000-3000
▲
□   Over 3000 people
■

Hamilton Accounts
£1 - £1000
£1000 - £3000
Over £3000

Railways in 1861

1 North East Hope Twp.
2 Shakespeare
3 Chesterfield
4 Philipsburg
5 New Dundee
6 Hayville
7 New Hamburg

Source: list of Hamilton customers, 30 Sept. 1857, 79/57936-9

soon became the trend.[50] The extent, though not the total volume, of the market was now established, and wholesalers faced heavy competition in starting up new accounts or capturing existing ones from rival firms. Retailers who had by about 1860 succeeded in building up and keeping a capital were in the minority, but there certainly were some. Their business was now much sought after, as is evidenced by the use of commercial travellers, the growing use of the Mercantile Agency by firms such as the Buchanans' as they sought names of potential customers, and the narrowness of wholesalers' profit margins on such first-class trade.[51] By the 1870s, moreover, many such established retail merchants would be able to secure direct banking accommodation, as the banks increasingly moved out from the larger centres. With this change and the rise of more specialized financial institutions such as mortgage companies, the long-credit system gradually came to an end in Upper Canadian wholesaling, and the wholesaler lost his central role in the credit-granting process.

Complicating the search for new customers and the battle to keep existing ones, for merchants in Toronto and Hamilton, was enhanced competition from Montreal. Merchants there had emerged relatively unscathed from the 1857 crisis, for the shorter credit terms of the market meant that their customers had to be better financed and more able to survive a crisis; no doubt Montreal firms had losses on their Upper Canadian trade, but not so many or so sudden as to force their own failure during the crisis. Now they confidently anticipated that the Grand Trunk Railway, completed to Toronto in 1856, would permit them to capture trade from Toronto and Hamilton.[52]

Although Toronto felt keenly this competition from Montreal, it was gradually able to rebuild its relative trading position. Factors here included its continued rise as a lumber port; the emergence in 1867 of the Bank of Commerce, a strong new bank dominated by Toronto merchants; the city's takeover of much of the trade formerly handled by the small ports along Lake Ontario; and its role as capital of the new Province of Ontario. To the extent that American goods were involved, Toronto had locational advantages in the import trade at least equal to Montreal's. Hamilton had closed the gap between its trading significance and Toronto's in the 1850s, but it had not overcome Toronto's lead, and Toronto still had a rather larger, more diversified commercial structure.[53] With the completion of the Grand Trunk across western Upper Canada in 1859, much of the west secured clearly better access to Toronto than to Hamilton, and this would further hamper Hamilton's merchants as they sought to survive in the 1860s. Hamilton had reached its limit as an independent centre in the import trade; in the 1860s and 1870s that trade would increasingly concentrate in Montreal and Toronto.[54]

In the Buchanans' case, fully half, in number and in terms of total obligations, of all the continuing accounts at Hamilton in 1857 were in the area that the Grand Trunk linked to Toronto (Figure 2, p 111). Existing customers were of course bound to them, and Hamilton, by debt, but there was little reason for new ones in the Grand Trunk area, especially east of Stratford, to look to Hamilton importers for supplies. The Buchanans might have moved their business, but the city itself could not move. Indeed, though he did not think very seriously of closing or moving the Hamilton branch, Isaac Buchanan expected the Montreal house to be the centre for much of the business's growth henceforth. The city of Hamilton, which had borrowed so heavily to encourage railroads and to build waterworks that it was bankrupt by the late 1850s, would learn in the 1860s and 1870s that the Great Western could serve to draw the western trade right past the city.

While the decennial censuses indicate that Hamilton's population was growing quite steadily between 1851 and 1871, local observers reckoned that population had peaked in 1858 and declined steadily over the next six years at least. The trends described here are likewise visible in the import figures. Both Toronto and Hamilton fell back relative to Montreal in the period from 1856 to 1862 and relative to their own import volumes of 1856 from 1856 to 1860 (Tables 12 and 13, p 179). Toronto's trade began to revive in the mid-1860s, however, and by the 1870s Toronto had clearly won the battle over Hamilton and regained the position it had occupied relative to Montreal in the mid-1850s. By the 1870s Hamilton was looking largely to industry rather than trade and finance for its future growth.[55]

There were in fact new business opportunities after 1857, for there was considerable growth in the Canadian economy – and in Anglo-Canadian trade – during the 1860s.[56] While the Canadian tariff was much increased in 1858 and 1859 primarily to procure greater government revenues, this had not reduced Canada's need for manufactured imports. Agriculture and lumbering remained the keys to Canadian prosperity, despite continuing growth of both secondary manufacturing and a more sophisticated service sector. For Upper Canadian agriculture, wheat remained the principal cash crop, but prices were lower than in the mid-1850s and production was more costly per bushel than it had been on virgin soil. New field crops such as barley contributed to farm incomes, however, and a growing livestock and dairying industry provided still more significant stimulus.[57]

Thus there was business to be done by traders, but in the competitive circumstances of the time, marginal differences in operating efficiency, location, and capitalization could be decisive to profit or loss. The economic changes of the time did not necessarily put money into the same hands as owed the Buchanans money, and general wholesalers like them did not necessarily have an advantage over smaller and more specialized competitors. As other mercantile roles diminished, the ability to buy and sell skilfully became ever more paramount, and this was not always done best in a large multi-department business. As the market widened and became more stable, it had become possible to secure larger volumes and substantial rewards in more specialized lines. As the large general firms of an earlier time disappeared or were wound up, they were not replaced. By the 1870s and 1880s, the more specialized merchant was completely in the ascendant in wholesaling, though his role in turn would soon be challenged by large integrated manufacturing firms and, in large urban areas, by department stores that had little need of wholesalers.[58]

Thus the pressure on the Buchanans' operations after 1857 came in part from longer-term trends that would limit merchants' roles in Upper Canadian trade and also, more specifically, the trading role of Hamilton. Such pressures exemplified parallel ones in the wider Atlantic world, and these were particularly evident in Glasgow, as it fell still further behind Liverpool as a trading port. This inevitably affected the position of overseas merchants in Glasgow. The relative decline of the Scottish cotton industry first began to become absolute in the 1860s as, in the tight competition accompanying the financial crisis of 1857 and the cotton famine of the early 1860s, Lancashire's locational advantages proved decisive.[59] Major growth in the British pig iron industry now shifted away from Scotland. Though Scottish production continued to increase in the 1860s and 1870s, a diminishing proportion of Scottish production went into the Atlantic trade; the trade between Glasgow and Canada had peaked in value in 1853-4 and did not again reach such levels until after 1866. As a result of the rise of the shipbuilding industry, Glasgow continued to grow rapidly. But the city's trade more and more consisted of the export of products of the city and its immediate hinterland, rather than the older entrepôt trade, in which the Buchanans were involved.*

* Some figures are available to illustrate the entrepôt nature of the Buchanans' trade; they suggest that Scottish sources supplied less than a third by value of the Buchanans' British goods. The following are the firm's purchases of Scottish dry goods expressed as a percentage of total British dry goods purchases for the year:

1836	20%	1839	21%	1845	28%
1837	30%	1841	26%	1847	31%
1838	24%	1842	25%	1849	31%

In 1855, the Glasgow office placed 23 per cent of the firm's British dry goods orders, 19 per cent of its grocery orders, and 21 per cent of its iron and hardware orders; the Liverpool office

Increasingly, personal factors, such as the preference of established traders to remain in Glasgow, were left as the sole reason for Glasgow to engage in the entrepôt trade. As such traders died, retired, moved, or went bankrupt, Glasgow's international entrepôt trade largely disappeared.[60]

When the American Civil War stopped the flow to England of raw cotton, the leading commodity in the North Atlantic trade, this severely affected cotton manufacturing in Britain for several years in the early 1860s. By cutting off the United States' chief staple export and by leading to major inflation in the north, the Civil War greatly enhanced the disruption of Anglo-American exchange rates and practices that the 1857 crisis had begun. Gold or grain became preferred methods of remittance, for the stronger firms at least. Cotton traders, once Liverpool's leading merchants, now had to seek new opportunities, for example in the Egyptian or Indian cotton trade, the Atlantic grain trade, areas of the British export trade, or the shipping industry.[61] Competition in the Anglo-American grain trade intensified, driving up advances and lowering commissions. Firms with capital therefore began to deal mainly on their own account because the risks of commission business were rising as profits fell. After the Civil War, this practice continued and was extended into the cotton trade. Both trades developed a system of futures trading when the Atlantic cable was completed and, secured by the futures system, large buyers and sellers found it easier to deal with one another directly. Increasingly the documentary bill replaced the older system where bills were based solely on the reputations of the names on them. The Anglo-American exchange system settled into a fully functioning mechanism in which the gold points really did indicate the exchanges.[62] Thus, after the Civil War many areas of the Anglo-American trade stabilized considerably; volume increased but because risks had been limited in many trades the mercantile function was much diminished, and mercantile opportunities therefore increased more slowly.[63]

For all in the Atlantic trades, even in Liverpool, just as for all in the Canadian trade, competition was significantly increased. Yet it must be noted that most such changes were relative rather than absolute and that many firms survived and prospered. Those with liquid capital could always seek other areas of opportunity, such as finance or the burgeoning Indian

handled paperwork, etc. for remaining orders, presumably placed in England. In 1867, of debts owed to dry goods suppliers by the firm, 31 per cent were owed to Scottish firms. Such figures, it should be noted, do not suggest any clear-cut decline in the role of Scottish goods in the firm's trade. See D. McCalla, 'The Buchanan Businesses, 1834-1872: A Study in the Organization and Development of Canadian Trade,' D.Phil. thesis, Oxford University, 1972, 204-17.

trade. Those tied to their trades and locations, such as the Buchanans, had to make the best of the new conditions. Both Glasgow and Hamilton were less and less the ideal locations for international trade, and this compounded the Buchanans' difficulties. Even in those cities, however, trade did not disappear and some firms survived; thus, managerial differences were important to the divergent fates of businesses sharing the same location. As of 1860 it remained to be determined whether the Buchanans' operation would survive the transition to the new era.

8
Isaac alone 1860-7

Peter Buchanan arrived in Liverpool on 10 October 1860. Within a few days, taking his oldest nephew, Peter T. Buchanan (who had begun mercantile training in the Glasgow office in February), he went with a group of friends to the shooting estate that he currently rented, Adamton, near Monkton, in Ayrshire. On 27 October, as they returned from shooting, Peter T.'s gun accidentally discharged, and the shot struck his uncle's right leg below the knee. At once Joseph Lister, the young surgeon whose great researches on antiseptic practice lay just in the future, was summoned from Glasgow. His prognosis was optimistic: it would not be necessary to amputate. But then tetanus developed, and on 5 November Peter died.[1] Much of Glasgow's trading community attended the funeral, for he had been well respected, and the tragic manner of his death aroused much sympathy. Writers of obituaries found little specific to say about Peter, however, other than that he was a man of integrity and character. A private, retiring man, he had few friends outside business, and he had taken relatively little part in Glasgow's civic, charitable, and social life.[2]

Peter's death deprived the business of its central figure. R.W. Harris, who now lived mainly in London, Canada, with his niece, died quietly there soon after, on 22 March 1861.[3] Of the men who had built the business, only Isaac Buchanan remained.

In the spring of 1860, aware of the vulnerability of the business, Peter had made a new will that provided for payments of capital that were very modest in proportion to the nominal value of his account.[4] His house in Glasgow was left to Jane Douglas, along with the income from a trust fund of £20,000stg to be invested securely outside the business. If George Douglas survived his wife, he was to receive £300 per year until his death. Ultimately the funds from this trust were to be divided equally among Isaac's children other than Peter T., who was left £5000 to be used to establish himself in business. Another £1200 in specific legacies were provided for. To the Douglases' evident chagrin, all the rest of the estate was left directly to Isaac.

As soon as he learned of Peter's death, Isaac undid some of the business changes so recently made.[5] First he offered partnerships to R.K. Masterton and to William Muir, who would move to Hamilton as manager of the grocery and hardware departments. Isaac felt that Muir's move would conciliate Harris's relatives by demonstrating that one of their number was represented in the business where most of Harris's interest was concentrated. Then Isaac united the Montreal and Hamilton firms. He planned to advertise Hamilton's hardware and grocery departments as extensions of equivalent departments at Montreal, because he thought they would attract more customers if visibly linked to the Montreal market, where prices were lower. By the new agreement, profits at Hamilton and Montreal were divided into 112 shares: Peter Buchanan and Company, 54; Leckie and Campbell, 18 each; Muir, 12; and Masterton, who lacked capital, 10. Peter Buchanan and Company was to build up the business's capital to $400,000.[6]

Isaac then left for Britain. He planned to live in Canada, where, he argued, the crucial decisions had to be made; as Wemyss alone was really qualified to take over in Glasgow, Isaac offered him a partnership in Peter Buchanan and Company, with one-third of its profits.[7] Already, however, there was tension between the two men, for Wemyss patterned his opinions after Peter's and faced the same problems in Glasgow. But Isaac, who had often been forced to accept his brother's views, would not accept them so readily when Wemyss proposed them.

Reflecting his disagreement with Peter, Isaac planned to expand the business and implement many of his long-cherished ideas. A good case could be made for this: some years of higher profits earned by an expanded business, carefully applied to reduction of borrowings, could end the business's decline, and new ideas could help the business sell its goods profitably. But Isaac's motives in 1860-1 were not really economic. As his wife* echoed it, his aim was 'to uphold in all its entirety [his] position without compromising its dignity one iota...'[8] While he was worried enough about a shortage of

---

* Agnes Buchanan emerged increasingly in these years as an important ally of her husband in business and politics; she often deputized for him in the office, wrote many letters on his behalf, and wrote some of his election literature. She was intensely loyal to Isaac's view of events and gave him full support.

capital to look, briefly, for a sleeping partner, he also bought his brother's house from Jane Douglas rather than see it sold outside the family. He transferred many customers' accounts from the old firm to the new at Hamilton and reallocated several suspense accounts to partners. The business had, he reckoned, a capital of about $800,000 after his brother's legacies were provided for. To expand, he needed all existing credits; as well, while in Britain, he opened a new credit, with Dennistoun, Cross and Company of London, the firm the Dennistouns had re-established after meeting all their 1857 obligations.

From 1860 to 1861, shipments to Hamilton were increased by 34 per cent, and there were increases in shipments to other locations and in North American purchases. Sales at both Montreal and Hamilton increased in a single year by forty per cent (Tables 1 and 2, pp 162-4). But at the end of 1861, the business's obligations were greatly increased over their level of twelve months earlier. In 1862, Hamilton had a further small sales increase, despite mixed economic conditions in Upper Canada. Collections, though, fell well short of 1861 sales, and Hamilton again increased its debt to Glasgow. This led in 1863 to a reduction in shipments and sales, but collections also fell, to a level equalling only 70 per cent of 1862 sales (Table 3, p 166). In the three years 1861 to 1863, Hamilton's sales exceeded collections by $400,000, and Hamilton's obligations to Glasgow increased by almost £50,000.[9] As a result, by 1864 the business at Glasgow began to encounter real difficulty at times in meeting its payments.

For all difficulties, Isaac Buchanan blamed commercial conditions in Upper Canadan – poor crops, low grain prices, and general uncertainty. Wheat prices in fact were low relative to those of the mid-1850s, but they seldom slid below $1.00 per bushel, and harvests were still larger in total volume than in most years of the 1850s. That it was possible to survive in these circumstances is indicated by the firm's other Canadian branches. Montreal sold heavily to Upper Canadians, but it consistently maintained its payments to Glasgow. The London business's hinterland was somewhat different from Hamilton's (Figures 2 and 3, pp 111, 120), and its accounts somewhat smaller, but it too depended on the agricultural prosperity of western Upper Canada. Sales there increased more moderately than Hamilton's, while the record of cash collections was very much better; the most glaring contrast was in 1863, when London collections equalled 98 per cent of 1862 sales (Table 3, p 166). Hope paid Glasgow each year for the previous year's shipments and met all capital payments required by the 1860 settlement.

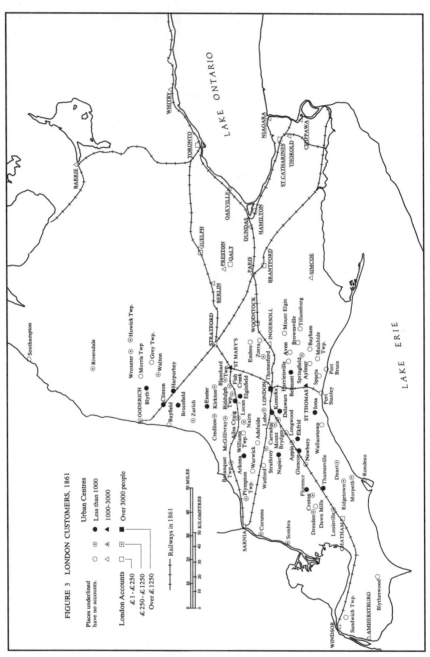

FIGURE 3 LONDON CUSTOMERS, 1861

Source: Adam Hope & Co., quarterly statement of accounts, 30 June 1861, 86/60887-91

Of course real problems faced the Hamilton business, but they were gravely compounded by Isaac's decisions. In 1861 at least, unchecked by Isaac, William Muir sold goods to many customers whose accounts were badly in arrears. By 1862 he was probably an alcoholic, was entirely untrustworthy, and was, moreover, thoroughly disliked by Harris's heirs, his wife evidently included. Eventually, in 1864, Isaac persuaded him to return with his wife and children to his family home in Scotland; there he was paid £15 per month to keep him out of the way.[10] Masterton proved more interested in sales than in collections, but although the partners later denounced him viciously, they were by then looking for a scapegoat. A capable enough employee, he did not become a satisfactory partner. To some extent this was because Isaac still treated him as an employee, telling him nothing of financial problems and issuing orders as before. In any case, for the promotion and lack of supervision of both men, whatever their contribution to the difficulties, Isaac alone was responsible. It is clear that he was conscious of at least some of his business's problems; until 1864, however, he pursued an erratic and often irrelevant attack upon them.

Isaac also continued his political career, although he frequently spoke of resigning from the Assembly.[11] In Hamilton he patronized many organizations – perhaps most notably the 13th Battalion of Volunteer Militia, which he organized in 1862 and commanded for two years – and his money found its way into a number of them. His prominence, purse, and local patriotism secured him re-election in 1861, 1863, and 1864. He and other Hamilton area members worked for several years on the issue of Hamilton's civic indebtedness; finally they secured creditors' agreement to and passage of a bill that settled the issue by recapitalizing Hamilton's debts and unpaid interest and temporarily reducing the rate of interest payable on them.[12] This was his chief cause of the period, the one that he saw as justifying his continued political activity.

He still spoke and wrote on his longer-term concerns, however. Protection and currency reform and liberalization were the chief among these, but he spoke also for the abolition of American slavery and continued to advocate a Canadian-American Zollverein. He opposed representation by population, stating that Lower Canadian votes were needed to preserve Canada's higher tariff levels. He was, in fact, a genuine independent, who did not seek office; rather arrogantly, he claimed that no party was sufficiently patriotic.[13] Yet his hostility to George Brown and 'political economy' of the Gladstonian variety pushed him some distance towards the Conservative camp. This and his reputation for independence served to bring him briefly to ministerial rank, as President of the Council in the short-lived Taché-Macdonald ministry of

March to June 1864. It is doubtful if he brought any particular support with him, not even the manufacturers; many of them could not have approved of his enthusiasm for extending Canadian-American reciprocity to manufactured goods.[14]

Despite such political activity, Isaac found time to launch a variety of new departures in the business in these years. In 1861 he took over several of Hamilton's backward accounts in larger centres, with a view to working off the arrears of debt that these firms owed.[15] Fearing that an overt takeover would arouse suspicions as to the stability of his business, in several cases he employed the former owners as managers and continued the businesses in their names to conceal the new ownership. These stores and at least one newly opened, in an employee's name, would, he hoped, sell for cash only, so that no further funds would be locked up in them. Thus, Isaac returned to an old idea that perhaps had greater merit: certainly by the later nineteenth century, some retail businesses, in cities at least, could attract cash customers successfully by offering lower prices; and businesses based on retail branch systems were also to grow in the last third of the century.[16] But good ideas unsupported by money and organization meant little in the business world. Moreover, if the original owner had not succeeded in reducing debts when he alone was liable for them, it is hard to see how he would do better when freed of such obligations. Isaac took up another of his old ideas in 1861 as well, importing goods in the fall for spring sale. In the railroad age, however, this idea had little place; Isaac simply tied up capital unnecessarily in stock.

Pursuing his theory that Canada's trade would centre more fully at Montreal, Isaac in 1862 authorized the house there to rent new, better located premises where stock could be displayed to more advantage, and in 1864 he agreed to doubling the size of the new store. Initially he proposed to help offset much higher store costs by renting out the old Lachine Canal premises, but he may have used them to house still further stock. Isaac planned also to move the Hamilton grocery and hardware businesses to Montreal. Though Campbell and Leckie thought Hamilton's lower class of customers would not suit Montreal, they agreed to try the idea. Then, without abandoning the idea, Isaac simply let it drop.

Peter Buchanan had explored the idea of securing tea consignments direct from China for their New York office with Isaac's brother-in-law, John Jarvie, who managed Jarvie, Thorburn and Company, the Shanghai house of the Glasgow firm of Buchanan, Hamilton and Company. In 1861, encouraged in part by the recent change in Canadian grocery duties to an *ad valorem* basis,* Isaac, Campbell, and Leckie developed the idea enthusiastically, but they planned to ship direct to Montreal. Such shipments would give great prestige to the firm, yet large outlays could be avoided because the trade could be done on joint account with Jarvie, Thorburn and Company, and bills used to purchase the tea would fall due only after Montreal had discounted bills received for its sale.[17] If Montreal was overstocked, the New York market could be used to dispose of the tea. Of all those consulted, only Adam Hope objected to the scheme.[18] New York, he argued, must remain the centre of the trade, especially after wartime disruptions had passed, and the risks involved were too great for the profit or prestige that might be gained. Tea sold at a large profit in the spring of 1861, and Hope suggested that firms would rush into the trade. Even so, Leckie purchased a large consignment in bond in New York, and on 5 November 1861, Montreal held its first tea auction. It was only a partial success, but Isaac and Leckie were now ready to try their first full cargo from China.

In the spring of 1862, a further large consignment from New York was purchased, and in the fall the first direct cargo, 370,000 pounds of tea costing over $200,000, arrived in Montreal. Further direct cargoes arrived in June 1863, spring 1864, and fall 1865. These six ventures, as a result of a very large profit on the final one, yielded some net profit.[19] The initial auction of teas for several of the cargoes realized good prices, but the remaining tea had always to be worked off privately, often at lower prices. Much of the spring 1864 shipment had to be reshipped to England or New York. Such disappointing profits for five years of tea operations are not hard to explain: five or more houses were competing for a share of the Montreal trade, and the proximity of the New York market limited price and hence profits. Although the Montreal firm did avoid large-scale outlay, there were risks in such business. For example, a huge inventory had to be carried in 1864-5; and when, early in 1865, Buchanan, Hamilton and Company failed, Wemyss had to meet almost £25,000stg in tea bills from the 1864 consignment that he had hoped to renew. He was fortunate to secure a special credit from William Connal and Company of Glasgow to cover this, Connal taking title to the tea as security.[20]

The tea trade, and one parallel venture in coffee with Buchanan, Watson and Company (of Glasgow and Brazil), indicated Isaac Buchanan's large ambitions even when his business was very vulnerable. It carried the Montreal house into a new business era, in which a large part of its sales was made

---

* Thus the business would pay duty on the price in Shanghai, not New York; until 1859, a specific duty was charged, regardless of where the tea was purchased.

at two or three auctions per year. But while volume increased to record levels (Table 1, p 162), profit margins were very narrow. With adequate capital support and more vigorous management, the Montreal house might have established itself firmly in the trade in the long-term; lacking these, it just held its own.*

By the end of 1864, Isaac's management was coming under increasing challenge by his partners, most especially Wemyss, who alone knew the details of Glasgow finance. The old business at Hamilton still owed the new about $175,000. It possessed real estate valued by Isaac and Wemyss at $130,000 and old accounts, totalling $580,000, estimated by Wemyss to be worth less than $200,000. Though the real estate at last began to seem saleable, Wemyss concluded that the old business could not be relied upon to yield a surplus of more than $100,000. After four years, the new firm had realized no capital from the old; worse still, any it had earned from its operations, some of which had shown good book profits, had been locked up in further backward accounts. The books seem to have shown the firm with more capital, as a result of various accounting arrrangements, and Isaac had gone on drawing sums from the business at a rate exceeding $25,000 per year.[21] He was either unaware of or preferred to ignore his lack of real capital when all accounts are analyzed together.

Since 1861, to avoid questions about Harris's estate, Isaac had paid out $47,000, about 20 per cent of Harris's nominal capital prior to the reorganization, to Harris's heirs, although it was not yet clear that Harris's account in the old business had any value. He had failed to make payments in the order specified by the will, however, and he had given Harris's trustees no accounts. When they learned that Isaac had not followed the will, they declared that they held him personally responsible for any losses that might result. The heirs in turn could not believe that their relative had left so little money, and in May 1864, they sued Harris's trustees in the Upper Canadian Court of Chancery. The case took several years before it was settled by a compromise, and it threatened at any time to expose the business's position. Isaac's management of the estate had needlessly complicated a difficult issue, and in the next few years he would spend much time and worry on the matter.

---

* After Buchanan, Hamilton and Company failed, Alexander Campbell was able to arrange a new joint account in tea with Gilman and Company of London and Shanghai. The Buchanans' half was supported by a special credit arranged in London with the Bank of British North America. Campbell to Isaac Buchanan, 21 Oct. 1865, 20/16596-8.

Peter T. Buchanan, even before his uncle's death, had shown little interest in business, and he made no further progress under Wemyss's tutelage. In 1862, Isaac brought his son to Hamilton where, nominally, he handled the cash in the store and worked for his father on political matters. In fact, Peter T. was given little responsibility, showed little interest or ability, and, because his father was constantly shifting his duties, was given no incentive to learn any job. Yet late in 1864, with Wemyss anxious to come to Canada, Isaac proposed to put his son in charge of the Glasgow office. The boy had, he said, shown 'a mind fitted for Finance & responsibility.'[22]

There is no better mind about our Establishment nor any one who has more the confidence & respect of the community as well as those about ourselves.

I feel that Peter's intimate knowledge of our Finance here, and the fact of my being able to trust him are great qualifications for the Glasgow office at the present time...[23]

Peter's uncle, John Jarvie, described the idea as 'rubbish,'[24] while Robert Leckie, currently visiting Scotland, recommended that 'a more elderly head in charge here would give more confidence to those interested with the firm...'[25] Isaac was projecting his own remembrance of himself 35 years earlier onto his son, while neglecting the enormous differences in situation and character. He seemed to believe that by declaring something to be true, he could make it so. In 1864, for example, he asserted:

The result of my present investigation leaves me with the same increased confidence as was always the case in former times of difficulty when my poor Brother & Mr Harris used to wonder how I always seemed to rise with the storm.

No firm ever stood so high as we do at this moment, and none probably will again ever do so – our position therefore is a great capital...[26]

Isaac's partners never accorded him quite the respect they had for Peter Buchanan, yet as a rich man, public figure, and founder of a great business, he had possessed much authority. In many respects Isaac was a most generous man; indeed this is one reason that he found it difficult to squeeze customers for payment. At the same time, he was often very high-handed in dealing with partners and employees, and he gave much offense in this way. He neither supervised his chief subordinates adequately nor gave adequate responsibility and power to them. Oppressed by the weight of decisions to be made and work to be done, he fell far behind on correspondence and postponed even minor decisions. As he paid little attention to detail, it is not even clear how much he knew of the business's real position. Hope wrote that he would like to discuss business matters, but Isaac ignored the request.

When the late Mr Harris was in his usual health I always looked forward with great pleasure to his annual investigation of the affairs of this business which embraced everything from the foundation *of the building itself* to the Stocks and final Balance of the Books, and many a useful hint he gave me...[27]

Detailed scrutiny and correspondence related to it had been Harris's responsibility. Isaac now had no such figure to rely on.

When Wemyss, alarmed at the growth of Glasgow's outstanding debts after 1861, called for new courses of action, Isaac accused him of trying to prejudice the banks against him so that Wemyss could take over the business. When others supported Wemyss, as in the matter of Peter T. Buchanan's business ability, Isaac accused them too of joining the conspiracy. By 1864, economic difficulties and Isaac's mismanagement had brought the business to the brink of bankruptcy.

The immediate cause of the difficulty was the closure of the New York exchange market for a time in the summer of 1864, although the failure of John Gladstone and Company in October slightly exacerbated the situation. The Buchanan firm had sold bills of exchange on Peter Buchanan and Company in New York first to make purchases there and later to facilitate the produce trade. Its reputation in the grain trade had permitted it to sell accommodation bills, notably in 1847 and 1857, to make up for deficiencies in collections. Though all 'accommodation' transactions were invariably condemned in the wake of commercial crises, drawing bills that were not directly and explicitly against particular transactions was a normal business practice. It was necessary for a business to be careful in its use of such paper, however, if it was to survive and sustain a high reputation. Thus, Peter Buchanan had always criticized Isaac strongly for being too ready to draw such bills, and after the firm's reliance on accommodation bills from 1857 to 1860, he had been determined to eliminate their use as soon as possible.[28] In 1861, that goal had been in sight; the average amount of such paper outstanding then at any one time was about £15,000.[29]

As Hamilton's debt to Glasgow grew thereafter, this figure mounted. Now David McGee's major job in New York was not to purchase goods or sell produce, though both functions continued to be of some importance, but to sell bills on Peter Buchanan and Company.[30] Over the next few years he found at least ten regular buyers, including such eminent firms as Brown Brothers.* Using the proceeds of this exchange, he bought bills on England from other bankers. The need to meet such paper raised Wemyss's monthly payments to hitherto unprecedented levels. In July 1862, he had to find £56,000, a record for any month in the firm's history, yet by the end of the year, this was the monthly average. In the summer of 1864, the New York exchange market was virtually closed; the firm survived only by heavy borrowing in Canada. When the market reopened, Isaac had to meet postponed North American payments, but he could only sell sixty-day paper instead of the usual ninety-day bills. Quickly Wemyss's average total monthly obligations passed £100,000. Early in 1865, the firm owed £112,000 on accommodation bills of exchange alone.[31]

Not all the firm's exchange was sold through New York, though it could not have operated on such a scale from Canada alone. To accommodate Hamilton, the Montreal firm sold a good deal of exchange, usually alternately to its two banks, the Commercial Bank and the Bank of British North America, using proceeds from one to buy at the other. Banking secrecy served to protect the business's reputation. At Hamilton, Isaac actually arranged direct trades of paper with the Gore Bank and the Bank of Upper Canada; both banks, now very weak, evidently saw such transactions as one way to keep up their business.[32] If they believed Isaac's explanations, it was likely because they also were using them.

As the amount McGee sold increased, and as he bought and sold even in quite unfavourable market situations, it became increasingly obvious that the firm was not primarily drawing against produce. Some of his buyers either did not or preferred not to notice, but others sought explanations. Isaac had a variety of plausible ones ready, and some accepted them. Others simply reduced their dealings with the business. Perhaps it was felt in New York that the Buchanan firm, like some other eminent mercantile houses, was becoming, increasingly, a banking rather than a commercial enterprise, yet it is difficult to believe this was true for most. It should be noted, however, that as late as 1866 the Mercantile Agency rated all three Buchanan houses in Canada A1A1; that is, each was said to command capital of over $500,000 and to have an unlimited credit rating – no more than two or three businesses in British North America stood higher, and few held the same rank.[33]

---

* Isaac's second son, Harris, entered Brown Brothers, New York in 1867 as a trainee clerk (his father paying a premium for this). David McGee to Isaac Buchanan, 3 Aug. 1867, 44/35795.

Wemyss's bankers, however, were well aware of what was happening, for most of this paper passed through the Union Bank. Alarmed at its near collapse in 1857, the Union directors had moved more actively into its management and had in 1862 appointed Charles Gairdner, a Glasgow accountant, to manage its affairs jointly with its present manager, James Robertson, who was a long-time friend of Peter Buchanan.[34] Gairdner increasingly pressed Wemyss to reduce his obligations to the bank. By late 1864, he strongly doubted Wemyss's explanations, and little but fear of a total loss induced him to keep the business going. His pressures led Wemyss in 1864 to propose going to Canada to investigate in detail the reasons for the difficulty. Considering this a challenge to his authority, Isaac refused. Wemyss pointed out that it was normal, in most businesses, for partners to meet,[35] and he won the backing of Campbell, Leckie, and Harris's trustees. This forced Isaac finally to look more closely at the business than he had in years. He resolved to anticipate Wemyss by merging the London and Hamilton businesses to extract capital from London and to secure Adam Hope's managerial skills at Hamilton.[36] Early in 1865, he at last resigned from the Canadian Assembly.

Isaac explained to Hope that the business's difficulties stemmed from a lock-up of capital in old accounts. As he had done so successfully in London, Hope was asked to manage goods operations at Hamilton to extract cash from these accounts and to develop a better connection. Much impressed by the size of the connection and the number of good accounts, Hope did not examine the overall state of the business, taking it to be safe enough. It meant a great deal to him to secure a full partnership in a large international business, including its Glasgow head office.[37] He planned to close his grocery and dry goods businesses at London and to bring his chief employees to Hamilton, and he hoped as well to keep many of his better customers. His wholesale and retail hardware business, because it completely dominated the London market, would be left open; it might also help to collect accounts that were being closed.

This proposal was made to Hope and accepted in December 1864, but it was not announced, even to the Montreal partners. Wemyss was told, and he found his bankers very pleased. Hope was known to be a capable manager for the circumstances. In March 1865, the closure of much of the business at London and the opening of the new firm of Buchanan, Hope and Company at Hamilton were announced. Hope moved to Hamilton soon after. Busied with customers' accounts, he was delighted with the position of the business during the spring sales season. But then he at last had time to survey all the firm's books and to learn just how weak it was. He reacted bitterly, but by closing his London business he had committed himself in Hamilton. He therefore insisted on an accounting of affairs between the new and old businesses. When Wemyss reached Canada in September 1865, leaving Alexander Campbell in charge at Glasgow, the three partners examined the state of the Hamilton business once again.

They concluded that another $200,000 in totally bad debts should be written off. Most of these accounts, Wemyss said, had been taken over from the pre-1860 business after Peter Buchanan's death; the worst of them, Hope considered, were the 'consignment' accounts, Isaac's retail branches. The write-off was dated 13 March 1865 and left Buchanan, Harris and Company with a loss for 1864 of $167,000. Hope valued remaining accounts at $736,000, while stock and other assets totalled $293,000. Hamilton owed Glasgow over $700,000 on current and exchange account and Canadian banks $227,000 on discounted paper; other debts brought liabilities about level with assets. At Glasgow, the books showed liabilities of £312,000 and assets of £369,000, but one of the assets, a 'capital loan' to Hamilton of £45,000, was not included in the above reckoning of Hamilton's debts.[38] If it is removed from Glasgow's assets, they are left exceeding liabilities by no more than the sum at credit of Glasgow suspense accounts, £13,000; in effect, the entire capital of about £45,000stg shown at Isaac's credit vanishes. All that was achieved by showing this sum at his credit was to allow him to draw interest on it. There was really no excess of assets over liabilities except for net capital at Montreal and sums realized at London.

The London business, though strongly entrenched in its own market, could not yield much capital to Hamilton. Capital accounts there in March 1865 were as follows: Isaac Buchanan, $123,000; Adam Hope, $59,000; C.J. Hope, $32,000; and reserve capital, $34,000. The hardware business at London was to be carried on under the name of Adam Hope and Company by C.J. Hope, who would receive forty per cent of its profits. His capital would stay in the business, as would $49,000 from Peter Buchanan and Company. The reserve capital account was likely to be needed to cover losses in winding up, so the net sum that could be realized from London was about $133,000, or not much more than ten per cent of Hamilton's liabilities.[39] A strong, well-capitalized business was being swallowed up by a larger and far less healthy one. It is hard to believe that Hope would have moved had he investigated fully first. His success in putting his business on a solid footing is an excellent indicator of the weakness of Hamilton management in the preceding eight years.

The other partners were unaware of Isaac's plans until the public announcement in March. Muir now ceased to be a partner; there is no evidence that he protested. Masterton was justifiably aggrieved, for there was no place for him in the new firm. The write-offs of 1865 left his account at a debit of $25,000, but he was able to negotiate a compromise settlement, essentially for leaving the business quietly; this paid him at least $10,000 and left him free of all liability to the firm.[40]

Hope demanded that he be guaranteed by Isaac and Wemyss against loss on several accounts: $82,000 lost on T.H. McKenzie's account, which had been pushed by Isaac over strong protests by his partners and despite considerable evidence of deceit on McKenzie's part; $105,000 drawn by Isaac since 1860 and charged against him in the books of the pre-1860 business; a further $161,000 owed by the pre-1860 business; $103,000 to cover debit balances against Muir, Masterton, and Campbell in the books of the post-1860 firm; and $100,000 to indemnify him against loss on any accounts taken over from the post-1860 business by Buchanan, Hope and Company. In return for this guarantee, Hope renounced his share of Montreal profits. Isaac and Wemyss agreed to use their shares from Montreal to cover certain of these debit balances.[41] Wemyss now had no capital and the figure at Isaac's credit was illusory, yet their accounts stood as security for guarantees and allowances to Hope exceeding $500,000. When Isaac in late 1865 proposed an amendment to permit him to put half his capital in one of his son's names, to secure a place in the business for a son in the event of his own death, Wemyss promptly pointed out that half of Isaac's current capital was very little indeed.

The complete new partnership agreement for Hamilton and Glasgow was finally signed on 19 October 1865 and back-dated to 13 March.[42] All three partners, rather than Isaac alone, now had to agree to a dissolution, and a ceiling of $12,500 was put on Isaac's spending. All partners were to stay out of politics. Profits and losses were to be divided 50 per cent to Isaac and 25 per cent each to Wemyss and Hope. Isaac could choose his place of residence, Wemyss agreeing to come to Canada if Isaac went to Glasgow, as Wemyss and Hope desired.

Isaac kept the Montreal partners free of Hamilton primarily to protect that business in the event of failure at Hamilton. Montreal might then provide a place to start a son in business. Even now the Montreal partners did not fully realize how desperate was the position at Hamilton, and they greatly resented Isaac's use of his power to dissolve the business unilaterally. This power, which Peter Buchanan had always given himself, evoked wonder two years later when public discussion of it occurred. Campbell and Leckie considered the write-offs at the closing of the combined Montreal-Hamilton business to be an effort by Hope to profit at their expense, and they objected to any implication that Hope and Wemyss were superior to them. Hence they insisted that Buchanan, Hope and Company's shares in the Montreal business be held in Isaac's name. No formal agreement was ever signed, but the Montreal partnership, known as I. Buchanan and Company, now consisted of Isaac Buchanan, with 30 shares held for himself and Wemyss; Peter T. Buchanan, whom Isaac wished to establish at Montreal, with 10 shares; Campbell and Leckie, each with 30; and F.B. Matthews, Montreal's long-time bookkeeper, now made a partner, with 12. Isaac pledged that he would supply $60,000 in capital, and he credited Montreal with this sum in the Glasgow books.[43] Thus, he restored the arrangement of separate interests at Hamilton and Montreal that he had rushed to abandon in 1860.

The negotiations that produced these changes left relations among partners very hostile indeed. If Hamilton, for the first time in over ten years, had capable and attentive management, the conflict among partners did much to offset the gain. Yet the merger did permit Canadian payments to Glasgow to improve while Glasgow's outlay was reduced from previous years. Thus the firm's gross contingency there dropped significantly in 1865; though assets were being reduced correspondingly as London accounts were wound up, the reduction in gross amounts convinced the bankers that the business was at last making progress.

In July 1866, the Hopes moved the hardware business to Hamilton as well, for Adam Hope had kept most of his better dry goods customers when he moved.* Two employees took over the London retail hardware business; a wholesale sample room was left open in London, and two travellers were employed to work from Hamilton. Adam Hope and Company moved into the Hamilton hardware premises, but the two firms remained distinct in order to take advantage of separate discount lines in Canada and the discount line for Adam Hope and Company acceptances in the Union Bank and also, no doubt, to protect the Hopes from a possible failure of the main Hamilton business. The hardware firm acquired Hamilton's good hardware customers. It was composed of C.J. Hope, with 30 per cent of profits, and Buchanan, Hope and Company.[44]

During the first part of 1866, Hamilton collections went well, as Hope applied great pressure to customers, and Wemyss was able to reduce banking obligations significantly, despite increased shipments to Hamilton. In May

---

* Among these was Timothy Eaton, then of St Mary's (London Quarterly Statement of Accounts, 29 Feb. 1864, 86/61134-8; T. & J. Eaton to Buchanan, Hope and Company, 17 Jan. 1868, 25/21372-3).

1866, Wemyss's obligations totalled about £205,000, of which £68,000 were due directly to suppliers; about a year earlier, he had owed £291,000, £71,000 of which were for goods. Thus, he had reduced his banking obligations by over £80,000. Hamilton had, however, postponed many local payments, and the widespread commercial pressures of the spring and summer added to its problems. There was little money for remittances in the second half of the year: Adam Hope and Company sent £10,000 to Glasgow while Buchanan, Hope and Company sent only £12,000. For the year, Hamilton's remittances just equalled shipments, although cash collections had exceeded sales by $100,000 (Table 3, p 166). In February 1867, Wemyss's banking obligations totalled £160,000, a substantial increase since May. Such a seasonal increase was not unusual, but Wemyss's creditors expected his obligations to decline steadily. Beyond these sums, Wemyss owed £30,000 to the Montreal business.

Isaac Buchanan now spent most of his time travelling between Montreal, Hamilton, and New York, apparently finding some satisfaction in the sense of action that this gave. When collections early in 1867 ran behind the rate of 1866, despite the increase in Hamilton sales in 1866, Isaac decided to go to Britain to seek a sleeping partner to furnish additional funds. Wemyss protested, warning that this would damage existing credits, that no such investor would be found unless Isaac grossly misrepresented the business's position, and that Isaac, as senior partner, would have to answer embarrassing questions that Wemyss could more easily evade. In London Isaac found it impossible to locate new funds, and in Glasgow he had a stiff interview with Charles Gairdner, who demanded detailed information about every aspect of the business. Wemyss and Isaac returned to Canada in April to secure this information. Campbell, who had moved his family to Scotland in an effort to economize, again took over the Glasgow office.

Spring sales and collections and hence remittances fell below expectations, and Campbell had gradually to raise his overdraft from the agreed ceiling. Gairdner was furious. When the partners undertook a special half-yearly balance for him, they concluded that all pre-1864 assets in the books of the pre-1865 businesses were worthless. At each succeeding valuation, these assets had been reduced, yet never by enough. The partners realized that the liabilities of the business significantly exceeded its assets, and they concluded that they had no choice but to ask their principal creditors for time to pay.

On 2 July, Wemyss offered a compromise to Gairdner that would see the business square its account with the Union Bank in 1873. The bank agreed, provided the Gore and Commercial Banks agreed and Wemyss lowered his overdraft to £27,500 by 30 September and furnished certain securities, including an insurance policy on Isaac Buchanan's life. The Gore Bank proved willing, but the Commercial, very near to its own bankruptcy, was reluctant. Rumours of the firm's difficulties circulated widely in Canada, and this contributed to a continuing weakness in collections. By September, the overdraft at the Union was £54,000; its directors refused to support the business any longer. Late in September, Hamilton and New York suspended payments, and Glasgow failed soon after.

As the business's position deteriorated, Isaac and his two partners quarreled ever more fiercely about every aspect of the business's difficulties. To Isaac, the situation was the result of the current depression in Canada. When remittances were slow late in 1866, he blamed the Fenian raids, the collapse of the Bank of Upper Canada, which reduced note circulation in Upper Canada, the rainy autumn of 1866, the attempt by the government of Canada to create a bank of issue, the hostile policy of the Bank of Montreal towards the Upper Canadian banks, the end of the Reciprocity Treaty, and the English financial panic.[45] It was an impressive catalogue, but it did not account for the long build-up of the situation, for the survival of competing businesses, or for Isaac's recurrent optimism.

Hope accused Isaac of misrepresentation in 1864-5, and said that Isaac's problem was lack of application, not lack of ideas;[46] he cited his own experience since 1857 to show that public causes alone did not explain Hamilton's problems. Hope and Wemyss insisted that, if the creditors accepted the request for delay, Isaac be kept from any real say in management; he would take nominal charge in Glasgow, employing David McGee as his office manager. Hope and Wemyss demanded the power to expel Isaac from the business if they chose.

The relative positions of partners are now entirely changed from those of the past, and some of us at least consider you as being solely answerable for our present humiliating position with our creditors.[47]

Isaac could never accept this; he preferred to see the business suspend. It is not surprising that the business did so little in its last months to avoid the rocks onto which it was drifting.

Despite Isaac's intention to separate Montreal and Hamilton, he thoroughly intertwined them in 1866 and 1867. During 1866, Montreal built up exceptional discounts and completed remittances to Glasgow much earlier than usual. To do so, Montreal postponed other payments until the last minute. In the fall, the sum at Hamilton's debit in Montreal was transferred to Montreal's credit in Glasgow so that more of Hamilton's collections could go into remittances. Hence Glasgow built up a larger debt to Montreal. Montreal also kept £20,000 in exchange on the circle for Hamilton, and in August 1867, to maintain payments in Glasgow, Campbell was forced to give Montreal's guarantee to the Union Bank to the amount of £10,000stg.

As he travelled back from Britain in April 1867, Isaac resolved to save Montreal from a possible suspension at Hamilton. Although he denied any intention of putting some of his resources beyond the reach of creditors, this clearly was his plan. On arrival, he went to Montreal and arranged a new partnership there, taking effect on 1 July. The old business was wound up, and a new business created consisting of Isaac, Campbell, and Leckie, each with 30 shares, Matthews with 20, and Peter T. Buchanan with 10.[48] Isaac reserved the right to transfer his shares to his son and abandoned the power to dissolve the business unilaterally. Wemyss, who travelled on the same ship as Isaac, heard nothing of this plan. He accused Isaac of attempting to defraud creditors and partners. In August, Isaac transferred his shares to his son Peter, who was to hold them for the entire family. It is hard to believe that a court would have upheld Isaac in this, but the matter never came to a formal test (see Table 9, p 175, however).[49] Leckie and Matthews were happy at any arrangement that promised to keep the business alive, if woefully under-capitalized, and their only complaint was that Campbell, to whom they were now very hostile, was not excluded.

At the time of the suspension, Wemyss again was in Canada to consult Hope; he rushed back to Britain carrying a power to act for Hope in most matters. Isaac followed a few weeks later. Meanwhile, the Union Bank sent an accountant, Robert Brown, to Canada to investigate. Sales and collections continued at Hamilton, though complicated by the suspension and increasingly by the loss of customers who sought better backing.

Finally, a meeting of twenty-five representatives of creditors was held at Glasgow on 21 November 1867 and it was decided to apply for sequestration under Scottish bankruptcy law. On 7 December, the first official meeting of creditors was held. Walter Mackenzie, a Glasgow accountant, was named trustee of the sequestrated estates, and Charles Gairdner, George Rainey, and James Campbell, all of Glasgow, were named commissioners of the estate. On 27 December, a meeting of creditors heard offers of composition by Isaac and by Hope and Wemyss, both sides wanting to carry on the business, and the creditors agreed to accept one of these; notification was sent to 74 creditors of this decision. A further meeting held 21 January 1868 accepted Isaac's offer. Later in the year all three partners were discharged, having furnished security for their payment of the sums owed (Hope's and

Wemyss's being the nominal sum of one penny in the pound on their personal estates.) The Canadian creditors had meanwhile agreed to come under Scottish law, provided two Canadian commissioners were named, and Plummer Dewar had been appointed official assignee of the estate in Canada. The American creditors, chiefly exchange bankers, accepted Scottish jurisdiction, primarily, it appears, because the firm possessed few assets in New York that could be seized.

When the partners' and the trustees' valuations of the estate were produced, the creditors were astonished at how poorly it had turned out. Some creditors had reservations at what they considered Isaac's unethical transfer at Montreal, but in the end they accepted his offer of 8/3 in the pound on his business estate and 3/6 on his personal estate (the latter consisting of that part of the business's debts not covered by the composition payments, plus a few minor claims). That Isaac's was the larger offer seems to have been the decisive factor. In effect he had offered slightly over ten shillings in the pound, whereas Hope and Wemyss offered 7/6 (Table 9, p 175). Isaac was determined to keep his business, if at all possible, in order to be able to support his family.

There were a number of contested accounts, including one claim by Peter Buchanan's trustees for sums at Peter's credit in Glasgow in 1860 (plus interest) that Isaac had never formally accounted for, which seems finally to have ranked on the estate. The sums paid the trustees from the business estate, minus some expenses, would yield £16,600 to Isaac and formed the basis for his offer on his personal estate; his real property, consisting of the Hamilton estate and the Montreal canal stores, was already considerably encumbered as security for various advances. Isaac's composition was to be paid in eight equal instalments, including interest on the last three, payments to be every six months commencing 24 August 1868. His payments in Britain were £10,740 each (of which £3090 went to Peter Buchanan's trustees and thence largely back to Isaac), and Canadian ones were about $15,000.[50] Thus he had to find and pay out over £85,000stg in the next four years from assets that he valued at slightly over £100,000. As security for the final instalment, he furnished his son Peter, whose inheritance would give him some capital; Michael James Jamieson, member of a mercantile family with whom the Buchanans had long been friends; and John Reid, a Glasgow merchant having some connection with Peter T. Buchanan.

During the bankruptcy proceedings, the partners offered explanations of what had occurred. Isaac now took a longer-term view than in 1866:

The suspension of Buchanan Hope & Co has no doubt its great origin in the fact that of the capital of Partners in the former Business of Buchanan Harris & Co (about

Seven Hundred Thousand dollars) nothing has yet been recovered. Its assets were the Debris of a thirty years business and although there were large allowances for bad debts these proved quite insufficient. But the overwhelming feature was that B. Harris & Co owed Peter Buchanan & Co and other foreign creditors and Banks an amount which with accumulating Interest has proved nearly double the amount at the credit of the partners ... And the case of Buchanan Harris & Co is the general rule rather than the exception here of Businesses which were wound up during the transition period when the country was going from a long credit system to one of short & definite credits.[51]

Isaac was aware that not all businesses that had operated before 1857 had since failed:

No House nor Bank having large debts out prior to 1858 have recovered much of them altho' some by a more active Business have made money enough to atone for this.[52]

Certainly a shorter-credit system was coming into being. Of $250,000 in customers' paper under discount at Hamilton in 1867, all but $20,000 was met at maturity, or far more than any estimate of business liabilities had assumed. Hope had been selling only to good customers, and it is in fact possible that narrow margins on sales to such customers could have yielded profits that were consumed by interest, in view of rates of eight and nine per cent per annum that the firm had frequently paid.[53] But of course Isaac's analysis did not go very far in explaining why a business as strong as his had fallen so far when ones that he and his partners had always thought much weaker carried on.

Wemyss and Hope attributed failure particularly to Isaac's political activity and his extravagance, but these were more a symptom of Isaac's failure to recognize the business's difficulties. Hope must have known that he was in part responsible for his own fate for not looking at all the books before signing his agreement with Isaac in 1864. He was a victim of Isaac's perennial and quite unrealistic public optimism about business prospects rather than of Isaac's wickedness. Anxious to preserve his own reputation, Hope now prepared to try to pay all the obligations of Adam Hope and Company out of its continuing operations. These amounted to between $80,000 and $100,000 due the bankruptcy estate for the sum at credit of Buchanan, Hope and Company, less certain set-offs; £34,500 in acceptances discounted in Britain or used as collateral for an advance from a major hardware supplier, Henry Rogers, Sons and Company; and possibly some further sums owing on hardware account (Table 9, p 175). All this far exceeded C.J. Hope's capital, but the evidence suggests that the Hopes, in partnership for some years with Wemyss, and with the Rogers firm's backing, succeeded: Adam Hope went on to considerable business prominence in the 1870s.[54] In this he was helped by the gradual emergence of Hamilton as a centre of industries in which iron and hardware were important supply items.

By early 1868, Isaac was in full control of the business estate and was making preparations to carry on in business. Committed to payments of capital at the rate of £20,000stg per annum, he had to try to build up a new capital at the same time as he worked off this obligation.

9
The final failures

When it was clear that he had won the right to continue the business, Isaac rapidly made arrangements for his new firms.[1] He promoted Andrew Anderson, a clerk and bookkeeper in the Glasgow office since 1860, to its managership. Anderson had never before been given independent responsibility, but Isaac planned to spend much of each year in Glasgow in any case.[2] Lack of capital compelled Isaac to confine the business to dry goods, and this department at Hamilton continued under the capable management of Alex Duncan, who had alternated with Kirkland as buyer since 1865. The whole of the old dry goods and grocery premises were retained, as were many of the old staff, although Isaac realized that the cost of such an establishment was high.[3] He planned to be in Hamilton at times, but managing partners there were to be Andrew Binny and Peter T. Buchanan, who would shortly come into his inheritance but whose fitness for business was not yet revealed to anyone except his parents. Binny, a young man, came originally from Edinburgh; he had once worked in the Buchanans' business in some capacity and currently worked in Liverpool. Either he or a relative had worked for the Guild family business in Honduras in the late 1850s.[4] For advice in Hamilton, Peter and Binny could also look to Dewar, who was now employed by the trustees of the bankruptcy estate, and to Agnes Buchanan. The new business was known as Buchanan and Company in Hamilton and Peter Buchanan and Company in Glasgow; Isaac held a two-thirds share of both, and Binny and Peter each had one-sixth.

The business's principal problem was its lack of capital. Occasionally, and fruitlessly, Isaac searched for a capitalist to support the business. Later he was to argue that the Hamilton bookkeeper had estimated even in 1868 that the old estate would fail by $75,000 to yield the sums required, but in 1868 he considered that the estate would yield a surplus of £10,000 to £20,000stg beyond what he had pledged to pay.[5] Although he proposed to go direct to manufacturers to obtain credit, he returned also to traditional mercantile suppliers and found them surprisingly willing to extend him their usual credit terms for spring shipments.[6] He would, however, need cash to pay them as their bills fell due, generally in six months, because he could not find further banking accounts such as the old business had relied on. As Canadian banks, particularly the fast-declining Gore Bank, would discount good commercial paper, funds could be raised in Canada after sales had been made; but it was necessary to sell only to those who would meet their bills in six months and to avoid overstocks of goods that would lock up capital. Buchanan and Company had to do a low-mark-up, low-risk, low-profit business.

Isaac aimed to create a new, more attractive mood in the Hamilton business. Thus, he hoped to send smaller, more frequent shipments from Britain, and he pledged in a circular to customers to have new stock every week. He planned to send out a team of three travellers to visit customers, take orders, and encourage new visits to the Hamilton store.[7] If initially this did not yield encouraging results, it was the trend in marketing and had to be followed. In all, Isaac considered that his reopening was successful; it was facilitated by a general shortage of goods in the Hamilton market in the spring of 1868. Shipments for the year totalled about £25,000stg, or less than half the comparable figure for the last relatively normal year 1866 (Table 2, p 164). Augmented by considerable purchases of Canadian and American goods, these permitted sales of $264,000 for the year, 21 per cent less than 1867's and 37 per cent below 1866's dry goods sales (Table 1, p 162).[8] Previously there had also been sales in the other departments as well; thus, 1868 sales were less than one-third of total sales at Hamilton in 1866, while it is doubtful if operating expenses had been reduced by anything like an equivalent sum.

Binny and Peter launched a campaign to liquidate remaining land-holdings, and at least one land auction was held in the spring of 1868. Cash to meet the first instalment to creditors was built up from collections and these sales. To avoid vexations caused by small creditors in Canada, payment was made in full to some of them in 1868. Also during 1868, a compromise was reached with Harris's heirs through the Ontario Court of Chancery, though at the cost of further payments to his estate.

Three separate firms had borne the name Adam Hope and Company in the past three years, the first down to 1865, the second, consisting of C.J. Hope and Buchanan, Hope and Company, from 1865 to 1867, and the third, consisting of the two Hopes and, perhaps, Wemyss, founded in 1868.

Accounts had still to be resolved among the three and between them and the parent firms of Buchanan, Hope and Company and Peter Buchanan and Company, but only after Isaac sued the Hopes did he secure a settlement. The Hopes kept possession of all the premises of the Buchanan operations in London and Hamilton for several months in 1868; thereafter they still held the hardware premises and continued to claim possession of all assets of the two earlier firms of Adam Hope and Company. As they had already agreed to pay the acceptances discounted in Britain (Table 9, p 175), the issue between Isaac and his creditors on the one hand and the Hopes on the other pertained to further sums due by Adam Hope and Company. There was a gap of $10,000 between the two parties' figures, and the Hopes also claimed certain sums collected since the suspension. Finally, they agreed to pay something near Isaac's calculations of what they owed, $95,000. This sum, equal to about twenty per cent of Isaac's net obligations to creditors, would be paid to Walter Mackenzie for the creditors in two instalments during 1871; it was, apparently, credited to Isaac's account before then.

Isaac now surrendered all claims to manage the liquidation of the old hardware firms and handed over the deeds to the hardware premises in Hamilton and London. The Hopes were free of further liability regarding the bankruptcy, provided they could find and pay out something over £50,000stg between 1868 and 1871. One small matter was left for the courts to arbitrate, but the final resolution of the year-long feud over the issues involved in separating the two firms proved surprisingly amicable. Of course both sides had every reason to compromise to protect their reputations and to increase the value of their assets.[9]

From the time it began, Isaac's new business was under pressure as it sought to maintain current business, to launch several new ventures, and to collect enough to meet composition payments. Sales in 1869 increased modestly over 1868, but competition in Hamilton and in the dry goods trade was very tight. Hamilton's weakening relative to Toronto and Montreal (Table 12, p 179) was signified by the failure of new wholesale firms to appear as a number of older firms failed or were wound up; thus, nearly all the firms that remained in the 1870s had clear predecessors in the 1850s.[10] Hamilton was said now to lack a satisfactory grocery wholesaler altogether. Travellers from large English manufacturers, Isaac said, further added to competition in some lines.[11] Hence profits could not be large. Overdue and bad debts began to mount once more, though how seriously it is difficult to judge; any lock-up in accounts posed problems for a capital-starved business. Near the time for payment of each instalment there was particular alarm. Isaac blamed his son and Binny for their failure to watch accounts closely, and it is clear that Peter could not cope with responsibility. Like his father when under pressure, he travelled ceaselessly but pointlessly. Binny may have been a good office manager; it is hard to know exactly what he did and how capably.

Alexander I. Mackenzie, who had formerly operated his own business as a customer of the firm and had then worked in the Hamilton firm's grocery department, was also involved in managing the Hamilton store, as 'general manager and cashier.'[12] Late in 1869, under mounting financial pressure, Isaac decided that another reorganization of the firm was needed and that Mackenzie should be promoted. Buchanan and Company was put into liquidation and a new firm known as Buchanans, Binny and Mackenzie was established. As Isaac now planned to stay in Hamilton, Andrew Anderson was promoted in Glasgow, and the firm there became Buchanan, Anderson and Company.[13]

When provision was made for bad debts and payment of the remaining instalments from its assets, Buchanan and Company showed no net gain.[14] Business was carried on under the new names for two years, the firm re-entered the grocery trade, and at least some profit was declared each year. But again financial pressure mounted, and to preserve its connection, again Isaac put his firm into liquidation. Another firm rose from the old in Hamilton early in 1872, under the management of A.I. Mackenzie's brother John, a Hamilton dry goods merchant who had just left the firm of Kerr, Brown and Mackenzie.[15] He had enough power to see that the firm name was changed to John I. Mackenzie and Company, and the only Buchanan officially in the firm was Isaac's fourth son, James, who was free from the earlier firms' liabilities and had a capital consisting of his modest expectations from Peter Buchanan's estate. Isaac, Peter, and Binny were all excluded, Binny protesting vehemently. Again the liquidation eliminated any previously declared profits. Buchanan, Anderson and Company were no longer to be the exclusive agents for the Hamilton business[16] and thus had little real business to do, and despite James Buchanan's association with the new firm, it was essentially Mackenzie's. Free of Isaac's liabilities to old creditors, he possessed the business's principal assets, its connection, its staff, and its links to British suppliers. These he was able to operate throughout the rest of the decade at least. Thus, control of the main branch of his business passed from Isaac's hands early in 1872; his reorganization, however, had done nothing to put extra money into his or his family's hands.

The Montreal business was kept from suspension in 1867 by Isaac's transfer of his share in it to Peter. Following the suspension, Isaac wished to resume his share in his own name, and the Montreal partners agreed, in return for setting off Montreal claims on the suspended business against Isaac's capital (Table 9, p 175). When all accounts between the old and new firms and their individual partners were squared, Isaac was left owing the business, now known as Buchanan, Leckie and Company, about $16,000, which he planned to make up through his share of Montreal's profits.[17] As Alexander Campbell's account was still overdrawn, the Montreal business really had very little capital: whatever was at Leckie and Matthews' credit minus sums at Isaac and Campbell's debit. This was not known outside the business, but Isaac's continuing connection led the Bank of British North America to cut off its lines of credit to the firm. The Bank of Montreal, however, thought enough of it to increase its credit support. In 1869, Isaac's son Harris was able to see a copy of the Mercantile Agency's report on the firms, and they showed Montreal with less than the highest rating but with an estimated capital of $100,000; Hamilton's rating, 'good,' was not as strong as Montreal's, but at least it was not unfavourable.[18] To secure a special advance to continue the tea trade, the Montreal firm now had to furnish sureties to the Bank of Montreal, these being supplied by a friend of Leckie and by Campbell's brother.

Montreal was frequently pressed tightly for funds in the next few years. Sales and profits fluctuated with the local market. After a poor spring, sales were good in the fall of 1868, but losses on a number of accounts reduced profit for the last half of the year to only $8588 on sales on $378,000, a rate of only 2.3 per cent.[19] This appears to have been a relatively typical year in the late 1860s and early 1870s. But the partners did not adjust their thinking adequately. Isaac went on drawing sums from the business, Campbell continued to build his overdraft, and from 1869 to 1871 the firm even operated a branch, Campbell, Matthews and Company, under Campbell's management, in London, England.

The branch was to seek consigners and to build a closer liaison with Gilman and Company, its tea suppliers; the firm also planned to draw exchange on the office from Montreal, although its banker, E.H. King of the Bank of Montreal, warned that this would seriously damage its credit.[20] It was a costly operation to establish and when it failed to earn any profit, it had to be abandoned. Campbell returned to Montreal, despite the tensions between himself and his partners. The branch was a further indication of commercial trends, however, London rather than Glasgow now being the essential centre for such trade, but the move from one city to the other when taken from weakness could not succeed.

By 1872 and 1873, the Montreal firm was only just solvent, according to the partners' best estimates; in 1873, a year of general economic crisis, it earned no profit at all.[21] The key to its survival was the support of Hennessy's, the principal of its still considerable group of consigners.[22] Every year Hennessy's agreed to let the account run well past its nominal due date, and such extra accommodation always seemed essential. Leckie and Matthews now resolved to expel Campbell from the business by putting the old firm into liquidation and forming a new one without him. He was relieved by the partners of any obligation for his overdraft, which totalled about $100,000, but he was left unemployed and permanently dependent on his brother George. At the same time, Isaac agreed to retire to save the firm from bankruptcy in case he again went bankrupt.[23] His account at Montreal remained at a debit of about $16,000. He sought an agreement to allow him later to rejoin the firm, now Leckie, Matthews and Company, but they refused. Thus, early in 1874, he too was, in effect, expelled from the business he had founded, just two months after he had helped to expel Campbell.

In 1876, Leckie and Matthews persuaded Robert Wemyss, who had just left an association with the Hopes that had allowed him to build up a capital of over £8000, to become their British agent. Within a year the business had to be wound up as insolvent, Wemyss's funds having vanished into it. He asserted that Matthews had lied to him about the state of the firm, and it is entirely possible that it really was insolvent in 1874.[24] Leckie died in 1881 in dire poverty, being supported by a few friends at the end.[25] Wemyss by then had moved to North America to seek work for himself and his sons. Thus the Montreal business ran down; after 1867 it had few dealings with the Hamilton firm, and Isaac played only a relatively small role in it. Had it been kept separate from the other houses, as Peter Buchanan had arranged, it probably had enough capital, if properly managed, to carry on indefinitely. But by 1867, it had been stripped of its capital, and management was inadequate to the difficult task of rebuilding the business thereafter. On the other hand, the slowness of its demise suggests how much an established reputation and connection meant in the business world.

Like the Montreal firm, the New York business gradually decayed in this period. David McGee had long wished to leave New York, and he took the occasion of the bankruptcy to do so and to quit the firm. Because the firm had had a presence in the New York market for over twenty years, Isaac could not bring himself to close there entirely.[26] He therefore had Peter rent a smaller office and left a clerk in it to handle any duties that were required. His son Harris, already working in New York, served as unofficial manager, and Isaac and Peter frequently visited New York. But in fact the office did little now that the Hamilton firm did not sell groceries and hardware. Against the advice of his wife and others, Isaac decided to change the office's location, expand its activities, and put Harris in charge when his engagement with Brown Brothers terminated in 1870. He therefore opened a new office under the name of Buchanan Brothers and Company; it was to buy produce on orders from Europe and various goods on order from Canada and to procure consignments and joint accounts to and from Europe.

Its principal venture was a joint account in wool from the Cape of Good Hope that Isaac arranged between the firms of James Jamieson and Company of Capetown and Buchanan Brothers and Company, with the further involvement in selling the wool of T.H. McKenzie's current firm, McKenzie and McKay of Hamilton.[27] Michael James Jamieson of the former firm's Glasgow office was a relative of Agnes Buchanan and a family friend in Glasgow, as well as partial guarantor of Isaac's final payment to his creditors. Raw wool was to be brought to New York or Montreal for sale to Canadian and American manufacturers, the accounts to be handled through the Glasgow offices of the two firms. Canadian and American manufactured goods would be shipped to the Cape in return. In preparation for the trade, Isaac's son James, aged seventeen, spent a month in a Sherbrooke woollen mill and then travelled to the Cape to learn more about wool buying. One wool cargo was shipped in late 1870 and yielded a good profit when sold, largely in Canada. Continuance of the trade was complicated by the decline of Isaac's main business, but at least one more cargo seems to have been shipped in 1871 or 1872.

This venture was scarcely enough to justify a New York office, and other consignments were harder to secure as business tended to move away from the consignment system. There was no capital available to attract trade in any case. Thus the New York office really worked only for the Hamilton house and one or two of its customers, and this business could have been done more economically by someone from Hamilton, for the railroad made New York much more accessible than it had been years ago when the first office there was opened. Isaac's reluctance to close an old operation and his lack of means to make the office pay thus cost him more money.

Isaac's sixth instalment to his creditors, amounting to £11,000stg net, was paid in February 1871 only because the two largest creditors, the Union Bank and the Merchants Bank, representing the old Commercial Bank, agreed to take the remaining real property (except the stores) of the old business in lieu of cash; they planned to sell the properties gradually to secure payment. But there was no money to meet the seventh instalment. In 1869, Isaac had renewed his effort to realize something from the Southern railroad. From W.A. Thomson, currently a principal promoter of the line (and a fellow advocate of monetary reform), he secured an acknowledgement of a debt of $80,000, in return for which Isaac surrendered his claim for $208,000, now of dubious value, against the Niagara and Detroit Rivers Railway Company; turned over maps, plans, charts, and other related material in his possession; and contributed time and some funds, possibly as much as $50,000, to Thomson's promotion. Thomson pledged to get some form of company security in this amount from whoever built the line if he did not do so himself.[28] Ultimately, in 1873 as it turned out, Isaac secured shares in the Canada Southern Railway Company with a par value of $80,000 from Milton Courtright, who was building the line. Most of Isaac's hope of avoiding a second formal bankruptcy rested on his realizing funds from this asset.

In August 1871, Isaac persuaded the creditors to postpone payment of the seventh instalment until the eighth fell due in February 1872. He now concentrated his efforts on Sir Hugh Allan's Merchants Bank, seeking to persuade it either to advance funds for the seventh instalment, $55,000, on the basis of his claim to railway stock; or to advance the funds for both instalments on the basis of almost all his remaining assets, which he valued, very optimistically as follows: shares in the Canada Southern, $80,000; assets of Buchanans, Binny and Mackenzie, $85,000; and his city and country properties in Hamilton, $30,000 beyond encumbrances.[29] Using all the very limited political influence he could still muster, Isaac pressed the bank to accept either scheme, but it rejected both. As a result, he was forced again to ask the creditors for time to meet both the seventh and eighth instalments. The British creditors agreed, provided Michael James Jamieson and Peter T. Buchanan paid the sums they were committed to meet. Jamieson resisted payment for a time until it was clear that Peter, who was sole guarantor of the instalment to the extent of £7000 and jointly liable with Jamieson for the sum of £3000, had no money left, but he then paid the trustee £3000. He had taken security from Buchanan Brothers and Company to help recompense himself in the event of his having to pay, but the funds that firm retained from the joint wool transactions may not have been large enough to meet this sum. As he also had a claim on Harris and James Buchanan's expectations from their uncle's will and on the trust assets of Agnes Buchanan, the latter from her marriage settlement and totalling up to £1700, it is clear that his payment would ultimately be repaid to him from the resources of Isaac's own family.

Isaac spent 1873 largely in efforts to raise funds on his railway stock, by sale or loan, but the line was mortgaged to the extent of $30,000 per mile, the stock was heavily watered, and the company was headed for bankruptcy. Down to 1874 at least, he realized nothing from this dubious asset. Buchanans, Binny and Mackenzie's assets failed to yield a surplus, though they did cover one bill for $20,000 that Isaac had reckoned among his assets.[30] The stores and the mountain estate, much of which was sold at this time (some of it to the provincial government for an inebriate asylum), perhaps yielded a surplus, but not a very large one. Isaac paid what he could and offered a variety of compromises to the creditors in 1874 and 1875; but they were slow to agree, because, Isaac was convinced, of the resistance of two Canadian banks, the Merchants and the Canadian Bank of Commerce, the latter of which had taken over the assets of the Gore Bank in 1869.[31] By 1874, the Bank of British North America was complicating the position by threatening to sue Isaac formally into bankruptcy.

By 1876, Isaac had left his mountain house and moved to rented quarters in Hamilton, and he had turned over all his assets to the creditors through Walter Mackenzie. The creditors were still slow to grant him a final release from his obligations; one or more may have felt personal rancour towards him, and others by now felt that he had deliberately misled them at one or several times in the past. Isaac had given Leckie, Matthews and Company a note for the sum at his debit when Buchanan, Leckie and Company was wound up. He denied that it was ever intended to be collected, but they refused to surrender it in 1877, and this too complicated his final discharge. In any event, after August 1871, Isaac operated entirely on sufferance from his creditors, and they did not grant him full discharge from his obligations until sometime in 1878.[32] It was a long and harrowing ordeal for him and his family.

After 1868, Isaac grew increasingly interested in highly speculative schemes that offered hope, however slight, of large returns on small investments. As in Buchanan Brothers and Company, he was the prime mover in most of these ventures, but he put most of them in the names of his sons. His children were each to inherit some £2000 to £3000 from his brother's estate following the death of both Douglases, and a number of these expectations were signed away in return for support for such new ventures.[33] None of the new businesses had much chance, because all lacked capital and neither Isaac nor his older sons gave adequate attention to the complex tasks involved in founding and slowly building up a new business.

Thus, Isaac and Peter began to invest in mining speculations. Isaac acquired whole or part interest in a series of highly touted properties, all for modest cash investments. Properties included several in Utah, another in North Carolina, and one at Thunder Bay, Lake Superior. Isaac then sought to sell these in Britain or Europe, but without success. If any of these were serious ventures, it is difficult now to know, but Isaac seems to have considered them all as potential working mines even if others did not.[34] Peter, besides his endeavours to sell mining stocks in Europe, involved himself in a costly and unprofitable coal mine in Scotland.[35] In the desperate search for new sources of wealth, Isaac further depleted such resources as the family had. A few thousand pounds lost in mining ventures represented a much larger portion of Isaac's wealth than would have been the case a few years earlier.

For a time Isaac considered entering the Canadian timber export trade, aiming to sell in South America or southern Africa rather than in traditional markets. He and his son Isaac R. acquired export rights for the sewing machines made by R.M. Wanzer in Hamilton, and Isaac R. sought unsuccessfully to sell these in Japan. Hoping to trade on his political connections, Isaac and his son Harris sought timber concessions from the federal government in the new province of Manitoba. Once more the aim was quick wealth, but this proved unattainable. Grants of land and timber were readily available, but only on identical terms to those granted to others, and western development proved much too slow in any event to satisfy Isaac's urgent requirements. Here, just as in the mining schemes, he was working with promoters and speculators who were almost unknown to him. He had little more to lose to such people, perhaps, but the chances of gain were equally slight. Late in 1873, he put his wife Agnes and his son James into a paint manufacturing business with another new acquaintance, H.M. Finlayson, under the firm name of the Buchanan Mineral Company. When Finlayson proved neither competent nor honest, it was too late to withdraw, and by 1876 such wealth as remained to Agnes and James was entirely lost.

One by one, Isaac's three oldest sons, Peter, Harris, and Isaac, embarked on business careers that proved unsuccessful. The two oldest became near-alcoholics and could not be trusted with money or any real responsibility. It is difficult to weigh the reasons for the difficulties that all three encountered, but their father had a good deal to do with this area of family failure as well. He and Agnes worried constantly at the need to launch their children in careers that had a future, but Isaac also needed funds immediately to support his family. He placed both Harris and Isaac R. in excellent commercial positions in New York, the latter in Seaman and Thompson, leading New York tea merchants. Both were dissatisfied with their rate of promotion, however, and Isaac encouraged them in this. None of the older boys were given much time to learn business techniques before, at their father's insistence, their small inheritances were signed away as security to creditors of the firms in which they were made nominal principals. Not only had their upbringing not prepared them for living on small incomes during their junior business years, but Isaac indulged them with continuing cash allowances and blinked repeatedly at Harris's and, especially, Peter's excesses and outright misdemeanours.[36] Though indulgent, Isaac was also an autocratic father, allowing little latitude to his sons in their business activities in connection with him; yet from time to time he expected them to shoulder great responsibilities and was invariably disappointed if they failed to do so. Again Isaac indicated how resistant he was to a realization of his circumstances. Granted that Harris and Isaac R.'s prospects for promotion to senior posts in the mercantile houses in which they trained were not great, and that the salary and status of junior clerk were not to be endured after an appropriate training period, it still appears that Isaac encouraged them to move far too quickly and without realistic consideraton of their position or their prospects. It should be noted, however, that Isaac R.'s problems were mainly the result of the break-up of the second tea firm in which he was employed and of serious illness while he was stationed by that firm in Japan as a tea-taster and buyer.

Clearly Isaac's management of affairs after 1867 was confused and unsuccessful. It is difficult now to judge whether a different set of strategies could have saved his business and his fortunes, though Hope's success and the ways in which funds were foolishly spent strongly suggest an answer, but that, of course, would have required Isaac to be a different person altogether. At any rate, by 1874, he was dependent on the paint business for an income. Its failure left him penniless, dependent for money on a testimonial organized by friends at his urging.[37] Claiming political ties with the Liberals, he begged the government of Alexander Mackenzie for even a modest postmastership. This was refused, but in 1878, with the return of John A. Macdonald to power, he was given a government post as an 'official Arbitrator of Canada'; this offered respectable employment and some income, arbitrating various disputes.[38] As well, Peter T. received a clerk's post in Ottawa from the Macdonald government. Isaac lived until 1 October 1883, when he died at Hamilton, in moderate but once more comfortable circumstances. His wife survived him, living until 1896, when she died at the age of 70.

In January 1877, following the failure of the paint company, James Buchanan fled Hamilton. Once or twice in the next few years he cautiously contacted his family to say that he was awaiting the expiry of the statute of limitations on the company's debts before he returned home, but for five years his parents knew little of his actions or his whereabouts. On leaving Canada, he had found his way to Oil City, Pennsylvania, where he got a job for a month as an extra assistant bookkeeper in a bank. He was re-engaged for a second month, then was asked to become private secretary to the bank's president, Captain J.J. Vandergrift, who was a major figure in the oil industry, with pipeline, property, and iron and steel interests as well. By 1882, James was acting as a manager or confidential assistant for Vandergrift and his allies in several businesses and was on his way to making a fortune in Oil City and, later, in Pittsburgh.[39] As a matter of honour, he began to repay the more legitimate, as he saw them, claims on the paint company. Then he began to rebuild the family fortune; he was able to employ three or four of his brothers in his business enterprises and, in 1900, using funds left him by Captain Vandergrift, to buy back the house, Auchmar, for his unmarried sisters. His success came too late for his older brothers to gain much from it, but for his mother and the family as a whole it represented financial salvation.

10

Conclusion: The Buchanans' business and the Upper Canadian business system

The character of those involved in the Buchanans' business, their strengths and weaknesses, their conflicts of judgment and personality, played major roles in its rise and fall. Central at every stage was Isaac Buchanan, whose energy, vision, and readiness to take risks had so much to do with building the business rapidly to its large scale. His initiatives, based mainly on his persistent faith that Upper Canada would expand, were for twenty years vindicated by its swift development. It is, however, doubtful if he fully understood this, or some of the other factors in his success, as was revealed when he was left in sole charge after 1860. Then the qualities that had made him one of the most prominent Canadian businessmen of his time proved insufficient or inappropriate for changed circumstances; his course thereafter, increasingly frantic and, finally, confused, had small chance of restoring his fortunes.

No less than his brother, Peter Buchanan was of utmost importance in shaping the business. Always a realist, as he showed in 1859-60, he combined this indispensable quality with ambition, imagination, and authority. From the firm's earliest days these variously supported, consolidated, or restrained his brother's initiatives. Yet it was his determination not to share his power with more junior partners and his pronounced family loyalty that provoked the firm's disruption early in the 1850s. Especially as they grew older, neither he nor Isaac proved at all adept at developing managers who could be given growing responsibility and who might some day be capable of taking over the firm and paying out their capital. Of course the firm's circumstances were very different by the early 1850s from those of a decade before, but even so it is hard to find the qualities of independence shown by Harris, Young, Hope, and both Laws in later partners and senior personnel – either they lacked such abilities, or their talents simply were not encouraged.

Managerial failures such as these, especially in the crucial mid-1850s, go some distance towards explaining the business's demise.

It was common for nineteenth-century observers to find the causes of business success or failure very much in the personal behaviour and characteristics of the businessman. Bankruptcies, for example, were attributed to foolishness or immorality, to 'utter recklessness,' 'unparalleled avidity,' or 'a vicious mode of business.'[1] Later writers of a hero-worshipping or a muckraking disposition have tended to continue this tradition,[2] and their approach has validity in that, in a competitive world, the character and abilities of the businessman often determined the fate of his business. But such an approach is inadequate both to a full understanding of the individual businessman and as a justification for studying him at all. To view one's protagonist too simply as hero or villain does not do justice to the complexities of human motivations and actions, and it reveals too little of the world in which the characters lived. Hence this study has sought to comprehend how decisions in the Buchanans' business were made, how they could have seemed logical or wise, how the world looked to those who made them. At the same time, it has sought to consider what the experience of the business can reveal about the North Atlantic, and especially the Upper Canadian, business worlds in which the partners operated.

The growth of the Buchanans' business highlights sometimes neglected factors underlying the emergence of independent wholesaling in and the urban structure of Upper Canada. Fundamental was competition in the fast-growing British business world, both within and between the major commercial centres such as Glasgow and Liverpool, because this produced a constant search for new business and a willingness to advance funds when suitable opportunities appeared from any part of the world. Such British credit underlay the Upper Canada trade and both helped to sustain and was reinforced by the local banking system of Upper Canada (which owed its existence in part to Upper Canada's political autonomy). Ample credit support was vital to the functioning of the distinctive frontier long-credit system. To succeed at that system, the wholesaler also needed thorough knowledge of his customers in order to control his risks, and this was best obtained in a location relatively close to his customers. At the same time, the distance to Montreal was sufficiently great that many retailers found it convenient to buy in Upper Canada if they could secure an adequate supply of goods and of credit nearer home.

Independent Upper Canadian wholesaling was, however, created not out of existing trade volumes and patterns but rather at the margin of the rapidly growing trading system. Some of that rising demand was met not from the established trading centre for Upper Canada, Montreal, but from newer centres, notably Toronto, Hamilton, and London. The crisis for the Upper Canadian system arose later, when the momentum of extensive growth slackened, and the competition among firms and among cities for a declining or more slowly growing total trade volume sharply intensified. It was then that Hamilton's independent importing role was sharply and permanently truncated.

Isaac Buchanan began operations in York at the beginning of that more than twenty-year period of almost uninterrupted frontier expansion. Expansion supplied both growing demand for goods in general and, more specifically, an ample supply of new customers, often in newly opening areas, to replace those lost. Equally, however, the rural economy required rapidly expanding credit, which firms such as the Buchanans' supplied. It is not true that, as has been argued, the Upper Canadian settlers were 'weighed down by ... the profits exacted by a rising and ambitious commercial and financial interest.'[3] Between merchant and customer, town and country, businessman and farmer, there was a reciprocal, albeit in some respects an unequal, relationship of mutual dependence. Merchants provided real services to the settlers and bore real risks. They relayed Upper Canadian demand to remote producers when they selected goods in British and American markets, arranged to have them finished, packed, shipped, transshipped, delivered, and displayed; and apart from the risk of loss or damage, against which insurance could be purchased, they bore the risk that they could not sell these goods profitably. In selling goods on long credits, they lent money, in effect, for about twelve months, and their customers in turn extended such credits to the farmers and tradesmen who comprised the largest part of the colony's population. Relatively few new settlers or businessmen were affluent enough not to need such credit; the long-credit system gave them the chance to begin and to continue operations without possessing large cash resources.

Merchants likewise provided a channel for colonial produce to find its way to markets in North America and overseas, a process that was virtually as lengthy and complex as the import process. This was evident in the Buchanans' trade in wheat and flour; and over the years they also handled many other Upper Canadian exports, among them ashes, staves (in small quantities), wool, butter, cheese, pork, whisky, and field crops other than wheat. Their business system permitted producers and country merchants to try out the markets for such products, some of which eventually became important exports from the Upper Canadian west.

Of course the merchant was not in business out of altruism. The Buchanans sought, and in their first twenty years received, substantial returns for their knowledge, investment, risks, and exertions. But they earned these because they provided goods and services that the community wanted relatively efficiently and skilfully. The farmer paid high prices for his manufactured and other imported goods by comparison with, say, a British consumer, but it was not a burdensome and monopolistic commercial system that imposed these. Rather they reflected risks and costs that were ultimately real and had to be borne by the consumer. This was virtually inevitable in the nature of the process by which a marginal economy first opened up.

Such firms as the Buchanans' had as a central role the linking of Canada and Britain. Britain's was an established, complex, rapidly evolving business world, while the largest Upper Canadian businesses in 1830 were, with two or three exceptions, essentially quite small general stores. From the beginning, the Buchanans operated one of Upper Canada's largest unincorporated businesses, yet even at its peak it was ordinary by the standards of the highest circles in Glasgow, Liverpool, and London. In Britain there was more competition for jobs, higher standards of commercial training prevailed, a substantial commercial hierarchy existed, and more wealth might be required to found an independent business. Not surprisingly, there were many who found the prospects offered by the colonies more attractive. This thinking underlay the Buchanans' strategy and, presumably, that of their employees and customers, most of whom were British-born. In some cases the Buchanans themselves hired and sent out personnel; more often, it seems, the individual found his own way to Canada and made his connections with the business there.

Both in business and in public life, different standards, in certain respects, prevailed in the two societies. Thus, Peter Buchanan and his business were expected to and did meet standards that many Upper Canadian-based firms could not match. In London, England, he was trusted at a time when the large Canadian company he represented, the Great Western, was still an unknown quantity.[4] His acceptability was the result of many factors, including wealth, knowledge, behaviour, education, friendships, and connections. And because his business ranked high, it was treated differently, notably in commercial crises, from smaller competitors.

The Buchanans experience vividly demonstrates the process of capital creation and accumulation that occurred in Upper Canada. Much fixed capital formation took place through the workings of the commercial system: the building of stores, mills, houses, and farm buildings and the wholesale and often overdone process of land subdivision and development depended significantly on the country merchant and the farmer being supplied with goods a year or more before they had to pay for them. Even so, it is possible to over-estimate the role of such firms as the Buchanans' as capital importers, despite the Buchanans' vital role in making the Great Western Railroad a reality. Peter and Isaac supplied £12,000stg initially, plus lines of credit in Britain that grew as their business grew, and they built these into a fortune for themselves and partners that, at its peak, was valued at twenty-four times that initial sum (Table 5, p 170). These funds were earned largely in Upper Canada; in effect, this capital was created there. But the process could not have worked without the kind of continuous links to the outside world that the business system provided.

If the overall trend in Upper Canada was one of economic expansion, the trade cycle was nevertheless of vital significance, its fluctuations and crises serving to adjust and to regulate the growing business system, to discipline the errant or unlucky and to reward the prudent or fortunate. The Buchanan firm emerged from the 1837 and 1847-8 crises relatively unscathed, indeed, it soon appeared, actually strengthened; by contrast, the 1857 crisis began the period of the firm's decline to failure. Between these major international crises, year-by-year variations in levels of business activity were of considerable consequence to profits and to the partners' strategic thinking. Such fluctuations were evidently closely tied to the international trade cycle, yet there were many factors particular to Upper Canada that helped to determine the precise impact of each on the economy and the business itself.

Downturns in the trade cycle were also an important precipitant of the failures that were so integral a factor in the Buchanans' business world. These bankruptcies reflected the insecurity of business life and the reality of business competition. To meet such circumstances, even the strongest business had constantly to adapt and to innovate, and even the strongest could fail. The frequent business talk of insecurity, the nervousness of the rich and powerful, had a reality underlying it, however incomprehensible this might have seemed to those outside the 'entrepreneurial class,' who saw it only in its outward manifestations of affluence and influence.[5] Failure did not, however, invariably put an end to a business career. Despite his bankruptcy at the relatively advanced age of fifty-four, Adam Hope was able to recover, and he died a prosperous man, a senator, a director of the Bank of Commerce, and president of the Hamilton Provident and Loan Society.[6] James Law and James Buchanan offer other examples from this account of men who overcame bankruptcy to prosper handsomely.

By the later 1850s, frontier expansion was reaching its limit, and a rural society and the urban system needed to serve it were now established throughout southern Upper Canada. At the same time, such technological developments of the era as the telegraph, the railroad, the Atlantic cable, and the steamship had growing impacts on business. And the rapid development of Canada's financial system began to reduce the wholesale merchant's role in the credit system. As a result, patterns of risk and opportunity for trade and investment in Upper Canada began to change. Increasingly, success in trade rewarded more specialized firms, concentrating on rather more limited roles than general wholesalers like the Buchanans had fulfilled. Such institutions were, ultimately, more efficient than the general firm could be. Similarly, those in more marginal locations now found it much harder to compete, as Hamilton's trading history after 1856 reveals.

In the creation of the institutions of the more complex economy that was emerging, such as building societies, mortgage companies, banks, railroads, and secondary manufacturing industries, the earlier generation of wholesalers played an important part.[7] Thus Isaac founded the Boards of Trade of both Toronto and Hamilton. John Young was a leading figure in the Gore Bank in its early years and later was a major force in the development of the Canada Life Assurance Company.[8] Adam Hope, in both London and Hamilton, was president of mortgage and savings companies that grew out of the rapid and successful development of building societies in Upper Canada in the 1850s.[9] In the late 1840s, Peter Buchanan actively assisted the Trust and Loan Company of Upper Canada in its search for British financial backing, and at the same time he was directly responsible for the Commercial Bank's securing accounts with and liberal drawing arrangements from the London Joint Stock Bank and the Western Bank of Scotland.[10] Yet because Peter and Isaac were so wealthy and because they were on excellent terms with the leading figures in the banks with which they dealt and received generous treatment from them, they had less incentive to found new financial institutions than had somewhat lesser Upper Canadian merchants. Because they dealt with so many Canadian banks, they did not want to form special ties with any one. This was illustrated in 1854, when R.W. Harris and Adam Hope rejected offers to be the senior local directors of the Bank of British North America in Hamilton and London.[11]

Similarly, it was their firm's eminence that permitted the Buchanans to be so involved in the direction of a major railroad system. Unlike most merchants, Peter and Isaac could treat with leading politicians, such as Francis Hincks and John A. Macdonald, and with the men who were becoming the great entrepreneurial specialists in railroads, such as Alexander Galt and Samuel Zimmerman, on an equal basis. Their aim, however, was simply to get the Great Western system built, and until Isaac's disastrous 1856 involvement, they avoided substantial or long-term commitments of funds to such projects, which were unlikely to yield the highest returns. In this, they were like other merchants; it was seen as the task of governments and foreign investors to own the shares and bonds of such companies, though some personal involvement might be accepted initially to persuade the others to take on the main burdens of supplying desired, but very risky and costly, facilities.[12]

The relationship of the wholesaler to the secondary manufacturing that Canada developed from the 1850s onward was more complex.[13] An import merchant had, evidently, no strong reason to favour local development of products that competed with his imports. As Adam Hope, replying to Isaac's complaint that he bought too much in North America, once put the matter,

I urge Mr Kirkland to avoid U.S. and Canadian goods as much as possible. True we can sell such goods, but our business is to import goods from England through our friends there and the fewer investments we make on this side of the water the better. I am constantly holding the same language to my Brother in connection with Hardware matters.[14]

But in fact the merchants, even had they wished to do so, could scarcely avoid contributing to the emergence of local manufacturing, where it could compete. Manufacturers usually required much circulating capital in relation to fixed capital, and in Canada just as in Britain they could draw on the resources of the mercantile and financial systems in various ways.[15] The Buchanans' imports of iron and hardware indicate this very well, for most of these items were in essence producer goods, not consumer goods. In selling pig iron on eight months' credit, the Buchanans were giving founders ample time to transform that iron into finished goods. Similarly, some of the hardware firms' customers were artisans and builders, not country merchants who sold to farmers. Isaac Buchanan's later experiments in wool imports also exemplify the role of the merchant as supplier of manufacturers' inputs. The same merchants, or others, might become involved in selling for manufacturers. Thus, Young, Law and Company eventually took over a cotton mill in Dundas to which they had advanced considerable sums, probably in the form both of raw materials and of advances on finished goods consigned for sale.[16]

Gradually, despite the philosophy expressed by Hope, Canadian textiles and hardware came to play a larger role in the business's stock, though despite Isaac's protectionist enthusiasm, they never composed a very large part of it.[17] Where the Canadian goods were competitive, they would be sold. This suggests that such major firms as the Buchanans' were essentially neutral in the process of manufacturing development. Yet at the margin there was pressure on some firms to experiment with raw material imports for sale on credit; for some to invest directly in manufacturing; and for some to find it profitable to explore the possibility of selling for producers in their hinterlands whose output began to exceed the demands of nearby markets.

In view of Isaac's long-time interest in politics, it is worth considering more explicitly the relationship between the business and government and politics. Plainly it was his wealth that permitted Isaac to indulge his interest in so independent a manner, but wealth could not make him a man of great influence and power on the political stage – if in fact this was what he really sought. Because he spoke so often and so candidly, however, his career reveals with particular clarity some of the myriad strands of local and private interests that we increasingly understand to have been a significant part of the functioning of the political system in mid-nineteenth-century Canada.

On the more general plane, governments affected the business world in many ways, and it is not surprising that many businessmen sought influence, whether solely for personal profit or as part of a more general desire for influence in society. The Buchanans considered that government expenditure, notably by the Royal Army in the late 1830s and by the provincial government, for public works, in the mid-1830s and early 1840s, played a vital role in stimulating the economy and in leading gradually to the creation of a more efficient transportation system. Banking policy was of considerable relevance, and not only in Isaac's eyes; the partners favoured policies that encouraged more liberal note issue and, in general, more independence from government regulation for the chartered banks. Isaac was probably an extremist in his enthusiasm for paper money,[18] but there is no doubt of the more general Upper Canadian resistance throughout the era to endeavours to centralize all banking control in one institution, such as a government bank of issue, or one city, Montreal.

Despite their resistance to dominance by Montreal, the Buchanans consistently supported policies that would first encourage and later maintain the Union. They opposed changes in the legislation that defined the imperial trading system, then very quickly learned to live with the changes. In these years too, many basic institutional matters of great concern to businessmen came before the legislature – laws on bankruptcy, usury, negotiable instruments, incorporation, and enforcement of and security on debts all had direct implications for the legal structure of the business system.[19] On most such issues the business community had opinions, though on some there were metropolitan divisions, and frequently such opinions greatly influenced governments. It should be noted, however, that throughout the period many issues arose to divide politics on other than class or economic lines. John Young, for example, generally voted Conservative, and he did not support the Free Kirk, despite his alliance with Isaac Buchanan; Adam Hope was a consistent free trader despite Isaac's protectionism. Finally, if the politics of development were so universally followed at local and provincial levels, it was probably because the enthusiasm for development and the assumption that promoting it was a vital role for governments to pursue greatly transcended the business communities of the province.[20]

The most evident concern drawing the Buchanans into the political process was the railroad issue in all its various ramifications – charters and their amendment, guarantees of bonds, municipal debts, and various patronage issues. They did not like this enforced situation, however, and Peter, Isaac, and Harris saw politics, after the Great Western was safely launched, as an essentially hostile milieu in which it was necessary to be constantly vigilant. This was the result above all of the close links among the government, the Grand Trunk, Montreal interests, contractors such as Gzowski and Zimmerman, and many local groups across the province. Business and government could, therefore, be highly antagonistic.

The two could also be almost entirely unrelated. The province and the municipalities collected a significant proportion of their tax revenues through the merchants, in the form of customs duties and property taxes, the latter including a rate charged on mercantile inventories; but provided the tax system was not used to favour another city, the essential mercantile interest was that the laws be enforced fairly, because the taxes were simply another mercantile cost, to be reflected in the final price of goods. In other words, most merchants in their everyday business lives could and did operate largely unregulated by government. It was other dimensions of their lives that were most likely to bring them into conflict or alliance with government.

As these points suggest, there is much to be learned from the history of a business, even a largely forgotten one which ended in collapse. Particularly important in the Buchanans' case are the significance and pervasiveness of credit relationships, the detailed information provided on Canadian business and urban structures in Upper Canada's age of extensive growth, and the more detailed economic chronology that an account like this relies upon. Because business has been so significant a part of Canadian society, such knowledge can only enhance our understanding of broader processes of social and economic change in nineteenth-century Canada, to the investigation of which the business historian, like the social, economic, and regional historian and the historical geographer, can contribute greatly.

Tables

TABLE 1
Sales 1835-66 (all figures £000cy)

Period	Hamilton Dry Goods	Groc	Hdwe	Total	Toronto	Montreal (sales to branches excluded)	London	Total Canadian sales (net)
Nov. 1835-Oct. 1836				-	42 a	-	-	42
Nov. 1836-Oct. 1837				-	na	-	-	na
Nov. 1837-Oct. 1838				-	49 b	-	-	49
May 1839-Oct. 1839				-	65 c	-	-	65
Dec. 1839-Nov. 1840	37 d	16 d	-	53 d	72 d	-	-	125
Dec. 1840-Oct. 1841	85 e	37 e	-	122 e	[75]*f	-	-	[197]
Nov. 1841-Oct. 1842	54	38	-	92	74 g	-	-	166
Nov. 1842-Oct. 1843	51	49	-	100	51 h	-	-	151
Nov. 1843-Mar. 1845	87	62	-	149	na		-	na
Apr. 1844-Mar. 1845						41 i		
Apr. 1845-Mar. 1846	128	42	17 e	187	-	48	-	235
Apr. 1846-Mar. 1847	88	28	19	135	-	na	-	na
Apr. 1847-Mar. 1848	80	23	19	122	-	na	-	na
Apr. 1848-Dec. 1848	57	17	14	88	-	na	-	na
1849	62	21	22	105	-	na	-	na
1850	76	28	30	134	-	52 j	-	186
1851	77	29	37	143	-	na	-	na
1852	75	36	35	146	-	na	46 k	na
1853	102	46	45	193	-	na	86	na
1854	121	63	54	238	-	na	117	na
1855	140	102	64	306	-	na	115	na
1856	119	90	51	260	-	[136]**m	109	[505]**
1857	77	69	33	179	-	83	75	337
1858	60	39	17	115	-	94 n	56 o	265
1859	60	28	15	103	-	98 p	65	265
1860†				132 q	-	90 r	na	na
1861				185	-	131 s††	83 t	399
1862				196 u	'-	220 v	80	496
1863				146	-	213 w	79 x	438
1864				na	-	175	na	na
1865				na	-	na	na	na
1866	104 y	57 y	71 y	232 y	-	na	-	na

a / Profit and loss account, 31 Oct. 1836, 83/59585-6

b / 'Different views of the advances obtained in 1837-38' (copy), 66/52102

c / Peter Buchanan to Isaac Buchanan, 9 Nov. 1839 (copy), 66/52179

d / Isaac Buchanan to Peter Buchanan, c.21 Dec. 1840, 9/8636

e / Memo in Peter Buchanan's handwriting entitled 'Jottings Accounts July 1860,' 82/59429-33

f / 'Some calculations regarding advances,' Nov. 1841, 83/59656

g / Profit and loss account, 1 Nov. 1842, 83/59705 A-B

h / Profit and loss account, Toronto, 1 Nov. 1843, 83/59775-6

i / Profit and loss account, Montreal, nd, 84/59922-3, 26

j / Profit and loss account, Montreal, 31 Dec. 1850, 84/60119

k / Peter Buchanan, note on London sales in his memo book for 1857-58, 90/63651

m / Memo of Montreal sales, Jan. 1858, 38/31146. See also Robert Leckie to Peter Buchanan, 23 Jan. 1858 (copy), 38/31214-15

n / Extracts from Montreal profit and loss account, 1858, 82/59423

o / Memorandum of London sales, 1858 and 1859, 82/59425

p / Peter Buchanan to Isaac Buchanan, 10 Mar. 1860, 15/12919-20

q / Isaac Buchanan to Alex Campbell, 23 June 1862 (copy), 19/16086

r / Montreal profit and loss account, 31 Dec. 1860, 86/60815

s / Alex Campbell to Isaac Buchanan, 20 Mar. 1862, 19/16053

t / Adam Hope to Isaac Buchanan, 3 Jan. 1863, 33/27344

u / Robert Wemyss to Isaac Buchanan, 17 June 1864, 60/47618

v / Statement of Montreal sales, 1862, 86/60999

w / Record of Montreal sales, 1863 and 1864, 86/61154-5. The 1864 figure is for 11 months only, but December was never a month for large sales.

x / Adam Hope to Isaac Buchanan, 1 Dec. 1863, 33/27414

y / Isaac Buchanan to David McGee, 7 Dec. 1866 (copy), 44/35663

* Estimate based on sterling cost of goods sold and knowledge of mark-ups applying

** Estimated figure in order to give a net sales figure for one of the peak years. Gross sales at Montreal for the year (£170,000) were reduced by 20 per cent on the assumption that a similar percentage of Montreal's sales went to the Hamilton and London branches in 1856 (when no net figure is available) and 1857.

† The firm changed its fiscal year in 1860 to end 30 Nov.; this practice continued thereafter. Thus, 1860 sales figures are for 11 months.

†† Montreal figure in 1861 includes sales to London.

TABLE 2
Shipments from Britain 1835-66 (£000stg)

| Year | To Hamilton | | | | To Toronto | To Montreal | To London | Total |
	Dry goods	Groc	Hdwe	Total				
1835	-	-	-	-	[23]* a	-	-	[23]
1836	-	-	-	-	[27] b	-	-	[27]
1837	-	-	-	-	[24]	-	-	[24]
1838	-	-	-	-	25 c	-	-	25
1839	-	-	-	-	72 d	-	-	72
1840	na	-	-	na	[60] e	-	-	na
1841	34 f	[10] g	-	[44]	45 h	-	-	[89]
1842	43 i		-	na	[40] j	-	-	na
1843			-	na	na	-	-	na
1844			-	na	na	-	-	na
1845	70 k		10 m	na	-	na	-	na
1846				na	-	na	-	77 n
1847				na	-	na	-	na
1848	30 o			na	-	7 p	-	na
1849	33 q			41 r	-	18 s	-	59
1850				[49]	-	[16] t	-	[65] u
1851	46 v			na	-	na	-	na
1852				na	-	na	na	na
1853				na	-	28 w	na	114 w
1854				100	-	70 x	43 y	213 x
1855				na	-	na	26 z	131 aa
1856				na	-	na	23 bb	na
1857	28 cc	-†	11 cc	38 cc	-	na	22 dd	na
1858		-		na	-	na	12 e	na
1859	24 ff	1 ff	4 ff	29 ff	-	35 ff	18 ff	82
1860	35 gg	-	6 gg	41 gg	-	na	23 hh	na
1861	47	-	8	55	-	na	26 ii	na
1862	46 jj	-	3	49 kk	-	27 mm	na	na
1863		-		37	-	na	22 nn	na
1864		-		na	-	na	29 oo	na
1865		-		na	-	na	na	na
1866	58 pp	-	22	80 pp	-	24 qq	-	104

* Estimates are generally those made by a partner during the shipping season. As many were made when shipments were relatively well advanced, they should be quite accurate; where wrong, they will err on the low side. Sources are often ambiguous as to whether packing and other such charges are included; where possible, they are excluded, to leave these as prices paid suppliers. As such charges did not normally exceed 10 per cent, the error from including charges in some figures is not large. If figures can be interpolated (eg, for Hamilton in 1850 and 1854) I have done so.

† After 1856, almost no further direct grocery orders were sent from Britain to London and Hamilton; virtually all were shipped to Montreal, which supplied the Upper Canadian houses.

a / 'Calculations of how the Business shd Pay,' 22 Aug. 1835, 13/11470

b / Order Book, 1835-38, 80/58644-774

c / 'Different views of the advances obtained in 1837-38' (copy), 66/52102

d / Memo re 1839 shipments, Peter Buchanan, 80/58810

e / Isaac Buchanan to Peter Buchanan, c.21 Dec. 1840, 9/8636. See also Peter Buchanan to Isaac Buchanan, 15 Dec. 1841, 13/11498.

f / 'Shipments to the different marks in 1841,' 83/59672

g / Payments schedule, Glasgow, 10 Feb. 1841, 80/58831

h / 'Some calculations regarding advances,' Nov. 1841, 83/59656. A somewhat lower figure (£38,000) is given in the source cited in note f, but I have favoured this one, as it comes from the end of the year; Peter Buchanan's letter (note e) also implies the higher figure.

i / Statement of shipments to Hamilton, 1842, 83/59724

j / Payments schedule, Glasgow, 8 Feb. 1842, 13/11519-20

k / Calculation of dry goods shipments, 1845, 63/50136. See also calculations re cost of 1845 dry goods shipments, 83/59836.

m / 'Statement of Cost & Charges of Hardware Imported 1845,' 83/59843

n / Extract from Peter Buchanan to R.W. Harris, 3 Mar. 1847 (copy), 67/52671

o / Peter Buchanan to R.W. Harris, 3 Nov. 1848 (copy), 67/52867-8

p / Peter Buchanan to R.W. Harris, 24 Oct. 1849 (copy), 67/53005

q / Peter Buchanan to James Law, 2 Nov. 1849 (copy), 67/53008

r / Peter Buchanan to James Law, 23 Nov. 1849 (copy), 67/53014. Finance statement, Glasgow, 1 Jan. 1850, 84/60131

s / Peter Buchanan to Buchanan, Harris & Co., 17 May 1850 (copy), 67/53094

t / Peter Buchanan to James Law, 22 Nov. 1850 (copy), 67/53125

u / Memos regarding new arrangements (copy), 67/53108

v / Peter Buchanan to Isaac Buchanan, 31 Oct. 1851 (copy), 68/53890

w / Peter Buchanan to R.W. Harris, 15 Dec. 1854, 14/12311. Also Peter Buchanan to R.W. Harris, 4 Nov. 1853, 14/12066

x / Peter Buchanan to R.W. Harris, 15 Dec. 1854, 14/12311. Minute of Peter Buchanan to R.W. Harris, 10 Nov. 1854 (copy), 68/54134

y / Adam Hope to Isaac Buchanan, 8 May 1855, 32/26515

z / Adam Hope to R.W. Harris, 31 Jan. 1857, 32/26732

aa / Finance statement, Glasgow, 1 Feb. 1856, 85/60338

bb / Table, quarterly statement amounts of London outstanding debts, 1858, 84/60163. Finance statement, Adam Hope & Co., 1 June 1857, 85/60447

cc / Peter Buchanan to Isaac Buchanan, 8 Jan. 1858, 15/12743. Row does not add because of rounding.

dd / '1858 Quarterly Statements Amts. London 1852 & 1858,' 84/60163

ee / Finance memorandum, London, 1 June 1859, 86/60728

ff / Peter Buchanan, memo re remittances, 11 Nov. 1859, 86/60688. Peter Buchanan to Buchanan, Harris & Co., 30 Dec. 1859 (copy), 68/54238

gg / Robert Wemyss to Isaac Buchanan, 6 May 1862, 59/47229-30

hh / Isaac Buchanan, memo re Adam Hope & Co. at end of 1860, 32/27080

ii / Adam Hope to Isaac Buchanan, 15 Nov. 1862, 33/27305

jj / Hamilton Dry Goods Department, Records of Imports, 1862, 29 Nov. 1862, 86/61019

kk / Robert Wemyss to Isaac Buchanan, 17 June 1864, 60/47619

mm / Alex Campbell to Isaac Buchanan, 12 Nov. 1862, 19/16152

nn / Adam Hope to Isaac Buchanan, 7 Jan. 1864, 33/27441

oo / Adam Hope to Isaac Buchanan, 8 Dec. 1864 (copy), 33/27642-3

pp / Robert Wemyss to Isaac Buchanan, 15 Dec. 1866, 61/48668-9

qq / Alex Campbell to Isaac Buchanan, 26 Nov. 1866, 20/16750-3

TABLE 3
Cash receipts, Hamilton & London, 1847-66 (cols. A, B, C £000cy)

Year	A Sales (nearest equiv. period)*	B Cash receipts†	C B-A	D B/A x 100	E B/A (prev. yr) x 100
Hamilton					
1846	135 a	na	-	-	-
1847	122	154 b	32	126%	114%
1848	88	136	48	155	111
1849	105	137	32	130	156
1850	134	163	29	122	155
1851	143	145	2	101	108
1852	146	159	13	109	111
1853	193	209	16	108	143
1854	238	205	-33	86	106
1855	306	247	-59	81	104
1856	260	254	- 6	98	83
1857	179	206	27	115	79
1858	115	147	32	128	82
1859	103	120	17	117	104
1860	132	137 c	5	104	133
1861	185	127	-58	69	96
1862	196	157 d	-39	80	85
1863	146	133	-13	91	68
1864	na	na			
1865	na	na			
1866	232	257 c	25	111	na
London					
1853	86	na	-	-	-
1854	117	80 f	-37	68	93
1855	115	94	-21	82	80
1856	109	103	- 6	94	90
1857	75	75	0	100	69
1861	83	71 g	-12	86	na
1862	80	76	- 4	95	92
1863	79	78	- 1	99	98

a / Table 1

b / Peter Buchanan, 'Jottings Accounts July 1860,' 82/59433

c / Isaac Buchanan to Alex Campbell, 23 June 1862 (copy), 19/16086

d / Robert Wemyss to Isaac Buchanan, 17 June 1864, 60/47618

e / Isaac Buchanan to D. McGee, 7 Dec. 1866 (copy), 44/35663

f / Peter Buchanan, note on London collections in his memo book for 1857-8, 90/63651

g / Adam Hope to Isaac Buchanan, 3 Jan. and 1 Dec. 1863, 33/27344-5, 414

* Source gives cash receipts by the calendar year, which only became the firm's fiscal year in 1849. See Table 1 for sales periods used for 1846-8.

† Hamilton collected a good deal on account of New York and Montreal, in early years at least, and the source does not distinguish such sums from those collected for sales at Hamilton. This helps to explain the persistent positive balance in early years in column c. I am assuming that this practice diminished or was even eliminated once the firms were separated in 1854; if it was not, then the subsequent negative figures in column c look even worse. The clienteles of the three houses overlapped and it was often simplest for the customer to pay at Hamilton, the nearest of the three; it was also the practice to transfer accounts that were not paid on time at the shorter credit terms that prevailed in New York and Montreal to Hamilton, which could supervise such accounts more closely and would require to know the customer's full indebtedness to the firm to do so to best advantage.

TABLE 4
Profits* declared 1834-56 (cols. A-K £ cy)

Period	Hamilton and Montreal**				Toronto	Total in Canada
	A	B	C	D	E	F
	Dry goods	Hamilton groc.	Montreal profit	Net profit declared	Net profit declared	
Nov. 1834-Oct. 1835				-	4329 a	4329
Nov. 1835-Oct. 1836				-	5330 b	5330
Nov. 1836-Oct. 1837				-	[2000]†	[2000]
Nov. 1837-Oct. 1838				-	8400 c	8400
Nov. 1838-Nov. 1839				-	[11000]†	[11000]
Dec. 1839-Nov. 1840				-	5018 d	5018
Dec. 1840-Oct. 1841	12513 e	3019 e	-	10277 e	[13000]†	na
Nov. 1841-Oct. 1842	4606	810	859 f	4148	4647 g	na
Nov. 1842-Oct. 1843	6668	3097	735	5330	5648 h	na
Nov. 1843-Mar. 1845	10694	5668	5467	12148	2255 e	na
Apr. 1845-Mar. 1846	7771	2642	4365	8072	-	8072
Apr. 1846-Mar. 1847	6894	2213	7964	11468	-	11468

Period	Hamilton	Montreal	London	New York		Glasgow	Liverpool (£ stg)
	G	H	J	K		L	M
Apr. 1847-Mar. 1848	na	[17500] j††	-		na	-11450 k	-
Apr. 1848-Dec. 1848	[8000] n	[7000] m	-		[15000] n		-
1849	[10000]o	na	-		na		-
1850	[16000]†††	4290 p	-	†††	[20000] q		-
1851	[7500]†††	3500 r	-	†††	[11000] s		-
1852	na	na	3482 t		23726 u		na
1853	na	14026 v	6000 w		na		2282 x
1854	16527 y	[9000] y	[7860] y	2217 z	[35500]	2102 aa	3523 bb
1855	na	5071 cc	na		na	1421	1982 dd
1856	na	8006 ee	na		na		749

a / Trial balance, old books, 30 Jan. 1836, 83/59567

b / Profit and loss account, Toronto, 31 Oct. 1836, 83/59585-6

c / Peter Buchanan to Isaac Buchanan, 5 Dec. 1838 (copy), 66/52103

d / Peter and Isaac Buchanan stock account, and profit and loss account, Toronto, 1 Dec. 1840, 83/59644

e / Hamilton profit and loss entries, 1840-47, 84/60053-8. The 1841 figure includes the period from Sept. to Nov. 1840 as well.

f / Montreal profit and loss account, 1842-47, 84/59917-27

g / Profit and loss account, Toronto, 1 Nov. 1842, 83/59705 A-B

h / Profit and loss account, Toronto, 1 Nov. 1843, 83/59775-6

j / James Law to Isaac Buchanan, 6 Mar. 1848, 37/30756-7

k / Memo, Glasgow, 22 Nov. 1848, 14/11866

m / Peter Buchanan to Isaac Buchanan, 13 Jan. 1849, 14/11848

n / Peter Buchanan to Robert Leckie, 12 Jan. 1849 (copy), 67/52904

o / Peter Buchanan to R.W. Harris, 24 Oct. 1849, and to John Young, 2 Nov. 1849 (copies), 67/53004, 11

p / Profit and loss account, Montreal, 31 Dec. 1850, 84/60119

q / Peter Buchanan to Isaac Buchanan, 1 Feb. 1851, 14/11885

r / Profit and loss account, Montreal, 31 Dec. 1851, 84/60153

s / Jottings re partners' capital, Peter Buchanan, Oct. 1851, 84/60148

t / Balance account, private ledger, Adam Hope & Co., 31 Dec. 1852, 84/60166

u / Memo, R.W. Harris, 21 Dec. 1853, 14/12045

v / Memo, net balance, Montreal, 31 Dec. 1853, 84/60196-7

w / Memo of balance, 31 Dec. 1853, London, 84/60231-3. See also Isaac Buchanan to Peter Buchanan, 10 Feb. 1855, 10/9041.

x / Peter Buchanan to R.W. Harris, 16 Dec. 1853, 14/12100

y / Isaac Buchanan to Peter Buchanan, 10 Feb. 1855, 10/9041

z / Balance, private books Isaac Buchanan & Co., New York, 31 Dec. 1854, 84/60213

aa / Profit and loss and stock accounts, Peter Buchanan & Co., 31 Dec. 1855, 85/60359

bb / Peter Buchanan to R.W. Harris, 2 Feb. 1855, 15/12348-9. Profit and loss account, Liverpool, 31 Dec. 1854, 84/60215

cc / Peter Buchanan to R.W. Harris and Isaac Buchanan, 1 Feb. 1856, 15/12510-11

dd / *Ibid.*; also profit and loss account, Liverpool, 30 Nov. 1856, 85/60417

ee / Alex Campbell to Isaac Buchanan, 19 Feb. 1857, 18/15546

* Before calculating profits, the partners credited all capital accounts with interest (at 5 per cent until 1847 or 1848, thereafter at 6 per cent).

** Figures in column A are for 'shipment account' carried to profit and loss. Those in column B are for grocery account transferred. No such figures are available for hardware. For the first three years I have removed the net Montreal profit (included at the time under grocery account at Hamilton) from the figure given in the source. I have not deducted Law's salary, which twice (1842 and 1843) was charged against this account. Because Montreal figures in column C are for a fiscal year ending 31 March, the 1843-5 figure for Montreal is for two full years. Deductions were made for contingencies and bad debts before the figures in columns D and E were calculated; hence rows do not total.

† Estimates for 1837, 1839, and 1841 are interpolated on the basis of capital figures (Table 5); profits of this order were required for partners' capital to have grown as it did.

†† Estimates for 1844–54, except as noted below, were made by partners in correspondence.

††† Hamilton figures for 1850 and 1851 are estimated by subtracting Montreal figures from totals; in effect, this includes New York profits in the Hamilton figure. There is no reason to assume that New York profits were very large; that for 1854 was almost certainly a maximum.

TABLE 5
Capital accounts 1835-56

A Toronto (£ cy)	31 Oct. 1835	31 Oct. 1836	31 Oct. 1837	31 Oct. 1838	30 Nov. 1839	30 Nov. 1840	31 Oct. 1841	31 Oct. 1842	31 Oct. 1843
P. and I. Buchanan	4834 a	7707 c	[10000] d	16540 e	25609 f	30650 h	41903 i	46440 j	51770 k
R.W. Harris	199 b	1266	na	3259	5583 g	6280	na	10638	na
Total	5033	8973	na	19799	31192	36930	na	57078	na

B In Canada (£ cy)	7 June 1844	31 Mar. 1845	31 Mar. 1846	31 Mar. 1848	31 Dec. 1850	Oct. 1851	31 Dec. 1856	C In whole business (£ cy) 31 Dec. 1856
Peter Buchanan	5003 m	7605 n	9518 o	13604 p	29435 q	36000 r	66000 s	193981 s
Isaac Buchanan	5003	4501	3521	-	-	-	32000	54434
R.W. Harris	4050	5411	6516	15058	29084	38000	56000	91816
George Douglás	1608	2969	1130	-	-	24000	-	-
John Young	8846	8792	7648	9704	19680	17500	-	-
James Law	1322	2866	3672	4790	13910	3700	-	-
R. Leckie	-	-	-	-	2173	-	12000	11873
A. Campbell	-	-	-	-	-	-	2000	1889
Adam Hope	-	-	-	-	-	-	10000	10021
C.J. Hope	-	-	-	-	-	-	5000	4534
Fred Lane	-	-	-	-	-	-	1000	626
Total partners' capital	25832	32144	32004	43156	94282	119200	184000	369174
Susp. acc'ts		9678	15763	35755	35025	25000	46000	46021
Total cap. acc'ts		41822	47767	78911	129307	144200	230000	415195

D Capital totals	1 Jan. 1835	30 Nov. 1839	31 Oct. 1843	1 Dec. 1845	31 Mar. 1846	31 Dec. 1856
Glasgow* (£ stg)	[12000] t	[13000] u	[17800] v	65600 x	114000 y	150000* s
Total in business (£ cy)	[15000]	[47000] u	[94000] w			369000

* 1856 figure for Glasgow and Liverpool

a / 'Balance of Profit and Loss in Old Books,' nd 83/59580

b / 'Trial Balance in the New Books,' 30 Jan. 1836, 83/59566

c / Balance, Toronto, 31 Oct. 1836, 83/59593-4

d / 'Memo of stock P & IB,' nd, in Isaac Buchanan notebook, 90/63599. This is Isaac's estimate for their capital at the end of 1837.

e / Peter Buchanan to Isaac Buchanan, 5 Dec. 1838 (copy), 66/52103

f / Peter and Isaac Buchanan stock account, and profit and loss account, Toronto, 1 Dec. 1840, 83/59644

g / Peter Buchanan to Isaac Buchanan, 12 Apr. 1840 (copy), 66/52193

h / Balance, Toronto, 1 Dec. 1840, 83/59642

i / 'P. & I. Buchanan's Stock Account,' Toronto, 1 Nov. 1842, 83/59705-6

j / Balance, 31 Oct. 1842, 83/59710. See also calculation of net worth, Isaac Buchanan, 1 July 1843, 83/59761-3.

k / 'P & I. Buchanan's Stock Account and Suspense Stock Account,' Toronto, 1 Nov. 1843, 83/59771-2

m / Statement of affairs in Hamilton, Apr. 1844; memo attached, dated 7 June 1844: 83/59797

n / Peter Buchanan to Isaac Buchanan, 1 June 1846 (copy), 66/52342

o / Peter Buchanan to Isaac Buchanan, 30 May 1846 (copy), 66/52337

p / Amended balance sheet, June 1848, 84/60083

q / Jottings by Peter Buchanan re partners' capital, Oct. 1851, 84/60148-9

r / *Ibid*. That these figures are quite reliable estimates is indicated by, eg, Peter Buchanan to Isaac Buchanan, 11 Apr. and 13 Dec. 1851, 14/11913, 65-6.

s / Calculation of capital at 31 Dec. 1856, 85/60394. Figures for capital in Canada of the three senior partners are approximate and are arrived at by deducting capital in British branches; see Balance, Private Books, Glasgow, and Balance Liverpool, 30 Nov. 1856, 85/60352, 413, 419.

t / Estimate based on figures for sales, profits, capital, and advances in 1835 and 1836

u / Peter Buchanan to Isaac Buchanan, 12 Apr. 1840 (copy), 66/52193. See also Isaac Buchanan to Peter Buchanan, c21 Dec. 1840, 9/8636.

v / Isaac Buchanan's estimate, 1 July 1843, 83/59761-3

w / Isaac's estimate (note v) converted to currency plus his and his brother's Canadian capital and estimates for Harris (£12,000) based on 1842 figure, Young (£7000) based on 1844 figure, and Douglas (£1600) based on 1844 also. The estimate should be within 10 to 15 per cent of the exact figure.

x / Calculation of obligations, Peter Buchanan, Dec. 1845, 83/59820. See also Table 6.

y / See Table 6.

TABLE 6
Estimated balance, 1 December 1845

A Peter Buchanan & Co. (£ stg)[a]		B Canadian Firms (£ cy)	
Assets		*Assets*	
Due from Canadian firms	£141000	Due from customers (net)	[£208000] b
Misc. assets (bills, advances		Real property (Montreal,	
produce, etc.)	19000	Hamilton and misc.)	19000 c
	160000	Inventory and produce	[58000] d
			[285000]
Liabilities		*Liabilities*	
Due suppliers	29000	Due P. Buchanan & Co.	
Due on bills drawn from Canada		(see column A)	176000
(against produce; for NY)	8000	Discounts (4 banks at	
Due to Glyns	2000	Hamilton, 1 at Montreal)	[50000] e
Due on banking credits (J. & A.		Due suppliers, on produce, etc.	[10000] d
Dennistoun, A. Dennistoun &			[236000]
Co., H.S. Floud & Co.)	16000	Partners' capital	32000 f
Due on cash advances (Guild;		Suspense and bad debts	16000 f
Buchanan, Watson; J. Watson*)	19000		[284000]
Due family members (Jane			
Douglas, Jean Buchanan, etc.)	5000		
Due in December (not broken		Total assets = £309000cy	= £247000stg
down) and on pig iron	15000	Total capital = 114000	= 92000
	94000	(ex susp.)	
		Net obligations = 178000	= 142000
P. & I. Buchanan, capital	59000		
R.W. Harris capital	7000		
	160000		

a / Summary of engagements, Peter Buchanan & Co., 1 Dec. 1845, 83/59820

b / Isaac Buchanan, memo on debts of supply account customers as of 1 Feb. 1846, 84/59974. Excluded are Hamilton's debts to Montreal. Figure is assumed to have been the same on 1 Dec., though this probably underestimates the actual figure. See Peter Buchanan to James Law, 28 Jan. 1848 (copy), 67/52660. This implies a higher figure; if so, North American payments were likely similarly higher.

c / Hamilton balance sheet, 31 Mar. 1846, 84/59907. The Montreal property was valued at about £8000 and it is added to the Hamilton figure.

d / Peter Buchanan, calculations of the weight of the Canadian business at 30 Oct. 1845 (dated Jan. 1845), 83/59818. These figures could well be too low (see note b), but no better ones are available.

e / Peter Buchanan (note d) anticipated a lower figure, £30,000, but this was certainly an under-estimate. One year later, Montreal's discounts were £18,000 (Montreal financial memo, 25 Dec. 1846, 84/59873). Two years later, in a commercial crisis, Hamilton's were £44,000 (John Young to Isaac Buchanan, 17 Dec. 1847, 63/50142). Such figures tended to stay relatively stable over considerable spans of time, but this figure really is only an educated guess.

f / Table 5

* James Watson was cashier of Peter's bank (now known as the Union Bank of Scotland); he had some £6000 invested in the firm at interest, and his son had now become a clerk in the firm's Glasgow office. Watson and Peter Buchanan were close friends.

TABLE 7
Approximate balance, 31 December 1857

A Glasgow and Liverpool Firms (£ stg)		B Canadian Firms (£ cy)	
Assets		*Assets*	
Due from Canadian firms	332000*	Due from customers, Mtl.	116000
Misc. assets (produce, bills)	12000	Due from customers, Ham. and	
		New York	365000
	344000	Due from customers, London	126000
		Inventory, Montreal	48000
		Inventory, Hamilton	60000
		Inventory, London	55000
Liabilities		Fixed property	40000
Due suppliers	62000		
Due Union Bank of Scotland			810000
(overdraft)	48000		
Due Union Bank of Scotland		*Liabilities*	
(Cdn bills discounted)	21000	Due to Glasgow and Liverpool	415000
Due on banking credit		Bank discounts, Montreal	30000
(Dennistoun, Cross & Co.)	12000	Bank discounts, Hamilton	86000
Due Glyns	4000	Bank discounts, London	15000
Due on H.B. Jackson drafts	9000	Other payments, Montreal**	25000
Due to Hennessy & Co.	16000	Other payments, Hamilton	17000
James Watson†	2000	Other payments, London	12000
Due on drafts against produce	4000	Other payments, New York	12000
Miscellaneous	1000	Miscellaneous	3000
	179000		615000
Partners' capital	166000***	Partners' capital	154000
	345000	Suspense accounts††	[41000]
			[810000]

Total assets = £825000cy = £660000stg.
Total liabs. = 424000 = 339000
Total capital = 362000 = 289000
(ex. susp.)

Peter Buchanan, 'General Position at Home & in Canada on 31 Dec. 1857 – or 1 January 1858,' 85/60642

* Includes accommodation bills drawn on Glasgow by the North American firms.
† Watson was the son of the firm's previous backer of the same name; he now worked as a senior clerk for the business in Hamilton, having earlier served in Montreal and Glasgow.
** Other payments, except for £13,000 due by Montreal to consigners, were to be made in North America. Some were probably due to other branches of the firm (chiefly to New York or Montreal); these would appear as assets for the appropriate firm above.
†† Figures do not quite balance because of rounding, though the original source includes some figures that were only approximate in any case. The figure for suspense accounts is my estimate to balance; it is reasonable in the light of other evidence (see Table 5).
*** Figure considerably exceeds that given in Table 5 for 31 Dec. 1856 chiefly because the basis of Peter Buchanan's calculation was different; in effect some lesser accounts are included here but not in 1856.

TABLE 8
Summary of reorganization 1860

Pre-reorganization			Post-reorganization		
A Glasgow (a)					
Partners' capital		£177,000			£61,000
Peter Buchanan	£112,000			£61,000	
Isaac Buchanan	24,000			-	
R.W. Harris	41,000			-	
B Montreal (b)					
Partners' capital (gross)		$136,000			$58,000
(net)		120,000			35,000
Buchanan, Harris			Isaac Buchanan	$28,000	
& Co.	$99,000				
R. Leckie	38,000			31,000	
A. Campbell	-16,000			-23,000	
Bad debt and suspense		31,000			59,000
			To pay R.W. Harris		
			and Peter Buchanan		34,000
C London (c)					
Partners' capital		$272,000			$121,000
Buchanan, Harris			Isaac Buchanan	$40,000	
& Co.	$191,000				
Adam Hope	38,000			38,000	
C.J. Hope	23,000			23,000	
William Muir	20,000			20,000	
			Suspense bad debts		48,000
			Reserve capital		40,000
			To pay out		128,000

a / Peter Buchanan & Co. to R.W. Harris, 27 Jan. 1860 (copy), 15/12878-9; and to Buchanan, Harris & Co., 17 Jan. 1860 (copy), 68/54241-4

b / Articles of copartnership, Montreal, 23 Aug. 1860, 73/55817-21. Montreal balance sheet, 31 Dec. 1859, and statement of capital in the Montreal business, 15 Aug. 1860, 86/60648, 770

c / Isaac Buchanan, position of Adam Hope & Co. at end of 1860, 32/27080. Articles of copartnership, London, 10 Aug. 1860, and separate agreement of same date re this, 73/55778-91, 809-11. Calculation of how Adam Hope & Co. could be carried on, 24 Nov. 1859; Peter Buchanan, statement re London business, August 1860; balance sheet, Adam Hope & Co., 30 Nov. 1860; 86/60697, 840, 878-80

TABLE 9
The bankruptcy estate 1867*

Due in Britain, for goods	£28,652	Stock	$158,768
Due on bills of exchange	35,500	Accounts	271,975
Union Bank of Scotland	59,039**	Premises	19,000
Due Canadian banks	30,264	T.H. McKenzie	10,592
Due Canadian banks for discounts		Adam Hope & Co.	95,025
not met at maturity	4,000***		555,360
Difference between value of		Cost to collect	
mortgages sold by firm and		and remit	42,500
actual value of property	2,481		512,860
Miscellaneous British		Equal to about	£102,600
open accounts	574		
Due on bills and open accounts		This equals 9/6 in the £ on the	
in Canada and United States	14,065	business estate, or 8/- in the £ if	
Due George Douglas	500	Peter Buchanan's trustees ranked.	
Due Isaac Buchanan & Co., Montreal	23,210†	Isaac Buchanan offered 8/3 and	
Due H.B. Jackson, Manchester	3,000	relied on funds from Peter Bu-	
Due Henry Rogers, Sons & Co.	7,006**	chanan's trustees to meet his offers	
Due Adam Hope & Co. in liquidation	1,128	on his personal estate.	
Total business debts	£209,419		
Due Peter Buchanan's Trustees	48,000††	Wemyss valued the estate at 8/9	
Due on Adam Hope & Co.		and Hope at 10/2, both omitting	
acceptances	34,500†††	Peter Buchanan's trustees. They	
Total possible obligations	£291,919	offered 7/6 in the £ for the estate.	

Principal source is Scottish Record Office, Record of Sequestration, Peter Buchanan &
Co., Accountant of Court's Process # 56 of 1869, esp. pages 84-96, 98, 100-9, 138, 163-73.

* There were discrepancies among the valuations of the estate and reckonings of liabilities; this statement follows Isaac Buchanan's except as indicated.

** These are somewhat higher than Isaac reckoned and are the sums that actually ranked on the estate.

*** All partners made higher estimates; this is the sum that actually ranked. The effect of these three changes is to leave total liabilities much as Isaac estimated.

† Opinion of counsel was solicited as to whether Isaac's capital in this firm, £12,329, now in Peter T. Buchanan's name, should be set off against this; in the end, a set-off of this and some other accounts with the firm was agreed to, and the Montreal firm's claim was dropped from the estate. (This of course reduced Isaac's assets, too.)

†† This claim, for sums at Peter Buchanan's credit in Glasgow in 1860 that Isaac had not formally accounted for, plus interest, was referred to counsel. It appears to have ranked on the estate, but the funds passed to Isaac and thus formed the basis of his offer of 3/6 in the £ on his personal estate.

††† This liability was for Adam Hope & Co. acceptances, mainly discounted at the Union Bank. Peter Buchanan & Co. was liable only if Adam Hope & Co. failed to meet this paper, and it did not in fact rank on the estate.

TABLES 10 TO 13: AN EXPLANATORY NOTE

By 1850, when the *Tables of Trade and Navigation* began to be published on an annual basis, the Canadian customs system was becoming better organized and more consistent; the number of customs houses had been much increased, the bonding system and arrangements for duty payments were relatively well established, and the categories under which imports were classified seem to have become more consistent. Fuller research than I have done would be required to make fullest use of the data contained in these tables, but I think they can serve to illustrate certain trends in city and business development. Figures given in the original source in £cy are converted to dollars at the standard rate of $4 = £1cy. The valuation of goods was the invoice value (at place of purchase).

These figures do not represent accurate total volumes for the 'independent' import trades of each port: 1 / because some importers in, say, Toronto or Hamilton, also purchased goods that had already been entered at customs, most often in Montreal; 2 / because importers such as the Buchanans might for various reasons enter their goods at customs at Quebec or Montreal although final sale was at Hamilton (there is not sufficient evidence on the firm's practices to permit more precise comment); and 3 / because a good many of Montreal's imports (chiefly from the United States) were entered at its outport, St Johns, on the Richelieu River. It should be noted, however, that there was an advantage to merchants in entering goods at point of sale, because this permitted maximum delay in paying duties.

If the various practices noted above were relatively constant from year to year, or changed in parallel manners, then these figures can serve to indicate in at least a rough way the relative positions of the major ports that imported manufactured goods. If such practices changed over time, but relatively gradually, then comparisons of one year at a port with the next one at the same port should also be relatively safely made. These are the principal uses made of these figures in this study. See, however, the note on Table 13.

Source notes, Table 10

a / *Journals*, 1849, App. z, 'Montreal Brokers' Circular'

b / 'Tables on the Trade of Toronto for the Year Ending Jan. 5, 1848,' Buchanan Papers, 90/63129

c / Israel D. Andrews, *Report on the Trade and Commerce of the British North American Colonies and upon the Trade of the Great Lakes and Rivers* (Washington 1853), US Senate, 32nd Cong., 1st Sess., Ex. Doc. 112, pp 419, 426, 430

d / Province of Canada, *Tables of Trade and Navigation*

TABLE 10
Value of imports entered at the Customs House,
leading ports,* 1841-74 ($000)

	Montreal	Quebec	Toronto	Hamilton
1841	8272 a	872 a		
1842	8084	868		
1843	5160	1608		
1844	9900	2624		
1845	10480	2848		
1846	9216	3004		
1847	8252	3188	740 b	
1848	5924	2504	789 c	941 c
1849	6184 c	1755 c	1315	1123
1850	6905 d	1976 d	2539 d	1583 d
1851	8804	2569	2714	2026
1852	8985	2591	2557	2361
1853	13526	4566	4660	3546
1854	15264	7017	5451	5106
1855	12256	2930	5606	4965
1856	16265	3486	6955	5400
1857	15525	3690	5085	3693
1858	12254	2783	3769	2102
1859	15554	3004	4019	2229
1860	15334	3359	4048	2377
1861	16198	6434	4619	2657
1862	20184	5337	4301	2894
1863†	18605	4984	4572	2720
1863-4†	21227	5410	5031	2621
1864-5	20253	4470	4329	2087
1865-6	24241	5082	6174	3435
1866-7	28139	5269	6964	3782
1867-8	24599	6176	6803	3129
1868-9	22561	5895	6473	3203
1869-70	24018	5534	7127	3587
1870-1	32080	5589	10295	3961
1871-2	37955	6853	12909	5208
1872-3	44064	6873	14851	5894
1873-4	41583	7422	14717	6220

* See note on Tables 10–13 above (p 176).
† Period changed from the calendar year to one running from
  1 July to 30 June. Hence these two overlap.

TABLE 11
Value of selected principal imports entered at the Customs House,* Hamilton, 1850-73 ($000)

	Cotton	Woollens	Silks, satins and velvets	Manufactures of hardware, iron, brass, and copper†	Tea	Sugar (brown or raw)†
1850	450	254	63	147	131	60
1851	496	328	125	249	149	66
1852	508	384	155	276	167	94
1853	701	603	181	329	206	122
1854	1053	814	252	447	199	173
1855	1002	667	210	412	244	235
1856	1200	634	231	406	289	247
1857	723	452	147	210	152	217
1858	363	170	31	70	171	156
1859	539	222	80	78	255	151
1860	687	277	95	104	131	174
1861	684	325	80	125	172	164
1862	604	325	62	129	236	166
1863	403	325	60	112	138	122
1864-5	339	334	27	78	112	165
1865-6	716	494	61	102	177	199
1866-7	674	703	60	163	212	143
1867-8	502	548	68	146	221	203
1868-9	532	428	52	141	218	110
1869-70	481	437	70	161	211	107
1870-71	634	551	103	198	214	157
1871-72	654	683	137	251	192**	178
1872-73††	517	746	120	349	na	229

* See note on Tables 10-13 above (p 176).
† These categories varied slightly over time, but always were the largest entry by far for their type of goods.
** Last year for a useful 'tea' category.
†† Such detailed breakdowns by port were not published after 1873.

TABLE 12
Relationships among value of imports
through selected Canadian ports 1850-74* (selected years)

Year	Toronto imports as % of Montreal's	Hamilton imports as % of Montreal's	Hamilton imports as % of Toronto's
1850	36%	23%	62%
1854	36	33	94
1856	43	33	78
1858	31	17	55
1860	26	16	60
1862	21	14	66
1865-6	25	14	66
1868-9	29	14	49
1873-4	35	15	42

* See note on Tables 10–13 above (p 176).
Source: all figures from Table 10

TABLE 13
Change in value of imports through selected ports at certain intervals*

	Hamilton	Toronto	Montreal
1858 relative to 1856	39%	54%	75%
1860 relative to 1856	44	58	94
1862 relative to 1856	54	62	124
1865-6 relative to 1856	63	89	148
1873-4 relative to 1856	137	212	255
1865-6 relative to 1860	144	154	158
1873-4 relative to 1860	312	364	272
1873-4 relative to 1865-6	216	248	172

* No allowance is made for price changes across these eighteen years; it is assumed that they were parallel in all ports. To the extent that the character of goods imported to the various ports diverged in later years, this assumption is weakened. In 1856, the character of imports was similar at all ports, though a greater and more specialized range of goods came through Montreal. By 1873-4, though this remained roughly true between Toronto and Montreal, Hamilton's shift towards industrialization was altering the character of local imports significantly.
Source: all figures from Table 10

Notes

The basis of this study is the Buchanan Papers (Public Archives of Canada, Ottawa, MG 24, D-16). Unless otherwise specified all manuscript references are to these papers. In the notes that follow, these abbreviations are employed:

BH Business History
BHR Business History Review
CHA Canadian Historical Association
CHR Canadian Historical Review
CJEPS Canadian Journal of Economics and Political Science
EcHR Economic History Review
JEH Journal of Economic History
Journals Journals of the Legislative Assembly of the Province of Canada
OH (*OHSPR*) Ontario History (Ontario Historical Society Papers and
    Records)
SHR Scottish Historical Review
SJPE Scottish Journal of Political Economy

CHAPTER 1: INTRODUCTION

1 Checkland, *The Rise of Industrial Society in England* 108
2 Bridgman, 'Isaac Buchanan and Religion, 1810-1883' (thesis); Baskerville, 'The Boardroom and Beyond,' (thesis); Neutel, 'From "Southern" Concept to Canada Southern Railway 1835-1873' (thesis)
3 Macmillan, ed., *Canadian Business History*; Porter and Cuff, eds., *Enterprise and National Development*, offer some samples of recent work in the field. See also Naylor, *The History of Canadian Business 1867-1914*.

4 Porter, 'Recent Trends in Canadian Business and Economic History' in Porter and Cuff, *Enterprise and National Development* 19
5 Porter and Livesay, *Merchants and Manufacturers*
6 Tulchinsky, *The River Barons* ix-xiii
7 Masters, *The Rise of Toronto, 1850-1890* 53; Careless, *The Union of the Canadas* 146. See also Armstrong, 'Toronto in Transition,' 450-2.
8 Payne, *British Entrepreneurship in the Nineteenth Century* 17-23. It is a pleasure to acknowledge Professor Payne's kind and most helpful advice and assistance, given some years ago when my research was at an early stage.
9 Creighton, *The Commercial Empire of the St Lawrence, 1760-1850*, Buck, *The Development of the Organization of Anglo-American Trade, 1800-1850*
10 Wilson, 'Problems and Traditions of Business History: Past Examples and Canadian Prospects' in Macmillan, *Canadian Business History* 307
11 Eg, Johnson, 'John A. Macdonald: The Young Non-Politician' 150-1; or the various articles in recent years by Donald Swainson, such as 'Business and Politics: The Career of John Willoughby Crawford'
12 H.G.J. Aitken, introduction to Tucker, *The Canadian Commercial Revolution, 1845-1851* xiv-xv
13 Fowke, 'The Myth of the Self-Sufficient Canadian Pioneer'
14 Eg, Careless, 'Somewhat Narrow Horizons.' Lower, *Great Britain's Woodyard* xiii
15 Albion, *The Rise of New York Port, 1815-1860*; Pred, *Urban Growth and the Circulation of Information* 203
16 McCalla, 'Peter Buchanan, London Agent for the Great Western Railway of Canada' in Macmillan, *Canadian Business History* 197-216
17 Wilson, 'The Entrepreneur in the Industrial Revolution in Britain' 131
18 See eg, Crouzet, editor's introduction in his *Capital Formation in the Industrial Revolution* 44-54.
19 Eg, Chambers and Bertram, 'Urbanization and Manufacturing in Central Canada, 1870-1890' 240. See also McCalla, 'The Decline of Hamilton as a Wholesale Centre.'
20 Katz, *The People of Hamilton, Canada West* 188-208

CHAPTER 2: FOUNDING THE BUSINESS

1 Smout 'The Development and Enterprise of Glasgow, 1556-1707' 194, 207-9. Campbell, 'The Anglo-Scottish Union of 1707' 475
2 The basic source for this and the next paragraph is Jacob M. Price, *France and the Chesapeake* I, 609-15, 649-77. See also Devine, 'Sources of Capital for the Glasgow Tobacco Trade,'; Soltow, 'Scottish Traders in Virginia, 1750-1775'; and two

articles by Price: 'The Rise of Glasgow in the Chesapeake Tobacco Trade, 1707-1775'; and 'Who Was John Norton?'

3 Campbell, *Scotland since 1707* 46-8

4 Devine, 'Glasgow Merchants and the Collapse of the Tobacco Trade, 1775-1783'; and *The Tobacco Lords* 161-7. M.L. Robertson, 'Scottish Commerce and the American War of Independence' 123-8. Checkland, 'Two Scottish West Indian Liquidations after 1793' 127. Anon. 'The Rise of Glasgow's West Indian Trade, 1793-1818' 34-6

5 Kellett, 'Property Speculators and the Building of Glasgow, 1780-1830'

6 Macmillan, *Scotland and Australia, 1788-1850* xvi, 5. I have benefited greatly from David Macmillan's advice on a number of points in this work.

7 Checkland, *Scottish Banking* 281-373. Campbell, *Scotland since 1707* 68-75, 82, 133-4, 137-43

8 Macmillan, *Scotland and Australia* xv-xvii, 5-7, 24, 69, 262. Stewart, *Progress of Glasgow*. Clapham, *An Economic History of Modern Britain* I, *The Early Railway Age, 1820-1850* 52

9 *Post Office Glasgow Directory*, 1807. The Mitchell Library in Glasgow has bound its directories in a continuous series; this source will henceforth be cited as *Glasgow Directory*. Peter Buchanan Sr to Duncan Buchanan, 12 June 1820 (copy), 8/6576

10 'Disposition of the Lands of Auchmar by Andrew Buchanan to Peter Buchanan,' 1813, 69/54350-61. Farmer, 'Calendar of the Buchanan Papers, 1697-1896, Presented to the Hamilton Public Library...' (typescript, Hamilton Public Library, 1962). See also Devine, 'Glasgow Colonial Merchants and Land, 1770-1815' in Ward and Wilson, eds, *Land and Industry*.

11 *List of Members of the Merchants House of Glasgow* (Glasgow 1891) 8. Buchanan, *Notes on the Members of the Buchanan Society, Numbers 1 to 366* 96. The Buchanan Society, *History, Rules, Bye-Laws, and List of Members* 2-13. Letters of Margaret Buchanan to Isaac Buchanan, 1831-3, 13/11191-221. Bridgman, 'Isaac Buchanan and Religion' 8-10

12 Ragatz, *The Fall of the Planter Class in the British Caribbean, 1763-1833* 286-337. Pares, *Merchants and Planters* 40-9

13 Correspondence between Peter Buchanan and Duncan Buchanan, 2 Feb. 1820 to 10 Feb. 1821, 8/6569-94. Letters from George Buchanan to Peter Buchanan, 18 Nov. 1820 to 16 May 1822, 8/6614-47. Letters from William Crichton to Peter Buchanan and to Peter Buchanan Jr, 18 Dec. 1820 to 3 July 1826, 22/18734-99. Letters from John Christie to Peter Buchanan Jr, 29 May 1827 to 4 June 1828, 22/18801-12. Partnership agreement, dated (incorrectly) 16 July 1822, between Peter Buchanan and Duncan Buchanan, 69/54364-6. Summary of Peter Buchanan's transactions, Nov. 1820 to Sept. 1823, 83/59511

14 A. Lapslie to Peter Buchanan, 23 Apr. 1829, 37/30670-8

15 Re Montreal and Quebec, see letters from Irvine, Leslie & Co. and Irvine, Macnaught & Co. to Peter Buchanan, 1 Mar. 1819 to 13 Sept. 1823, 34/28569-651. Re Jamaica, see letters from James & Ben Buchanan & Co. to Peter Buchanan and to Peter Buchanan Jr, 19 Oct. 1822 to 3 Sept. 1827, 11/10027-10179. Re Berbice, see Charles Lyle correspondence, 29 July 1820 to 31 Dec. 1829, 40/32396-32520; and Robert Semple letters to Peter Buchanan, 9 Mar. 1826 to 18 May 1832, 54/43022-145. Re South American markets, see Brown, Buchanan & Co. letters to Peter Buchanan, 15 May 1824 to 27 Apr. 1826, 4/2419-24; and 23 Jan. 1823 to 10 Feb. 1826, 8/6519-50; and Brown, Watson & Co. to Peter Buchanan, 12 Mar. and 11 June 1825, 5/2677-83. Re Haiti, see Ure, Smart & Co. letters to Peter Buchanan, 11 Dec. 1823 to 12 Jan. 1826, 58/45982-46019

16 John Buchanan to Margaret Buchanan, 23 May 1822, 13/11091

17 Isaac Buchanan to the Trustees and Executors of Peter Buchanan, 1834, 69/54401-6

18 Peter Buchanan Jr to Peter Buchanan, 3 June 1822, 13/11325. John Buchanan to Peter Buchanan Jr, 29 Jan., 20 and 23 Feb., and 25 May 1822, 13/11023, 29, 34-5, 42, 94

19 Newspaper clipping, 1 Jan. 1827, 77/57209. *Glasgow Directory*, 1825, 116; 1827, 112; 1834-5, 118. Draft partnership agreement, Robert Laing and Peter Buchanan (nd), 69/54375-8. Peter Buchanan to Isaac Buchanan, 22 June and 21 Sept. 1830, 10 and 19 Mar., and 14 Apr. 1831, 13/11346-7, 53-4, 74, 82-5, 90-1

20 Peter Buchanan to Isaac Buchanan, 28 May 1830 and 5 Dec. 1831, 13/11341-4, 11410-12. Isaac Buchanan to Peter Buchanan, 5 Oct. 1833, 9/8615-16

21 Morgan, *Sketches of Celebrated Canadians and Persons Connected with Canada* 553-4. Notman and Taylor, *Portraits* I, 383. Guild & Woodburn to Peter Buchanan, 21 Dec. 1825, 11/10128-30. Peter Buchanan to Isaac Buchanan, 22 June 1830 and 10 Mar. 1831, 13/11346, 77

22 Bailyn, ' "Hedges" *Browns*'

23 Macmillan, *Scotland and Australia* 8

24 Platt, *Latin America and British Trade, 1806-1914* 3-38. Jenks, *The Migration of British Capital to 1875* 44-9, 57-8

25 Jenks, *Migration of British Capital* 65-81. Gayer, Rostow, and Schwartz, *The Growth and Fluctuation of the British Economy 1790-1850* I, 215, 251; II, 747, 784. Potter, 'Atlantic Economy, 1815-60' in Pressnell, ed., *Studies in the Industrial Revolution* 236-41, 260-77

26 Albion, 'New York Port and Its Disappointed Rivals, 1815-1860.' Edwards, *The Growth of the British Cotton Trade, 1780-1815* 107-25. Cohen, 'The Auction System in the Port of New York, 1817-1837.' Perkins, *Financing Anglo-American*

Trade 13-37. Williams, 'Liverpool Merchants and the Cotton Trade, 1820-1850' in Harris, ed., *Liverpool and Merseyside*

27 Clapham, *Econ. Hist. of Modern Britain* I, 155

28 Invoices of goods consigned to Montreal by William Guild, 16 and 18 Aug. 1828, 83/59524, 27-30. Rankin, *A History of Our Firm* 91-107. Macmillan, *Scotland and Australia* 8

29 'Articles of Copartnership betwixt Wm. Guild & Co. of Glasgow and Isaac Buchanan. Montreal Canada, 1 May 1830,' 69/54394-5. Peter Buchanan to Isaac Buchanan, 22 June 1830, 13/11346

30 Parker, 'The Towns of Lower Canada in the 1830's' in Beckinsale and Houston, eds, *Urbanization and Its Problems*. H.A. Innis, 'Unused Capacity as a Factor in Canadian Economic History' in his *Essays in Canadian Economic History* 146. Ouellet, *Histoire économique et sociale du Québec, 1760-1850* 389-412. North, 'Ocean Freight Rates and Economic Development 1750-1913.' Cross, 'The Dark Druidical Groves' (thesis) Chapters 1-4

31 Chapman, *A Statistical Sketch of the Corn Trade of Canada*. Jones, *History of Agriculture in Ontario, 1613-1880* 47-8, 85-108, 123. Burton, 'Wheat in Canadian History' 213. Fowke, *Canadian Agricultural Policy* 78-80. Pentland, 'The Role of Capital in Canadian Economic Development before 1875' 462; and 'Further Observations on Canadian Development' 405-6. Ouellet and Hamelin, 'La Crise agricole dans le Bas-Canada, 1802-1837.' Le Goff, 'The Agricultural Crisis in Lower Canada, 1802-12' 20-7. McIlwraith, 'The Logistical Geography of the Great Lakes Grain Trade, 1820-1850' (thesis) 30-46

32 *Census of Canada, 1870-71* IV (Ottawa 1876). See also J.D. Wood, 'Introduction: A Context for Upper Canada and Its Settlement' in Wood, ed., *Perspectives on Landscape and Settlement in Nineteenth Century Ontario* xxv

33 Jones, *History of Agriculture* 67-84. Harris and Warkentin, *Canada before Confederation* 118-38

34 Aitken, *The Welland Canal Company* 14-16, 23. Aitken, 'A New Way to Pay Old Debts' in Miller, ed., *Men in Business* 72-5. Innis, 'The Changing Structure of the Canadian Market' in *Essays in Canadian Economic History* 283-5

35 Firth, *The Town of York, 1815-1834* xxvi. Preston, *Kingston before the War of 1812* lxv-lxxviii. Cruikshank, 'A Country Merchant in Upper Canada, 1800-1812'

36 Breckenridge, *The Canadian Banking System 1817-1890* 22-35, 42-8, 62-8. Hammond, *Banks and Politics in America from the Revolution to the Civil War* vii-ix, 647-54

37 Peter Buchanan to Isaac Buchanan, 21 Sept. 1830, 13/11353. Isaac Buchanan to Peter Buchanan, 7 and 20 Feb. and 27 Aug. 1833, 9/8480, 84, 8598

38 Isaac Buchanan to Peter Buchanan, 4 Dec. 1832, 9/8472-3. Peter Buchanan to Isaac Buchanan, 5 Dec. 1831, 13/11413

39 Isaac Buchanan to Peter Buchanan, 4 Dec. 1832 and 20 Feb. 1833, 9/8472-3, 84
40 Armstrong, 'Toronto in Transition' 367-86; and 'Metropolitanism and Toronto Re-examined, 1825-1850.' Acheson, 'The Nature and Structure of York Commerce in the 1820s.' Firth, *The Town of York, 1815-1834* xxvi, xxxiv, lxxxii, 75-6, 82-4. Robertson, *Landmarks of Toronto*, I, 81-2; III, 21, 127-49
41 Morgan, *Sketches of Celebrated Canadians* 555
42 Isaac Buchanan to Peter Buchanan, 4 and 30 May, 8 July, and 14 Sept. 1833, 9/8536, 46, 80, 8607-8
43 This account of the formation of the business itself depends mainly on the 1830 to 1834 correspondence between Peter and Isaac Buchanan: 9/8472-8616; 13/11335-459.
44 W. Guild to Isaac Buchanan, 5 Aug. 1833, quoted in Isaac Buchanan to Peter Buchanan, 14 Sept. 1833, 9/8608
45 Isaac Buchanan to Peter Buchanan, 30 May and 14 Sept. 1833, 9/8546, 8603. Italics his
46 Isaac Buchanan to Peter Buchanan, 1 July 1833, 9/8560-1. Italics his
47 Agreement between R. Laing and P. Buchanan, 5 Apr. 1834, 69/54410-13
48 Gayer *et al.*, *British Economy 1790-1850* I, 242-4, 263-5. Matthews, *A Study in Trade Cycle History* 16-18, 128-36
49 69/54418-19
50 Account of the estate of Peter Buchanan, legal form registered 1 Feb. 1859 by Peter Buchanan Jr, 37/25707-10. R. Hill to Isaac Buchanan, 13 Feb. 1861, 31/25704. Isaac Buchanan to the Executors of Peter Buchanan, 4 Jan. 1834, 69/54401-6. Isaac Buchanan to Peter Buchanan, 7 June 1833, 9/8548. Jean Buchanan to Isaac Buchanan, 16 Nov. 1838, 12/10974-5
51 Isaac Buchanan to Peter Buchanan, 1 July 1833, 9/8562
52 Peter Buchanan to Isaac Buchanan, 14 June 1835 and 21 Jan. 1839 (copy), 13/11468, 66/52122. Jean Buchanan to Isaac Buchanan, 16 Nov. and 4 Dec. 1838, 8 and 14 Jan. 1839, 12/10974-83. Devine, 'Sources of Capital for the Glasgow Tobacco Trade' 122-6
53 Hidy, *The House of Baring In American Trade and Finance* 212, 239
54 Kennedy, 'The Union Bank of Scotland Ltd.' 18
55 Isaac Buchanan to Peter Buchanan, 14 Sept. 1833, 9/8602. See also R.W. Harris to Peter Buchanan, 3 Dec. 1858, 30/25304; and D. McCalla, 'R.W. Harris' in *Dictionary of Canadian Biography* IX 368-9.
56 *Glasgow Directory*, 1835-6, 49, 311-17

CHAPTER 3: SUCCESS IN TORONTO 1835-9

1 Quoted in Innis and Lower, eds, *Select Documents in Canadian Economic History, 1783-1885* 250

2 Jones, *History of Agriculture* 123. Burton, 'Wheat in Canadian History' 215. Creighton, *The Commercial Empire* 282-3, 308, 312

3 Breckenridge, *The Canadian Banking System* 57-62

4 Duncan Cameron to Joseph Gordon, 20 May 1836; printed in MacDermot, ed., 'Some Opinions of a Tory in the 1830's' 234

5 'Calculations of how the Business should Pay,' 22 Aug. 1835, 13/11470-1. Lee, 'The Concept of Profit in British Accounting, 1760-1900' 15-16. Pp 26-9 of this chapter are based primarily on the following runs of material for 1835-6: Peter Buchanan, 13/11463-87; financial memoranda and accounts, 80/58465-774, 83/59566-97.

6 Draft Memo of Partnership, Partnership Agreement, 31 Oct. 1835, 69/54425-6, 32, 35-6

7 Memo re terms for Price and Davidson, Toronto, 3 Oct. 1836, 69/54441-4. Isaac Buchanan to Peter Buchanan, 13 Dec. 1838 (copy), 64/50343

8 Brown, 'The Durham Report and the Upper Canadian Scene' 139. Dent, *The Last Forty Years* I, 105. Middleton, *The Municipality of Toronto* II, 782. Robertson, *Landmarks of Toronto* III, 127. Morgan, *Sketches of Celebrated Canadians* 558-9. Armstrong, 'Toronto in Transition' 325, 352, 358-9, 381, 480-2. Peter Buchanan to Isaac Buchanan, 19 Mar. 1831 and 5 Dec. 1838 (copy), 13/11387, 66/52104. The Board of Trade was not incorporated at this time, but it was heard from on a variety of issues.

9 Peter Buchanan to George Douglas, 8 Oct. 1838 (copy), 66/52050

10 Pp 29-33 are based primarily on the following runs of correspondence for 1837-8: R.W. Harris, 30/24879-929; Isaac Buchanan (letterbook), 64/50276-353; and Peter Buchanan (letterbooks), 66/52040-60, 112-17.

11 McGrane, *The Panic of 1837* 93

12 Breckenridge, *The Canadian Banking System* 68-75, 79

13 Creighton, *The Commercial Empire* 283, 312-13, 322-3, 341

14 Peter Buchanan to Isac Buchanan, 9 Nov. 1839 (copy), 66/52174

15 Isaac Buchanan to Peter Buchanan, 16 Dec. 1837, 9/8630

16 R.W. Harris to Peter Buchanan, 15 Apr. 1838, 30/24925

17 Burton, 'Wheat in Canadian History' 215

18 Morgan, *Sketches of Celebrated Canadians* 558-9

19 R.W. Harris to Isaac Buchanan, 4 Feb. 1838, 30/24901-2. Peter Buchanan to Isaac Buchanan, 5 Dec. 1838 (copy), 66/52104

20 Isaac Buchanan, 'Memorandum for Mr Harris,' 12 Apr. 1838, 30/24920-3. Peter Buchanan to Isaac Buchanan, 21 Dec. 1838 (copy), 66/52111

21 R.W. Harris to Peter Buchanan, 22 Mar. 1838, 30/24917

22 Peter Buchanan to Isaac Buchanan, 5 Dec. 1838 (copy), 66/52103. Table of Discounts, 1839-42, nd, 83/59663

23 Peter Buchanan to Isaac Buchanan, 21 Dec. 1838 and 31 Mar. 1840; to Robert
    Laing, 2 May 1840 and 5 Oct. 1843; and to R.W. Harris, 27 Apr. 1844 and 31
    Dec. 1847 (copies): 66/52110, 52190, 52085, 52215, 52236-7; 67/52647. Isaac
    Buchanan to Peter Buchanan, 29 Oct. 1841 (copy) and 10 and 13 Nov. 1847:
    64/50659-60; 10/8846, 50. Isaac Buchanan, memos, 8 Sept. 1843 (copy),
    64/51232. Evans, *The City* 10
24 Clapham, *An Economic History of Modern Britain*, II, *Free Trade and Steel
    1850-1886* 343
25 Peter Buchanan to Jane Douglas, 25 Feb. 1839 (copy), 66/52065. Emphasis his.
    Robertson, *Landmarks of Toronto* II, 753
26 Pp 33-7 are based primarily on the following runs of material covering 1839
    and early 1840: R.W. Harris, 30/24931-51; Isaac Buchanan (letterbooks),
    64/50355-444; Peter Buchanan (letterbooks), 66/52061-84, 118-94; financial
    memoranda and accounts, 80/58806-18, 47-92, 83/59615-28.
27 Gayer *et al.*, *British Economy 1790-1850* I, 293-4, 348. Jenks, *Migration of British
    Capital* 89-98. Matthews, *Economic Fluctuations in Great Britain, 1833-1842* 21-2,
    137-40
28 Peter Buchanan to Isaac Buchanan, 21 Dec. 1838 (copy), 66/52110. Re Moly-
    neux, Witherby and Co., see Williams, 'Liverpool Merchants and the Cotton
    Trade' 190, 206.
29 Gayer *et al.*, *British Economy 1790-1850* I, 244, 251, 263, 282, 294. Matthews,
    Economic Fluctuations in Great Britain 1833-1842 21-2, 137-9, 151, 201
30 Montreal Brokers' Circular, 25 Mar. 1849, printed in *Journals*, 1849, App. z.
    Burton, 'Wheat in Canadian History' 213-15. Easterbrook and Aitken, *Canadian
    Economic History* 283-6
31 Creighton, *The Commercial Empire* 341
32 Peter Buchanan to Isaac Buchanan, 9 Nov. 1839 (copy), 66/52175
33 *Ibid.* 52172
34 Eg, Clapp, *John Owens* 41, 126-7; Marriner, *Rathbones of Liverpool 1845-73*
    206-7; Lee, *A Cotton Enterprise, 1795-1840* 145-9
35 Partnership agreement, 13 Feb. 1840, 69/54434
36 Isaac Buchanan to Peter Buchanan, 28 Feb. 1840 (copy), 64/50410
37 Payments schedules, Glasgow, 5 Sept. 1840 and 10 Feb. 1841, 80/58827, 33.
    Peter Buchanan to Isaac Buchanan, 15 Dec. 1841 and 6 Apr. 184[2],
    13/11497-501, 492. Obligations of Peter Buchanan & Co. Dec. 1845, 83/59820.
    H.B. Jackson to Peter Buchanan, 6 Jan. 1846, 35/28715-18
38 Wilson, *Gentlemen Merchants* 243-6. Edwards, *Growth of the British Cotton Trade*
    149-57
39 R.W. Harris to Peter Buchanan, 30 Jan. 1842, 30/25037

40 Peter Buchanan to Isaac Buchanan, 3 Aug. 1845, 13/11656. See also Isaac Bucha-
nan to Peter Buchanan, 16 Nov. 1841 (copy), 64/50680; Peter Buchanan to Isaac
Buchanan, 6 June 1839 (copy), 66/52153; List of Bills on the Circle, Glasgow, 1
July 1846, 84/59938.

41 Peter Buchanan to Robert Laing, 2 May 1840 (copy), 66/52085-6

42 Habakkuk, 'Fluctuations and Growth in the Nineteenth Century' in Kooy, ed.,
Studies in Economics and Economic History 262, 268-9

43 Peter Buchanan to R.W. Harris, 8 Dec. 1854, 14/12304-5. See also Isaac
Buchanan to Peter Buchanan, 18 Nov. 1838 (copy), 64/50317; Peter Buchanan
to James Watson, 24 Dec. 1842 (copy), 66/55205.

44 Isaac Buchanan to P. Witherby, 12 June 1840 (copy), 64/50569-70

45 Eg, Peter Buchanan to Isaac Buchanan, 15 May 1857, 15/12702-3

46 Peter Buchanan to R.W. Harris, 15 Feb. 1842 (copy), 13/11527-9. See also memos, James Law, Feb. 1848, 63/50151-60; memo by Mr Birrell on the business
at London, 28 Mar. 1851, 4/1846-53.

47 Peter Buchanan to Isaac Buchanan, 7 Feb. 1842 and 17 Sept. 1845, 13/11521,
671-2. James Law to John MacKay, 4 Feb. 1848 (copy), 63/50162

48 Peter Buchanan to R.W. Harris, 15 Feb. 1842 (copy), 13/11527-8. See also
Robert Leckie to Isaac Buchanan, 17 Aug. 1857, 38/31198-202; R.K. Masterton
to Peter Buchanan, 17 Nov. 1859, 47/37904

49 Peter Buchanan to Isaac Buchanan, 28 Jan. 1851 (copy), 66/52533-4

50 Isaac Buchanan to Peter Buchanan, 13 Dec. 1838, and to John Young, 11 May
1840 and 11 June 1841 (copies), 64/50343, 63/50045-6, 64/50842. John Young
to Isaac Buchanan, 13 Sept. 1845, 63/50126. Peter Buchanan to Isaac Buchanan,
8 Feb. 1842, 13/11525

51 Eg, Sir George Arthur to Lord Sydenham, 6 Mar. 1841, in Sanderson, ed., *The
Arthur Papers*, III, 363 (#1809)

CHAPTER 4: GENERAL WHOLESALERS
AT HAMILTON 1840-5

1 Pp 42-5 are based primarily on the following material covering early 1840 to
early 1841: R.W. Harris, 30/24952-25009; John Young, 63/50045-65; Isaac
Buchanan (letterbooks), 64/50445-581; Peter Buchanan (letterbook),
66/52085-101; financial memoranda and accounts, 80/58819-35, 83/59629-56.

2 Peter Buchanan to Isaac Buchanan, 12 and 23 Feb. 1839 (copies), 66/52131, 36.
Isaac Buchanan to Peter Buchanan, 16 Oct. 1839 (copy), 64/50438

3 Johnston, *The Head of the Lake* 125, 135-7, 183-4. Gardiner, 'The Hamiltons of
Queenston, Kingston and Hamilton' 27-32. Campbell, *A Mountain and a City* 93.
Ross, *A History of the Canadian Bank of Commerce* 172-86, 209

4 McCalla, 'John Young,' *Dictionary of Canadian Biography* X, 720-2. Rankin, *A History of Our Firm* 108, 121

5 Peter Buchanan to Captain Trevelyan, 29 July 1840 (copy), 66/52090. See also W.H.G. Kingston, *Western Wanderings or, a Pleasure Tour of the Canadas* I (London 1856) as quoted in Hamilton *Spectator, One Hundredth Anniversary Edition...1846-1946*, 15 July 1946, p 7: 'I had never seen anything in England at all to be compared to these colonial general stores' (describing Isaac's store in 1853).

6 *Montreal Herald*, 3 Feb. 1868. Another source suggests he was only 24: James Law, passport to France, 1849, 37/30754. Bond to the City Bank of Montreal, 65/54449-51. Peter Buchanan to ?, 5 Jan. 1839 (copy), 66/52062

7 McCalla, 'The Canadian Grain Trade in the 1840's' 96-8. The spelling of Molyneux, used in the present study, is the correct one (see Williams, 'Liverpool Merchants and the Cotton Trade' 190); the Buchanans sometimes spelled it Molyneaux.

8 R.W. Harris to Peter Buchanan, 18 Oct. 1840, 30/24981. *Journals*, 1849, App. Z

9 John Young to Peter Buchanan, 26 Oct. 1840, 63/50052-3

10 Peter Buchanan to Jane Douglas, 23 Dec. 1839 (copy), 66/52082-4. Morgan, *Sketches of Celebrated Canadians* 556-8. Dent, *The Last Forty Years* I, 105, 125, 138. *The Arthur Papers* III, items 1351, 1661, 1664, 1678, 1692, 1702, 1704, 1752, 1768, 1773, 1778, 1798, 1809, 1816, 1831, 1859, 1888. Abella, 'The "Sydenham Election" of 1841.' Middleton, *The Municipality of Toronto* I, 210-12. *Journals*, 1841, App. S, Report on the late election riots at Toronto. Notman and Taylor, *Portraits*, I, 388-9

11 Isaac Buchanan to Peter Buchanan, 26 June 1841, 9/8655. Pp 46-9 are based primarily on the following material covering 1841 to 1843: Isaac Buchanan, 9/8640-8719, and (letterbooks) 64/50604-51258; Peter Buchanan, 13/11492-11605, and (letterbook) 66/52196-223; R.W. Harris, 30/25010-110; John Young, 63/50067-108; financial memoranda and accounts, 83/59656-793.

12 *Journals*, 1841, *passim*. See also Breckenridge, *The Canadian Banking System* 85-8

13 Isaac Buchanan to Peter Buchanan, 21 (2 letters) and 29 Oct. 1841, 3 May 1842 (copies), 64/50653-63, 51072-3

14 Jane Douglas to Isaac Buchanan, 8 Aug. 1840, 17 and 31 Mar. 1841, 12/10615-18, 27-30, 32-5. George Douglas to Isaac Buchanan, 2 Jan. and 2 Apr. 1841, 24/20192, 198-201

15 Gayer *et al., British Economy 1790-1850* I, 282, 294, 296, 327n. Matthews, *Economic Fluctuations in Great Britain, 1833-1842* 30, 141-2, 151

16 *Journals*, 1849, App. Z. Jones, *History of Agriculture* 134-5

17 Breckenridge, *The Canadian Banking System* 88-93

18 Gayer *et al., British Economy, 1790-1850* I, 244, 282, 294-6, 307, 314, 325-7, 329, 348. Matthews, *Economic Fluctuations in Great Britain, 1833-1842* 30, 141-2, 151.

Jenks, *Migration of British Capital* 103, 107, 126-30. Smith and Cole, *Fluctuations in American Business 1790-1860* 61, 73-7

19 *Journals*, 1849, App. z. Jones, *History of Agriculture* 134-6. Ouellet, *Histoire économique* 446-50

20 R.W. Harris to Isaac Buchanan, 24 Oct. 1842, 30/25074-5

21 Easterbrook and Aitken, *Canadian Economic History* 289-91. Creighton, *The Commercial Empire* 348. Jones, 'The Canadian Agricultural Tariff of 1843'

22 Isaac Buchanan to Agnes Jarvie, 17 Aug. 1842; to Peter Buchanan, 17 June and 2 July 1843; calculation of his net worth (nd): 5/3118-19; 9/8692-3, 8705-19; 83/59761-3

23 Pp 50-6 are based primarily on the following material covering 1844-5: Isaac Buchanan, 9/8720-84, and (letterbooks) 64/51270-96; Peter Buchanan, 13/11615-98, and (letterbook) 66/52212-311; R.W. Harris, 30/25112-21; James Law, 37/30724-47; John Young, 63/50115-36; financial memoranda and accounts, 83/59795-857.

24 'Sketch of Capital of Firm at Home, Dec., 1845,' 83/59820

25 'Statement of Affairs in Hamilton, April, 1844,' 83/59797

26 Isaac Buchanan to Parker and Linley, 11 May 1846 (copy), 66/52354-6. Memo of Buchanan, Harris and Co. hardware purchases, spring 1846, 84/59985

27 Campbell, *Scotland since 1707* 121-3; 'The Growth and Fluctuations of the Scottish Pig Iron Trade, 1828-1873' (thesis) 86, 166-8; and 'Developments in the Scottish Pig Iron Trade, 1844-1848'

28 Peter Buchanan to Isaac Buchanan, 7 Mar. 1842, 13/11540. Campbell, *Scotland since 1707* 121-2. Macgeorge, *The Bairds of Gartsherrie*

29 Extra, Toronto *Banner*, 1 Jan. 1844, in Public Archives of Ontario, Mackenzie-Lindsey Collection, Box 25 G, File 3854. Morgan, *Sketches of Celebrated Canadians* 579-80. Dent, *The Last Forty Years* I, 362. Bonnycastle, *Canada and the Canadians in 1846* II, 35-7. Campbell, *A Mountain and a City* 97

30 Bridgman, 'Isaac Buchanan and Religion' 27-58. Notman and Taylor, *Portraits* I, 387, 396-7. Isaac Buchanan, account current with Isaac Buchanan and Co., Nov. 1843 to Mar. 1845; and private account, Hamilton, 1 Apr. 1845 to 31 Mar. 1846: 83/59832-3; 84/59969-72

31 Creighton, *The Commercial Empire* 347, 358-9, 363-4. Albion, 'New York Port and Its Disappointed Rivals.' Clark, *The Grain Trade in the Old Northwest* 49-50, 53-6, 104-11, 119-20, 172-81

32 Draft circular re New York Office, 15 Aug. 1845, 77/57211-12

33 Agreement between Peter Buchanan and Co. and ... Dennistoun and Co. (NY) ..., 12 July 1845, 70/54536-8

34 R.W. Harris to Isaac Buchanan, 15 May 1845, 30/25114

35 Peter Buchanan to Isaac Buchanan, 20 May 1845, 13/11635. Fashion was always a fundamental part of the trade; see, eg, Coleman, 'Textile Growth' in Harte and Ponting, eds, *Textile History and Economic History* 8-9.

36 See also Lee, 'The Concept of Profit' 6, 34-6.

37 Gayer *et al.*, *The Growth and Fluctuation of the British Economy 1790-1850* I, 314, 320-1, 325-6, 329

38 *Journals*, 1849, App. z. Jones, *History of Agriculture* 134-6

39 Peter Buchanan to Isaac Buchanan, 30 May 1846 (copy), 66/52337

40 'View of P.B. and Co.'s Engagements, Dec., 1845'; 'Estimate of the weight of the Canadian business at Oct. 31, 1845,' Jan. 1845: 83/59820, 818

41 Isaac Buchanan to Peter Buchanan, 13 June 1844, 9/8720

42 Isaac Buchanan, current account with Buchanan, Harris and Co., Nov. 1844 to Mar. 1845, 83/59828. For the material re personnel, see list of Hamilton salaries as at 31 Mar. 1846, 84/59960-1, 63.

43 McCalla, 'The Canadian Grain Trade in the 1840's' 103

44 McCalla, 'Peter Buchanan, London Agent' 197-200

45 For a conflicting view of Peter Buchanan, see Baskerville, 'The Boardroom and Beyond' 127-9.

46 See the 1846 Toronto directory in Robertson, *Landmarks of Toronto* III, 173-256.

CHAPTER 5: INDEPENDENCE 1846-51

1 See eg, Campbell, *Scotland since 1707* 81-96; Oakley, *The Second City* 76-8.

2 Clapham, *Economic History of Modern Britain* II, 521-2. Baines, *History of the Commerce and Town of Liverpool* 743-5, 755; and *Liverpool in 1859* 12-48. Poole, *The Commerce of Liverpool* 15-24. Williams, 'Merchanting in the First Half of the Nineteenth Century.' Marriner, *Rathbones of Liverpool* 17-18

3 Bremner, *The Industries of Scotland* 286-8. Marwick, 'The Cotton Industry and the Industrial Revolution in Scotland' 216-18. Mitchell, 'English and Scottish Cotton Industries,' 112-14. Robertson, 'The Decline of the Scottish Cotton Industry 1860-1914' 117-19

4 Hyde, *Liverpool and the Mersey* 55; and *Cunard and the North Atlantic 1840-1973* 7-15

5 Checkland, *Scottish Banking* 463-97. Campbell, 'Edinburgh Bankers and the Western Bank of Scotland.' Clapham, *Economic History of Modern Britain*, II, 341-3. Cameron, conclusion in Cameron *et al.*, *Banking in the Early Stages of Industrialization* 292-3, 313

6 Strang, *The Progress of Glasgow* in his *Statistics of Glasgow* 3,4

7 *City of Hamilton Directory*, 1853, 4; 1862-3, 14. Title and publishers of Hamilton directories varied somewhat; all references are to the series found under this general title at the Hamilton Public Library.

8 *City of Hamilton Directory*, 1856, 3-4. See also Smith, *Canada, Past, Present and Future* I, 223; Armstrong and Hultin, eds, 'The Anglo-American Magazine Looks at Urban Upper Canada' in *Profiles of a Province* 52-3

9 Creighton, *British North America at Confederation* 13-21. Lower, 'The Assault on the Laurentian Barrier, 1850-1870' 294-303. Jones, *History of Agriculture* 85-108, 176-8, 196-9, 202-5. Urquhart and Buckley, eds, *Historical Statistics of Canada* 384-5. Kelly, 'Wheat Farming in Simcoe County in the Mid-Nineteenth Century.' Re agriculture and the wheat staple, see also Caves and Holton, *The Canadian Economy* 41-6, 169-81.

10 Pentland, 'The Role of Capital in Canadian Economic Development before 1875' 463-5. Hartland, 'Factors in Economic Growth in Canada' 13-14

11 Campbell, *A Mountain and a City* 97, 110, 120. Stevens, *Canadian National Railways* I, 99-115. Currie, *The Grand Trunk Railway of Canada* 161-9

12 Smith, *Canadian Gazetteer* 76

13 *City of Hamilton Directory*, 1856, 75-169

14 *Brown's Toronto General Directory 1856* 246-311. See also Harris and Warkentin, *Canada before Confederation* 148-56.

15 Lovells' *Canada Directory for 1857-58* 425-41

16 Pp 64-9 are based largely on the following runs of material covering 1846 and 1847: Isaac Buchanan, 10/8791-8861; Peter Buchanan, 14/11700-810 and (letterbooks) 66/52320-80, 66/52506-11, 67/52536-671; R.W. Harris, 30/25123-38; James Law, 37/30750-7; John Young, 63/50142-162; financial memoranda and accounts, 84/59871-60088.

17 James McIntyre to Isaac Buchanan, 26 Jan. 1846, and Isaac Buchanan to James McIntyre (copy), 3 Feb. 1846, 45/36055-66

18 Isaac Buchanan to Peter Buchanan, 7 Mar. 1846, 10/8791-3. Italics his. For examples of his views in 1846-7, see Isaac Buchanan to D.H. Forbes, 24 July 1846, and to Lord George Bentinck, 9 Jan. 1847 (copies), 26/22113, 3/1669-76; and the following, all found in the Mackenzie-Lindsey Collection, Box 25 G, File 3854: open letters, Isaac Buchanan to Lord George Bentinck, 9 July 1847, published in *Scotch Reformers' Gazette*; to Lord Elgin, 26 Oct. 1846; to Members of the Canadian Parliament, 17 Apr. 1847; to W.H. Merritt, 28 Feb. 1846; to the editor, Greenock *Advertiser*, 24 Apr. 1847.

19 Peter Buchanan to Isaac Buchanan, 9 and 11 Mar. 1846, 14/11708-9, 17-18

20 Gayer *et al.*, *British Economy 1790-1850* I, 306-29. Ward-Perkins, 'The Commercial Crisis of 1847' 77-88

21 *Journals*, 1849, App. z

22 Creighton, *The Commercial Empire* 361-3. Tucker, *The Canadian Commercial Revolution* 158

23 Much of the remainder of this section is drawn from my paper 'The Canadian Grain Trade in the 1840s' 104-6. Its principal manuscript sources are those cited in n16, above

24 Evans, *The Commercial Crisis, 1847-1848* 67-108, lxxxix-ci
25 Pp 69-71 are based on the following materials, mainly from Jan. to Aug. 1848:
Isaac Buchanan, 10/8863-8922; Peter Buchanan, 14/11816-36 and (letterbooks)
67/52682-843; John Young, 63/50165-191; and two draft partnership agreements, Isaac Buchanan and R.W. Harris, 28 Jan. 1848, and R.W. Harris and Peter
Buchanan, 24 Feb. 1848, 70/54579-90.
26 Peter Buchanan to Isaac Buchanan, 2 Apr. 1830; and to R. Leckie (copy), 30
Sept. 1853: 13/11335-9; 38/30979-82
27 Peter Buchanan to R. Leckie (copy), 11 July 1848, 67/52825. Italics his
28 Hughes, *Fluctuations in Trade, Industry, and Finance* 8, 11, 28-9, 74, 80, 121, 287
29 *Journals*, 1849, App. z. Jones, *History of Agriculture* 136
30 Pp 71-5 are based largely on the surviving copies of the correspondence of
Peter Buchanan from Aug. 1848 to mid-1850: 14/11837-81, 67/52848-53099
(letterbook), and correspondence journal, 67/53288-549. See also John Young to
Isaac Buchanan, 27 Apr. 1849; James Law to Peter Buchanan, 27 Sept. 1848; and
some miscellaneous accounts: 63/50193-4; 37/30773-6; 84/60071-138.
31 Peter Buchanan to Isaac Buchanan, 28 Jan. 1851 (copy), 66/52534. See also Peter
Buchanan to Isaac Buchanan, 12 Feb. 1851, 14/11887-8.
32 Material in this section on the firm's grain trade is drawn largely from McCalla,
'The Canadian Grain Trade in the 1840s' 106-8.
33 Jones, *History of Agriculture* 136, 176-86. Tucker, *The Canadian Commercial Revolution* 158-9. Careless, *The Union of the Canadas* 132-5. Andrews, *Report on the
Trade and Commerce of the British North American Colonies* 77-9, 413-14, 428-33
34 Agreement between Peter Buchanan and John Birrell, 15 May 1851, 70/54697-8
35 Peter Buchanan to James Law, 22 Nov. 1850, and to R.W. Harris, 29 Nov. 1850
(copies), 67/53125, 72
36 Peter Buchanan to Isaac Buchanan, 1 Feb. 1851, quoting Harris, 14/11885.
Emphasis his
37 McCalla, 'Peter Buchanan, London Agent for the G.W.R.' 201-3
38 Reid, *Glasgow Past and Present* I, 10. This passage was evidently written in 1851,
when this part of the work was first published. See also *List of Members of the
Merchants House* 10; *Glasgow Directory*, 1850-1, App., 66; 1852-3, 64; Buchanan,
Members of the Buchanan Society 131; Peter Buchanan to John Black Jr, 13 Jan.
1847 (copy), 66/52380; List of Paintings and Wines owned by Peter Buchanan,
sold 13 Oct. 1864, 86/61177-9; Catalogue of Peter Buchanan's pictures, auctioned 4 Apr. 1868, 107/70646-55.
39 Pp 75-9 are based on the following material covering the period from fall 1850
to the end of 1851: Isaac Buchanan, 10/8927-92; James Law, 37/30787-812;
Peter Buchanan, 14/11882-968 and (letterbooks) 66/52413-26, 66/52517-35,
67/53100-222, 68/53618-988; financial memoranda and accounts, 84/60140-52.

40 The circular announcing this and some of the essays submitted are in the Buchanan Papers, 119/76762-77315.

41 Peter Buchanan to Isaac Buchanan, 19 Feb. 1851, 14/11898-9

42 Contract of copartnership, 8 Apr. 1851, 70/54660-8

43 Contract of copartnership, 12 Sept. 1851, 70/54714-18

44 Hamilton Public Library, Adam Hope, Letters to His Father, 1834-7 (typed copies of three letters). Hamilton *Evening Times*, 8 Aug. 1882. Toronto *Globe*, 9 and 11 Aug. 1882. Hamilton Public Library, Reference Department Files, 'Adam Hope,' 'Hope Family.' Adam Hope to Isaac Buchanan, 12 Feb. 1848 and 10 Dec. 1853, 31/26140-1, 26216

45 Quarterly statement of accounts, Hamilton, 31 Jan. 1841, 83/59648-9. Adam Hope to Isaac Buchanan, 26 Nov. 1845, 31/26131-4. Peter Buchanan to Hope, Birrell & Co., 4 Nov. 1846 (copy), 31/26138

46 Miller, *A Century of Western Ontario* 16-18, 29-37; and 'The Fat Years and the Lean' 73-5. Armstrong and Hultin, '*The Anglo-American Magazine*' 56. Smith, *Canadian Gazetteer* 100-1. F.H. Armstrong, 'John Birrell,' *Dictionary of Canadian Biography* x, 68

47 Proposed Arrangements for a Business in London, Peter Buchanan and Adam Hope, 15 Apr. 1851; agreement between John Birrell and Peter Buchanan, 15 May 1851; agreement between R.W. Harris and Adam Hope, 7 Oct. 1851; agreement between Adam Hope and Co. and W. & R. Simson, 1 Jan. 1852: 70/54692-3, 697-9, 720-6, 735-7. Adam Hope to Isaac Buchanan, 23 Sept. 1853, and to R.W. Harris, 28 Jan. 1854, 31/26182, 32/26234

48 James Law to Isaac Buchanan, 17 Jan. 1852, 37/30821

CHAPTER 6: THE FIRM SPLITS 1852-6

1 Hartland, 'Factors in Economic Growth' 13-14. Creighton, *British North America at Confederation* 13-21

2 Hughes, *British Economic Development, 1850-1860, passim*

3 Michell, 'Statistics of Prices' in Michell and Taylor, *Statistical Contributions to Canadian Economic History* 55. Careless, *The Union of the Canadas* 132-45

4 Hughes, *British Economic Development, 1850-1860* 86

5 Michell, 'Statistics of Prices' 59. Jones, *History of Agriculture* 198

6 Peter Buchanan to Isaac Buchanan, 10 Dec. 1852, 14/12025

7 Peter Buchanan to R.W. Harris, 7 Mar. 1853 (copy), 14/12038. R.W. Harris to Isaac Buchanan, 8 Apr. 1853, 30/25190

8 R.W. Harris to Peter Buchanan, 11 Nov. 1853 (copy), 30/25195. Robert Leckie to Isaac Buchanan, 19 Oct. 1853, 38/30987

9 Peter Buchanan to Isaac Buchanan, 3 Sept. 1852, 14/11994

10 Peter Buchanan to Isaac Buchanan, 9 Dec. 1853, 14/12088
11 Pp 82-6 are based largely on the following runs of partners' correspondence:
Isaac Buchanan (Oct. 1853 to June 1854), 10/8999-9018; Peter Buchanan (Mar.
1853 to July 1854), 14/12038-253, and partial correspondence journal (1853),
68/54116, 24-6; Alexander Campbell (Feb. to July 1854), 18/15388-420; R.W.
Harris (Nov.-Dec. 1853), 30/25200-220; Adam Hope (July 1853 to May 1854),
31/26173-217, 32/26225-331; Robert Leckie (Sept. 1853 to Sept. 1854),
38/30979-31056.
12 Agreement between John Young and James Law, and Peter Buchanan, R.W.
Harris, Isaac Buchanan, and Robert Leckie, 14 Sept. 1853, 70/54815-16. Prospective finance memorandum, Peter Buchanan, 9 Nov. 1853, 84/60188
13 Re Hennessy's: Peter Buchanan & Co., Correspondence Journal, 5 Feb. 1850,
67/53549; Peter Buchanan to James Law, 8 Nov. 1850, to A. Hennessy, 15 Jan.
and 15 Feb. 1851, and to Isaac Buchanan, 2 May 1856 (copies), 67/53166,
66/52517-19, 413-14, 63/49811; Jas. Hennessy & Co. to Peter Buchanan & Co.,
4 Apr. 1857 (copy), 30/25548-9. Re Bairds': Peter Buchanan to R.W. Harris, 8
Sept. 1848, and to James Law, 25 Jan. 1850 (copies), 67/52850, 53041; James
Law to Isaac Buchanan, 5 Apr. 1852, 37/30837. Re role of consignments at Montreal: memo, Montreal Sales, 1856-7, 90/63633; Alex Campbell to Isaac Buchanan, 20 Mar. 1862, 19/16053; Isaac Buchanan to D. McGee, 27 July 1864 (copy),
43/35115
14 A. Kirkland to Buchanan, Harris & Co., 14 July 1854, 37/30123
15 Peter Buchanan to R.W. Harris, 25 May 1855, 15/12403. Adam Hope to Isaac
Buchanan, 15 Apr. 1856, 32/26622-3
16 Peter Buchanan to Isaac Buchanan, 20 Nov. 1852, 14/11997
17 R.W. Harris to Peter Buchanan, 11 Nov. 1853 (copy), 30/25198. History of
Titles, Mountain Property, 1802-73, 78/57604-10. Account books, Clairmont
Park, to 1 July 1854, 84/60237-45, 51, 77-86, 88-93. MacRae and Adamson, *The
Ancestral Roof* 179-81. Bailey, *Traces, Places and Faces* 25-8.
18 Eg, Peter Buchanan to Isaac Buchanan, 2 Jan. 185 [2] (copy), 68/53979
19 Peter Buchanan to R.W. Harris, 7 Mar. 1853 (copy), 14/12038. Jean Buchanan to
Isaac Buchanan, Mar. 1832 and 24 Mar. 1833, 12/10940-7
20 Partnership agreement, Montreal, 10 Nov. 1853, 70/54830-7
21 Circular, 2 Jan. 1854, 77/57221-2
22 Eg, Peter Buchanan to R.W. Harris, 23 Nov. 1853, 15/12487-8
23 Pp 86-94 are based on the abundant correspondence among partners for the
period early 1854 to the end of 1856: Isaac Buchanan, 10/9028-212; Peter Buchanan, 14/12163-323, 15/12326-677; Alex Campbell, 18/15421-2, 433-535; R.W.
Harris, 30/25227-77; Adam Hope, 32/26302-711; Robert Leckie, 38/31066-126;
George Borthwick, 4/2015-110; financial memoranda and accounts,
84/60211-275, 85/60294-441.

24 Peter Buchanan, Correspondence Journal, letter to R.W. Harris, 10 Nov. 1854, 68/54134

25 Peter Buchanan to R.W. Harris, 28 Oct. 1853, 14/12060

26 Peter Buchanan to R.W. Harris, 8 Dec. 1854, 14/12305

27 Peter Buchanan to R.W. Harris, 22 Feb. 1856, 15/12561

28 Notman and Taylor, *Portraits* 384. See also Bailey, *Traces, Places and Faces* 29, 32.

29 See, eg, Bridgman, 'Isaac Buchanan and Religion' 100-4.

30 See, eg, Keefer, *Philosophy of Railroads and Other Essays* 159-62.

31 Benedict, *The Great Southern Railway of Canada*. Neutel, 'From "Southern" Concept to Canada Southern' 25-81. McCalla, 'Peter Buchanan, London Agent for the Great Western Railway' 214. Baskerville, 'The Boardroom and Beyond' 246-65

32 Isaac Buchanan to Peter Buchanan, 17 July 1856, 10/9135

33 C.J. Brydges to Isaac Buchanan, 7 Aug. 1856, 5/3051

34 Peter Buchanan to R.W. Harris, 2 Sept. 1856, 15/12643

35 Peter Buchanan to Isaac Buchanan, 15 Aug. 1856 (copy), 15/12630

36 Eg, Letter to the Editor by 'Observer,' *Hamilton Spectator*, 30 Mar. 1861, found in Alex Campbell to Isaac Buchanan, 3 Apr. 1861, 19/15999

37 H.C. Barwick to Buchanan, Harris & Co. and Adam Hope & Co., 4 Dec. 1856, D. Davidson to Alex Campbell, 8 Dec. 1856, and Campbell to Davidson, 9 Dec. 1856 (copy), 3/1332-7. I. Buchanan, Harris & Co. to D. Davidson, 19 Jan. 1857 (copy), 32/26729. Isaac Buchanan to Peter Buchanan, 9 Oct. 1856 and 22 June 1857, 10/9190, 9255. Alex Campbell to Peter Buchanan, 19 and 23 Jan. 1857, 18/15541-2, 618-21

38 Peter Buchanan to Isaac Buchanan, 1, 19, and 22 May 1857, 15/12696-8, 63/49882-3, 15/12706-12

CHAPTER 7: DEPRESSION AND
REORGANIZATION 1857-60

1 Pp 95-7 are based largely on the following runs of material covering 1857 and the first four months of 1858: Peter Buchanan, 15/12678-781; Alexander Campbell, 18/15537-613, 644-7; Adam Hope, 32/26721-828; Robert Leckie, 38/31139-221; financial memoranda and accounts, 85/60442-523.

2 Smith and Cole, *American Business 1790-1860* 97-100, 107-15, 130-5. Van Vleck, *The Panic of 1857* 62-74, 83

3 Clapham, *Econ. Hist. of Modern Britain* II, 368-70. Evans, *The History of the Commercial Crisis* 33-7, cxxxvii-ix. Hughes, 'The Commercial Crisis of 1857' 215-17. Callender, *The Commercial Crisis of 1857* 12-14

4 Office of the Mercantile Agency, 'To Our Subscribers' 443

5 Evans, *History of the Commercial Crisis, 1857-58* 187-9, cxix-xxvi, cxxxii-iii

6 Hughes, *British Economic Development 1850-1860* 74-5, 108, 111-12, 132-40
7 Michell, 'Statistics of Prices' 59
8 Peter Buchanan to Isaac Buchanan, 8 Jan. 1858, 15/12743
9 Pp 000-000 are based primarily on the following material covering the period from spring 1858 to the end of 1859: Peter Buchanan, 15/12785-872; his letterbooks, 68/54150-96, 224-40, 249-96; his notebooks, 90/63494-531, 624-742; Alexander Campbell, 18/15629-40, 648-701; Adam Hope, 32/26866- 930; Robert Leckie, 38/31225-67; financial memoranda and accounts, 85/60525-644, 86/60646-730.
10 J. Gairdner to Messrs Buchanan & Co., 9 Feb. 1858, 26/22640
11 Lists of personnel are found in Peter Buchanan, notebook, 90/63630-1, 36-7, 93. See also memo on Hamilton dry goods department, 15 Dec. 1862, 86/61014. Re Liverpool, see, eg, George Borthwick to Isaac Buchanan, 29 May 1861, 4/2129-30; Robert Wemyss to Isaac Buchanan, 10 Jan. 1867, 61/48701. Re New York, F. Lane to Isaac Buchanan, 13 Jan. 1859, 37/30512. On reduction, see Isaac Buchanan, memo regarding London Balance, 7 Feb. 1859 (copy), 91/64414-16.
12 Memo of agreement between T.H. McKenzie and Buchanan, Harris & Co., 2 Oct. 1860, 73/55858-60. Re property securities, see P. Dewar to Isaac Buchanan, 10 Dec. 1860 and 18 May 1865 (copy), 23/19398-9, 747.
13 Peter Buchanan to Isaac Buchanan, 24 Mar. 1860, 15/12934
14 Peter Buchanan to Isaac Buchanan, 31 Dec. 1859, 15/12871
15 For pp 101-5, see in particular Isaac Buchanan's correspondence for 1857-9: 10/9230-444.
16 Toronto *Leader*, 16 Mar. 1857. For the significance to Isaac of Zimmerman's death, see George Wythes to Peter Buchanan, 17 Apr. and 16 May 1857, 63/49866-7, 873-5.
17 Proceedings and report of both are in *Journals*, 1857, App. 6. For proceedings in the Assembly, see *Journals*, 1857, *passim*. See also Neutel, 'From "Southern" Concept to Canada Southern' 82-107.
18 Report of the Select Committee to Investigate and Report on the Position of the Woodstock and Lake Erie Railway and Harbour Company, *Journals*,1857, App. 6
19 Eg, Isaac Buchanan to Peter Buchanan, 22 June 1857, 10/9251-4
20 Toronto *Globe*, 28 May 1857
21 Isaac Buchanan to ?, 20 Jan. 1857 (copy), 10/9214-16
22 Barnett, 'An Election without Politics' 153-62
23 'The Question of Money,' *Canadian Merchants Magazine* I (Apr.-Sept. 1857) 126-9; 'What Parliament Must Do for the Province,' *ibid*. II (Oct. 1857-Mar. 1858) 468-84. Buchanan, *National Unthrift*. Buchanan, *The Relations of the Industry of Canada* 483-95. Dent, *The Last Forty Years* II, 392-3

24 Campbell, of course, had been a banker. See Alexander Campbell to Peter Buchanan, 21 Dec. 1857, 18/15566.
25 *Journals*, 14 Mar. 1859, 197. Province of Canada, Legislative Assembly, *Newspaper Reports of Debates* (Canadian Library Association microfilm) 14, 17, 18, and 21 Mar. 1859
26 *Ibid.*, 9 Aug. 1858; 2, 3, and 4 May 1859. Neutel, 'From "Southern" Concept to Canada Southern' 101-5
27 Isaac Buchanan, undated memo, probably from 1859, 15/12849
28 Isaac Buchanan to Peter Buchanan, 18 Apr. 1859 (copy), 10/9394
29 Peter Buchanan to Isaac Buchanan, 8 Apr. 1859, and to R.W. Harris, 27 May 1859 (copies), 15/12846, 854-6. R.W. Harris to Peter Buchanan, 30 July 1859 (copy), 30/25313. Alex Campbell to Isaac Buchanan, 24 Aug. 1866, 20/16689-95
30 Peter Buchanan, notebook, 1859, 90/63509
31 Peter Buchanan to Isaac Buchanan, 16 May 1860, 15/12950
32 Pp 105-9 are based largely on the following materials covering Jan. to Oct. 1860: Isaac Buchanan, 11/9450-9541; Peter Buchanan (Feb. 1859 and after), 15/12829-978; his letterbook, 68/54199-217, 241-4; Alexander Campbell, 19/15705-896; Adam Hope, 32/26940-27063; Robert Leckie, 38/31278-324; financial memoranda and accounts, 86/60712-876.
33 Articles of copartnership, Montreal, 23 Aug. 1860, 73/55817-21. Extract from Montreal Profit & Loss Account, 31 Dec. 1859, 82/59423. Montreal balance sheet, 31 Dec. 1859 and statement of capital in the Montreal business, 15 Aug. 1860, 86/60648, 60770
34 Isaac Buchanan, Position of Adam Hope & Company at end of 1860, 32/27080. Articles of copartnership, London, 10 Aug. 1860 and separate agreement of same date re this, 73/55778-91, 809-11. Peter Buchanan, statement re London business, Aug. 1860, 86/60840. Balance sheet, Adam Hope and Company, 30 Nov. 1860, 86/60878-80. Calculation of how Adam Hope and Company could be carried on, 24 Nov. 1859, 86/60697
35 Eg, Peter Buchanan to Isaac Buchanan, 2 Jan. 185 [2] (copy), 68/53977
36 Jottings on Hamilton accounts, Peter Buchanan: 82/59429; 90/63699-700
37 P. Dewar to Isaac Buchanan, 31 Dec. 1860, 23/19427-8. Private memo, Isaac Buchanan's appeal against tax assessment for 1859, 26 May 1860, 86/60844-5. Peter Buchanan, Glasgow finance memorandum, 1 Aug. 1860, 82/59414-15
38 Eg, Peter Buchanan to Isaac Buchanan, 15 Oct. 1858, 15/12798-900. Re Wemyss, see also *List of Members of the Merchants House* 65.
39 Peter Buchanan notebook, 1860, 91/64412. Partnership agreement, Hamilton, 2 Oct. 1860, 73/55840-56
40 Peter Buchanan to Isaac Buchanan, 17 Feb. 1860, 15/12907

41 F. Lane to Isaac Buchanan, 9 and 1 Feb. 1860 (copies), 37/30528-9. Alexander Campbell to Isaac Buchanan, 19 May 1860, 19/15810-11. David McGee to Isaac Buchanan, 11 Feb. 1865 and 9 Feb. 1866, 44/35313, 450-3. Agreement between Forrest Brothers and Isaac Buchanan, 27 Feb. 1860, 73/55279-30. Valuation of land in Chicago, 25 Feb. 1860, 78/57541. Isaac Buchanan to Peter Buchanan, 15 Feb. 1860, 11/9465-8

42 Peter Buchanan to Isaac Buchanan, undated copy of letter in reply to one from Isaac to Peter dated 12 Sept. 1860, 11/9527-30

43 For borrowed capital, see Robert Wemyss to Isaac Buchanan, 14 Nov. 1860 and 27 Nov. 1861, 59/46846, 47107-8. Capital memorandum, 31 Dec. 1858, 86/60695.

44 For this term, see Dales, *The Protective Tariff in Canada's Development* 154-8.

45 Breckenridge, *The Canadian Banking System* 121-54. Anonymous, 'Glyns and the Bank of Upper Canada.' Pentland, 'The Role of Capital in Canadian Economic Development before 1875' 472-4. Creighton, *British North America at Confederation* 11-21

46 Harris and Warkentin, *Canada before Confederation* 148-56

47 George Borthwick, 'Remarks upon Analysis of Outstandings at Hamilton, 30 June, 1856,' 85/60441

48 List of Toronto and Hamilton customers, 1842, 79/57943-5. List of Hamilton customers, 1857, 79/57936-9

49 Quarterly statement of accounts, London, 31 Dec. 1854, 84/60221-4. Quarterly statement of accounts, London, 30 June 1861, 86/60887-91

50 Eg, McDougall, 'Immigration into Canada, 1851-1920' 172

51 Innis, 'The Changing Structure of the Canadian Market' in *Essays in Canadian Economic History* 285. Robert Leckie to Isaac Buchanan, 25 July 1862 and 14 Feb. 1863, 38/31442-4, 506-7. Isaac Buchanan to Alexander Campbell, 9 Nov. 1861; and to Robert Wemyss, 11 Nov. 1861 and 9 Feb. 1864 (copies): 19/16041-4, 59/47081, 60/47537. Isaac Buchanan to ?, nd [1862] (copy), 59/47343. Adam Hope to Isaac Buchanan, 1 Dec. 1863, 3/27414-15

52 Robert Leckie to R.W. Harris, 27 Oct. 1856, and to Peter Buchanan, 21 May 1859, 38/31120-1, 31253. Peter Buchanan to H.B. Jackson, 5 Dec. 1859 (copy), 68/54183

53 Masters, *The Rise of Toronto* 56-124. Jones, *History of Agriculture* 231-49. Spelt, *Urban Development in South-Central Ontario* 101-37. Wiman, *Annual Report of the Board of Trade*

54 McCalla, 'The Decline of Hamilton as a Wholesale Centre' 247-51

55 Lister, *Hamilton, Canada* 75. Campbell, *A Mountain and a City* 120-1. Johnston, *The Head of the Lake* 201

56 Firestone, 'Development of Canada's Economy, 1850-1900' 222-9, 234-7. Morton, *The Critical Years* 6-7
57 Jones, *History of Agriculture* 216-88
58 Porter and Livesay, *Merchants and Manufacturers* 7-12, 116-29. Hyde and Marriner, 'The Economic Functions of the Export Merchant' 215-26
59 Robertson, 'The Decline of the Scottish Cotton Industry.' Slaven, *The Development of the West of Scotland* 108-11
60 Campbell, *Scotland since 1707* 109-11, 225-36. Bremner, *The Industries of Scotland* 287-8. Rankin, *A History of Our Firm* 28. *James Finlay & Company Limited* 37-9. Checkland, *The Upas Tree* 1-8
61 Jenks, *Migration of British Capital* 214-23. Marriner, *Rathbones of Liverpool* 34-8. John, *A Liverpool Merchant House* 28-36. Hyde, *Shipping Enterprise and Management, 1830-1939* 11-38
62 Davis and Hughes, 'A Dollar-Sterling Exchange, 1803-1895' 60-3, 69. Marriner, *Rathbones of Liverpool* 60-2, 77-80, 111-16. Clapham, *Econ. Hist. of Modern Britain* II, 312-22. Perkins, *Financing Anglo-American Trade* 9. For the rise in respectability of the documentary bill see, eg, David McGee to Isaac Buchanan, 8 Mar. 1861 and 9 May 1867, 43/34505-7, 44/35729-30; Adam Hope to Isaac Buchanan, 8 Apr. 1864, 33/27483; Alex Campbell to Isaac Buchanan, 11 Feb. 1865, 20/16615
63 Eg, Killick, 'Risk, Specialization and Profit in the Mercantile Sector' 13

CHAPTER 8: ISAAC ALONE 1860-7

1 George Douglas to Isaac Buchanan, 30 Oct. and 6 and 13 Nov. 1860, 24/20622-39
2 Hamilton *Spectator*, 22 Nov. 1860; Glasgow *Courier*, 8 Nov., reprinted in *Spectator*, 26 Nov. 1860. Other Glasgow newspapers printed only the announcement of his death.
3 Hamilton *Spectator*, 25 and 27 Mar. 1861
4 Scottish Record Office, Edinburgh, Trust Disposition and Settlement by Peter Buchanan, 24 May 1860, registered 13 Nov. 1860. Isaac Buchanan to Alex Campbell, 10 Apr. 1861 (copy), 19/16004-5
5 Pp 118-26 are largely based on the abundant correspondence covering the period November 1860 to the end of 1864: Agnes Buchanan, 6/3985-4328, 7/4376-4722; Isaac Buchanan, 11/9550-9614; Alexander Campbell, 19/15905-16491; Plummer Dewar, 23/19459-732; Adam Hope, 33/27091-644, 739; Robert Leckie, 38/31349-524, 541-5; Robert Wemyss, 59/46844-47493, 60/47503-938; accounts and financial memoranda, 86/60882-61181. Where

especially pertinent, a few more specific citations from this material are provided. Most of Isaac Buchanan's letters from the period after 1860 are to be found under the name of his correspondent.

6 Partnership agreement, 5 Dec. 1860, 73/55893-908

7 Draft partnership agreement between Isaac Buchanan and Robert Wemyss, 29 Nov. 1860, 73/59961-9

8 Agnes Buchanan to Isaac Buchanan, 3 Jan. 1861, 6/3987

9 Robert Wemyss to Isaac Buchanan, 17 June 1864, 60/47618-19

10 Isaac Buchanan to George Douglas, 13 June 1862 (copy) and Douglas to Isaac, 23 June 1862 and 15 Aug. 1864, 24/20783-8, 795-802, 858-864. Robert Wemyss to Isaac Buchanan, 12 Jan. and 10 June 1865, 60/47969-70, 61/48234-5. Agnes Buchanan to Isaac Buchanan, 27 May 1864, 7/4507-12. Isaac Buchanan to William Muir, 19 Feb. 1864 (copy), 49/39644-50

11 This account of Isaac's politics is most heavily based on *The Relations of the Industry of Canada ..., passim*, a compilation of speeches, letters, etc. from this period. There is a good deal of material on elections and Hamilton politics in Agnes Buchanan's correspondence for the period. See also Campbell, *A Mountain and a City* 121-3, 136-7, 147; Johnston, *The Head of the Lake* 211, 217-18, 220, 255-8; Ross, *History of the Canadian Bank of Commerce* I, 231-2.

12 Eg, Robert Wemyss to Isaac Buchanan, 25 Apr. and 31 July 1863, and 22 and 29 Sept. 1864: 59/47420, 450; 60/47681, 700-1. P. Dewar to Isaac Buchanan, 6 Mar. and 9 Apr. 1861, 23/19460-1, 472. Province of Canada, *Statutes*, 27 & 28 Vict. c.72, 'An Act to Reconstitute the Debenture Debt of the City of Hamilton...'

13 Eg, Isaac Buchanan to George Douglas, 21 May 1862 (copy), 24/20773-4

14 Morton, *The Critical Years* 143

15 Agreements between Buchanan, Harris & Co. and Duncan Macpherson and John W. Baine (both 13 Sept. 1861), Alexander Mitchell (1 Oct. 1861), Duncan Macfarlane (15 Oct. 1861), and James McIlwraith (16 Jan. 1862), 73/56072-82, 84-8, 56123-9. Robert Wemyss to Isaac Buchanan, 29 Mar. 1865, 60/48122

16 Wilson, *John Northway* 53-93. Stephenson, *The Store that Timothy Built* 19-23. Lebhor, *Chain Stores in America, 1859-1959* 23

17 Peter Buchanan to F. Lane, 28 Oct. 1859 (copy), 68/54260. Peter Buchanan, notebook, 1859, 91/63779. Robert Leckie to Isaac Buchanan, 11 Mar. 1861, and Isaac to Leckie, 10 Apr. 1862 (copy), 38/31369-73, 404-5. Alex Campbell to Isaac Buchanan, 16 Jan. 1865, 20/16510

18 Adam Hope to Isaac Buchanan, 19 Oct. 1861, 33/27181-2

19 Alex Campbell to Isaac Buchanan, 16 Jan. and 2 Dec. 1865, 20/16510, 623-5

20 Robert Wemyss to Isaac Buchanan, 30 Dec. 1864 and 13 May 1865, 60/47937-8, 48172-4

21 Draft answer to complaint in Chancery, in the case of *Muir* v *Rainey*, 4 May 1864, 77/57361-5. Robert Wemyss to Isaac Buchanan, 30 Sept., 13 Oct., and 1 Dec. 1864, 60/47704, 725, 839-41

22 Isaac Buchanan to Alex Campbell, 4 Nov. 1864 (copy), 19/16434

23 Isaac Buchanan to Robert Wemyss, 7 Nov. 1864 (copy), 60/47770-1

24 Quoted in Robert Wemyss to Isaac Buchanan, 22 Dec. 1864, 60/47888

25 Robert Leckie to Isaac Buchanan, 25 Nov. 1864, 38/31542

26 Isaac Buchanan to Robert Wemyss, 15 Oct. 1864 (copy), 60/47791-2

27 Adam Hope to Isaac Buchanan, 18 Feb. 1862, 33/27212 (italics his). See also Hope to Isaac, 1 Apr. 1863, 33/27373-4.

28 Peter Buchanan to Isaac Buchanan, 5 Aug. 1856, 15/12620. Prospective Finance Memo, Glasgow, 1 Mar. 1860, 82/59408-9

29 Robert Wemyss to Isaac Buchanan, 17 June 1864, 60/47617-18

30 For the New York exchange business, see the David McGee correspondence, from 1860 to 1867, 43/34350-35121, 44/35122-863. The Campbell and Wemyss correspondence cited in n5, above, is also pertinent.

31 Glasgow finance statement, 17 Feb. 1865, 87/61232-3

32 Alex Campbell to Peter Buchanan, 19 June and 28 Dec. 1857; to Isaac Buchanan, 30 June 1863, 14 and 15 Oct., and 21 Dec. 1864: 18/15557-60, 573; 19/16198-201, 399-403, 490-1. Isaac Buchanan to Alex Campbell, 9 Dec. 1864 (copy), 19/16479. Agnes Buchanan to Isaac Buchanan, 21 Mar. 1867, 7/5094-5. Perkins, *Financing Anglo-American Trade* 177

33 *The Mercantile Agency Reference Book ... 1866* esp. 153, 212, 241

34 Checkland, *Scottish Banking: A History* 528, 544-5

35 Robert Wemyss to Isaac Buchanan, 4 Aug. 1864, 60/47650-1

36 Isaac Buchanan to Robert Wemyss, 12 Dec. 1864 (copy), 60/47875-8. Adam Hope to Isaac Buchanan, 12 Dec. 1864, 33/27739. Pp 000-000 are based largely on the following material from 1865: Agnes Buchanan, 7/4768-4895; Alexander Campbell, 20/16509-625; Plummer Dewar, 23/19733-52; Adam Hope, 33/27670-742; Robert Leckie, 38/31536-7, 548-86; Robert Wemyss, 60/47940-48207, 61/48223-358; financial memoranda and accounts, 87/61192-265.

37 Adam Hope to Isaac Buchanan, 8 Sept. 1864, 33/27563

38 Memo on takeover at Hamilton, 13 Mar. 1865, 87/61192-3. Abstract of balance of private books, balance of public books, Peter Buchanan and Co., 31 Mar. 1865, 87/61203, 5. Statement showing probable liquidation of old business, 87/61213. Balance of public and private ledgers, Peter Buchanan and Co., 30 Nov. 1865, 87/61253, 59

39 Balance of new and old firms of Adam Hope and Co., 30 Nov. 1865, 87/61257, 64. 'Paper referred to in agreement of 19 Oct. 1865 between Isaac Buchanan, Adam Hope and Robert Wemyss,' 74/56359

40 Agreements between Buchanan, Hope and Co. and R.K. Masterton, 16 and 20 June 1865, 74/56379-81, 85-7
41 Agreement between Isaac Buchanan, Robert Wemyss, and Adam Hope, 19 Oct. 1865, 74/56448-53. Agreement between Isaac Buchanan and Robert Wemyss, 25 Oct. 1865, 74/56476-8. Abstract of Buchanan, Harris and Co. profit and loss account, 31 Mar. 1865; calculations by Robert Wemyss regarding the capital of the new firm; partial balance sheet of Buchanan, Hope and Co. 30 Nov. 1865; trial balance of Buchanan, Hope and Co., 30 Nov. 1866: 87/61196, 211, 261-2, 300-1
42 Partnership agreement and related contract, 19 Oct. 1865, 74/56448-53, 55-72
43 Draft partnership agreement, Montreal, 8 Mar. 1865, 74/56334-6
44 Agreement between Buchanan, Hope and Co. and Adam Hope and Co., Mar. 1866 (copy), 74/56486-7. Bill of Complaint in Chancery, *Buchanan* v *Hope*, 1868, 77/57429. Pp 131-7 are largely based on the following material for the period 1866 to March 1868: Agnes Buchanan, 7/4971-5696; Isaac Buchanan, 11/9625-44; Alex Campbell, 20/16588, 16636-903; Plummer Dewar, 23/19754-85; Adam Hope, 33/27744-945; Robert Leckie, 38/31593-660; Robert Wemyss, 61/48377-954; financial memoranda and accounts, 87/61266-369. Also important is Scottish Record Office, Edinburgh, Record of Sequestration, Peter Buchanan and Co., Accountant of Court's Process #56 of 1869.
45 Isaac Buchanan to Alex Campbell, 1 Dec. 1866, and to Robert Wemyss, 3 Dec. 1866 (copies), 20/16759-61, 61/48660
46 Agnes Buchanan to Isaac Buchanan, 28 Feb. 1867, 7/5075-81
47 Robert Wemyss to Isaac Buchanan, 8 June 1867, 61/48811
48 Isaac Buchanan, memo re partnership agreement, 23 Apr. 1867, 75/56585-8
49 Agreement between Isaac Buchanan, Agnes Buchanan, and P.T. Buchanan, 20 May 1867, 75/56579-81. Isaac Buchanan to Alex Campbell, 17 Dec. 1867 (copy), 20/16887-8. See Glasgow *Herald*, 20 Dec. 1867, p 6, for discussion of this during bankruptcy proceedings.
50 Scheme of Division among the Creditors, 87/61383
51 Isaac Buchanan to ?, 10 Oct. 1867 (copy), 11/9640
52 Isaac Buchanan to John Buchanan, 24 Oct. 1867 (copy), 13/11153
53 P. Dewar to Isaac Buchanan, 11 Nov. 1867, 23/19782-5. Robert Wemyss to Isaac Buchanan, 5 May 1864 and 9 Feb. 1866, 60/47597-8, 61/48393
54 McCalla, 'Adam Hope,' *Dictionary of Canadian Biography* XI

CHAPTER 9: THE FINAL FAILURES

1 Partnership agreement, Hamilton and Glasgow, 21 Jan. 1868, 75/56681-9
2 The basic sources for this chapter are a number of often lengthy runs of material, of which the following are the principal: Andrew Anderson (1868-74),

1/250-416; Andrew Binny(1868-72), 3/1729-1843; Agnes Buchanan (1868-83), 7/5418-6001, 8/6070-6508; Isaac Buchanan (1868-83), 11/9647-9740; Isaac R. Buchanan (1869-83), 11/9741-10026; James I. Buchanan (1869-83), 12/10219-538; Peter T. Buchanan (1868-83), 16/13292-866, 17/13867-14799; Alex Campbell (1868-82), 20/16894-17140; P. Dewar (1868-74), 23/19794-852; Robert Leckie (1868-77), 38/31661-724; John I. Mackenzie (1872), 45/36363- 81; Walter Mackenzie (1871-3), 45/36501-44; Robert Wemyss (1868, 1880-2), 61/48941-49028; financial memoranda and accounts (1868-75), 87/61368-491. Most surviving copies of Isaac Buchanan's letters are filed in series with his correspondents'. More specific citations are also made from these sources where appropriate.

3 Isaac Buchanan to Agnes Buchanan, 18 Jan. 1868, and to A. Binny and P.T. Buchanan, 7 Oct. 1869 (copies), 7/5516-17, 3/1811-12

4 Peter Buchanan to H.B. Jackson, 5 Dec. 1859 (copy), 68/54184. Isaac Buchanan to Robert Wemyss, 26 Feb. 1866 (copy), 61/48434-5. Agnes Buchanan to Isaac Buchanan, 12 Mar. 1868, 7/5676. James I. Buchanan to Isaac Buchanan, 6 Oct. 1870, 12/10352-61

5 Isaac Buchanan to Alex Campbell, 1 Jan. 1868 (copy), 20/16894-6. Memo by Isaac Buchanan on causes of second failure, 11 Sept. 1873, 45/36538

6 Isaac Buchanan to A. Binny and Peter T. Buchanan, 23 and 29 Apr. 1868, 3/1770, 76-7. List of furnishers and their terms, fall 1871, 87/61462

7 Agnes Buchanan to Isaac Buchanan, 2 Jan. and 16 Apr. 1868; to P.T. Buchanan, 8 Feb. 1868; memorandum regarding travellers, 10 Feb. 1868: 7/5418-19, 5737-8, 5561, 5587-8. Isaac Buchanan, memorandum on the spring trade, 1868, 90/63484-6

8 Estimate of probable dry goods stock at 1 Jan. 1868; memo of Hamilton sales, 1868-9: 87/61438, 40-1

9 The case was *Buchanan* v *Hope*, in Chancery. Plaintiff's Bill of Complaint, nd, and reply of C.J. Hope, 14 Aug. 1868, 77/57428-31, 47-52. Memo of agreement, 24 Oct. 1868; question for court, 26 Oct. 1868; final compromise, 31 Oct. 1868: 75/56812-13, 15-16, 18. Memo re obligations of Adam Hope and Company, nd 87/61374, 77. Robert Wemyss to Isaac Buchanan, 12, 16, and 23 Oct. 1868 (copies), 61/48959-63, 69-70, 87-8

10 Eg, *City of Hamilton Directory*, 1871-2, 104

11 Isaac Buchanan to George Douglas, 31 Mar. 1875 (copy), 24/21009

12 *City of Hamilton Directory*, 1868-9, 226. See also Buchanan, Harris and Co. to A.I. Mackenzie, 25 Oct. 1861, 45/36291; Isaac Buchanan to Robert Wemyss, 7 Mar.

12 1864 (copy), 60/47552; P. Dewar to Isaac Buchanan, 11 Nov. 1867, 23/19782-5.

13 Partnership agreement, Hamilton, 1 Dec. 1869; Isaac Buchanan, draft memos to bankers about this agreement, nd; Isaac Buchanan, draft of agreement with Andrew Anderson, nd: 75/56890-901, 911-13, 915, 916

14 Balance of private books, Buchanan and Company, 30 Nov. 1872; statement of assets and liabilities of Buchanan and Company, nd: 87/61464-6, 477. Balance sheet, Buchanans, Binny and Mackenzie, 31 July 1873; statement of assets and liabilities of this firm, 31 July 1873; memos re its assets and liabilities, 13 Sept. 1875: 87/61474-6, 479-80, 488-9

15 *City of Hamilton Directory*, 1871-2, 104, 239; 1872-3, 109, 153, 159-60

16 Andrew Anderson to Isaac Buchanan, 15 Feb. 1872, 1/347

17 Partnership agreements, Montreal, 26 June 1868, and memo of same date re this, 75/56761-7, 769

18 Harris Buchanan to Isaac Buchanan, 16 Sept. 1869, 9/7990

19 Balance of profit and loss account and memo of closing entries, Buchanan, Leckie and Company, 31 Dec. 1868, 38/31670-3, 668-9, 674

20 Alex Campbell to Isaac Buchanan, 2 July 1868, 20/16909-16

21 Alex Campbell to Isaac Buchanan, 7 Feb. and 21 Sept. 1872 and 22 July 1873 (copy), 20/17038, 98-9, 115

22 Eg, Isaac Buchanan to Isaac R. Buchanan, 18 Mar. 1872 (copy), 11/9810-13

23 Partnership agreement, Montreal, 23 Jan. 1874; waiver to Campbell, 21 Jan. 1874; memo by Isaac Buchanan on the Montreal business, nd; memorandum explaining Isaac Buchanan's retirement, 20 Mar. 1874: 76/57140-1, 47, 51, 43. Memo by Isaac Buchanan re his dispute with Leckie and Matthews, nd, 91/64006. Buchanan, Leckie and Company to Isaac Buchanan, 25 Feb. 1874, 38/31720

24 Robert Wemyss to Isaac Buchanan, 24 Feb. 1880, 61/48997-49000

25 George Campbell to Isaac Buchanan, 25 Jan. 1881, 20/17225-34

26 Isaac Buchanan to P. Witherby, 2 May 1868 (copy), 63/49564. Copy of New York office lease, 75/56752

27 Isaac Buchanan to Isaac R. Buchanan, 19 Sept. and 19 Oct. 1870 (copy), 11/9770, 72-5. Agreement between M.J. Jamieson and P.T. Buchanan, Aug. 1870; two memos re an agreement between Buchanan Brothers and Company and McKenzie and McKay, 23 Mar. 1871: 76/56979, 57018-19, 20-1

28 Andrew Binny to Isaac Buchanan, 18 Oct. 1869, 3/1815-16. Agreement between Isaac Buchanan and Walter Mackenzie, 18 July 1870, 76/56960-5. Neutel, 'From "Southern" Concept to Canada Southern' 111-30

29 Isaac Buchanan to Alex Campbell, 4 May 1872, and to Isaac R. Buchanan, 22 June 1872 (copies), 20/17093-4, 11/9833-4

30 Isaac Buchanan to Alex Campbell, 14 Feb. 1872, and to Walter Mackenzie, 21 June 1873 (copies), 20/17049-50, 45/36524-8

31 Eg, Isaac Buchanan to Sir Hugh Allan, 25 Jan. 1875 (copy), 1/202

32 Copy of final discharge, 76/57177

33 Scottish Record Office, Edinburgh, Unextracted Process CS 249/493, Peter Buchanan's Trustees against Jane M. Buchanan and others. Scottish Record

Office, Court of Session, *Minute Book*, vol. 96 (1876-7) 652-3. See also Jane
Buchanan to Isaac Buchanan, 21 May 1878, 12/10934-7; Isaac Buchanan to
George Douglas, 31 Mar. 1875 (copy), 24/21007

34 Isaac Buchanan to Isaac R. Buchanan, 22 Apr. and 22 May 1873 (copies),
11/9885, 90-1

35 Material relating to P.T. Buchanan's coal speculation, 1872, 26/22347-62. Scottish Record Office, Court of Session, *Minute Book*, vol. 93 (1873-4) 384, 459.
Scottish Record Office, Unextracted Process CS 250/5567, John Reid against
Peter Toronto Buchanan and Others.

36 Eg, Isaac Buchanan to Sir Hugh Allan, 4 May 1881 (copy), 1/208-9. Isaac Buchanan to Isaac R. Buchanan, 22 May 1873 (copy), 11/9890-1. Jane Buchanan to
Isaac Buchanan, 21 May 1878, 12/10934-7

37 Isaac Buchanan to George Campbell, 2 Oct. 1875 (copy), and Campbell to Isaac,
7 Oct. 1875, 20/17204, 214-19. Isaac Buchanan to John Barry, 10 Oct. 1876, and
to Leckie, Matthews and Company, 29 May 1877 (copies), 2/1308-9, 38/31724

38 Morgan, ed., *The Dominion Annual Register and Review, 1883* 304

39 Isaac R. Buchanan to Isaac Buchanan, 19 Apr. 1877, 11/10014-15. James I.
Buchanan to Isaac Buchanan, 16 and 18 Sept. 1882, 12/10510-14, 16-19. Isaac
Buchanan to ?, 22 Mar. 1883 (copy), 11/9737-40. 'Jacob Jay Vandergrift,' *Dictionary of American Biography* X, part I, (New York [1959]) 179. 'James Isaac
Buchanan,' *Who Was Who in America* I, *1897-1942* (Chicago 1943) 159-60.
Farmer, 'Calendar of the Buchanan Papers.' Hamilton Public Library, Reference
Department, clipping files on the Buchanan family. James I. Buchanan, *Memorial
of Eliza Macfarlane Buchanan*.

CHAPTER 10: THE BUCHANANS' BUSINESS
AND THE UPPER CANADIAN BUSINESS SYSTEM

1 Evans, *The History of the Commercial Crisis, 1857-58* 33; and *The Commercial
Crisis, 1847-48* 82. See the appendices to both for ample evidence that businessmen, too, employed such terms. For a Canadian example, see *Monetary Times*, 1
Oct. 1875, 381-3. This is an account of the failure of Moffat Brothers and Company, successor to another of Toronto's large general mercantile firms of the
1850's (Moffat, Murray and Company).

2 Eg, Baskerville, 'Donald Bethune's Steamboat Business' 148-9; or 'The Boardroom and Beyond' 128

3 Brown, 'The Durham Report and the Upper Canadian Scene' 138. See also Naylor, 'The Rise and Fall of the Third Commercial Empire of the St Lawrence' and
Teeple, 'Land, Labour, and Capital in Pre-Confederation Canada' in Teeple, ed.,
Capitalism and the National Question in Canada 6-9, 59-62.

4 Samuel Laing to Peter Buchanan, 12 Dec. 1854, 37/30466-7
5 Katz, *The People of Hamilton, Canada West* 188. Bliss, *A Living Profit*
6 Toronto *Globe*, 9 Aug. 1882
7 For an overview of the financial institutions involved, see Neufeld, *The Financial System of Canada* 36-47.
8 Ross, *A History of the Canadian Bank of Commerce* I, 179, 205, 208-10. Hamilton Public Library, Alexander W. Roy Scrapbook of Newspaper Clippings, 13
9 Hamilton Public Library, Reference Department, Adam Hope file
10 Peter Buchanan to James Law, 15 Sept. 1848; to F. Harper, 15 Dec. 1848; to John Young, 10 Aug. 1849; and to R.S. Atcheson, 31 Dec. 1850 (copies): 67/52852, 893, 971-2; 66/52381-2. Re the Trust and Loan Company, see also Creighton, *John A. Macdonald* 157-65, and Neufeld, *The Financial System of Canada* 182.
11 Alex Campbell to Isaac Buchanan, 24 Feb. and 10 Mar. 1854; Isaac Buchanan to Alex Campbell, 17 Mar. 1854 (copy): 18/15388-91, 94, 99. Adam Hope to R.W. Harris, 13 and 22 June 1854, 32/26345, 52
12 Peter Buchanan to R.W. Harris, 27 Sept. 1850 (copy), 67/53119-20
13 For the significance of this issue, see, eg, MacDonald, 'Merchants against Industry'; and Naylor, *A History of Canadian Business* I, 38, II, 278, and *passim*.
14 Adam Hope to Isaac Buchanan, 2 Mar. 1860, 32/26964
15 Pollard, 'Fixed Capital in the Industrial Revolution in Britain'
16 Agnes Buchanan to Isaac Buchanan, 18 Nov. 1867, 7/5263-4. *City of Hamilton Directory*, 1871-2, 336. 'Indenture between Joseph Wright ... and Young Law & Co ...' nd, 69/54348
17 Contemplated order for Canadian dry goods, fall, 1860; memo of dry goods orders, spring, 1863; abstracts of dry goods inventories, Hamilton, 30 Nov. 1862 and 11 Mar. 1865: 86/60818, 61022, 61016; 37/30225-6. A. Binny to Isaac Buchanan, 2 Apr. 1868, 3/1741-2
18 Isaac Buchanan, *The Relations of the Industry of Canada* 91, 95n, 98-9, 269, 446-9
19 Risk, 'The Nineteenth-Century Foundations of the Business Corporation in Ontario.' I have benefited greatly from discussions with Professor Risk on nineteenth-century commercial law and practice and their wider implications. McCalla, 'The Commercial Politics of the Toronto Board of Trade, 1850-1860'
20 Waite, 'The Edge of the Forest' 4-9

Select bibliography

This study depends very much on one primary source, but is informed by an extensive range of literature which served to define the context within which the Buchanans are seen. To keep this bibliography to a reasonable length, I have limited it largely to works actually cited in the notes. For the abbreviations employed see p. 181

PRIMARY SOURCES

Manuscripts
Hamilton Public Library, Hamilton
- Adam Hope, letters to his father, 1834-7 (typescript)
- Farmer, Mary H. 'Calendar of the Buchanan Papers, 1697-1896, Presented to the Hamilton Public Library ...' (typescript, Hamilton Public Library, 1962)
- Reference department files re Adam Hope and the Hope family and Isaac Buchanan and the Buchanan family
- Roy, Alexander W., scrapbook of newspaper clippings
Public Archives of Canada, Ottawa
- Baring Papers (MG 24, D-21), vol. I
- Board of Railway Commissioners Records (RG 1, E-6), vols. I, II
- Buchanan Papers (MG 24, D-16)
- Glyn, Mills and Co. Papers (MG 24, D-36), vols. A541-2
Public Archives of Ontario, Toronto
- Mackenzie-Lindsey Collection, Box 25G, File 3854
Scottish Record Office, Edinburgh
- Court of Session, Minute Book, vols. 93 (1873-4) and 96 (1876-7)
- Record of Sequestration, Peter Buchanan and Co.; Accountant of Court's Process #56 of 1869

- Trust Disposition and Settlement by Peter Buchanan, 24 May 1860, registered 13 Nov. 1860
- Unextracted Process CS 249/493, Peter Buchanan's Trustees against Jane M. Buchanan and others
- Unextracted Process CS 250/5567, John Reid against Peter Toronto Buchanan and Others

Directories

The Mitchell Library in Glasgow has bound its directories of the city in a continuous series, cited here as *Glasgow Directory*; all relevant volumes (which are virtually annual for the Buchanans' period) have been consulted.

The Hamilton Public Library possesses a good series of Hamilton directories, cited here as *City of Hamilton Directory*; all its volumes for the period from 1853 to 1883 have been consulted.

A variety of other directories have been consulted. Those actually cited are
- *Brown's Toronto General Directory 1856* (Toronto 1856)
- Lovell's *Canada Directory for 1857-58* (Montreal 1857).

Newspapers and magazines

Contemporary newspapers and magazines were consulted only for a few specific dates and incidents. Those cited include the Hamilton *Spectator* and *Evening Times*, the Montreal *Herald*, the Toronto *Globe* and *Leader*, the Glasgow *Herald*, and the (Toronto) *Monetary Times*. The *Canadian Merchants Magazine* (Toronto 1857-9) was fully consulted.

Records of the Legislative Assembly

All volumes of the *Journals* of the Legislative Assembly of the Province of Canada for the period 1841 to 1873 have been consulted. The most important items actually cited are listed.
- Report on the late election riots at Toronto, 1841, Appendix s
- Montreal Brokers' Circular, 25 Mar. 1849; 1849, Appendix z
- Report of the Select Committee to Investigate and Report on the Position of the Woodstock and Lake Erie Railway and Harbour Company; Proceedings of the Standing Committee on Railroads re the Great Southern Railway; 1857, Appendix 6
- Tables of Trade and Navigation, annual, 1850-73

Newspaper Reports of Debates of the Assembly (microfilmed under that title by the Canadian Library Association) have been consulted for 1857-65.

Other printed primary sources

Andrews, Israel D. *Report on the Trade and Commerce of the British North American Colonies and upon the Trade of the Great Lakes and Rivers* (Washington 1853)
Armstrong, F.H. and N.D. Hultin, eds. '*The Anglo-American Magazine* Looks at Urban Upper Canada on the Eve of the Railway Era' in Ontario Historical Society, *Profiles of a Province* (Toronto 1967) 43-58
Baines, T. *History of the Commerce and Town of Liverpool* (London 1852)
– *Liverpool in 1859* (London 1859)
Benedict, R.G. *The Great Southern Railway of Canada: Letter to the Railway Committee in Favor of the Extension Claimed by the Woodstock and Lake Erie Railway* (Quebec 1855)
Bonnycastle, Sir R.H. *Canada and the Canadians in 1846*, 2 vols. (London 1846)
Bremner, D. *The Industries of Scotland* (Edinburgh 1869)
Brown, P.L., ed. *Clyde Company Papers*, 6 vols. (London 1941-68)
Buchanan, Isaac *Can the British Monarchy be Preserved?* (np 1848)
– *A Government Specie Paying Bank of Issue and Other Subversive Legislation Proposed by the Finance Minister of Canada* (Hamilton 1866)
– *Letters Illustrative of the Present Position of Politics in Canada written on the occasion of The Political Convention which met at Toronto, on 9th Nov., 1859* (Hamilton 1859)
– *Moral Consequences of Sir R. Peel's Unprincipled and Fatal Course, Disquiet, Overturn, and Revolution* (Greenock 1850)
– *National Unthrift, or, The Cup of British Prosperity as It Unfortunately Is...* (Hamilton 1860)
– *The Relations of the Industry of Canada with the Mother Country and the United States...*, H.J. Morgan, ed. (Montreal 1864)
Buchanan, James I. *Memorial of Eliza Macfarlane Buchanan* (Pittsburgh 1928)
Buchanan, Robert J. *Canada: A Patriotic Address* (Hamilton 1907)
Buchanan Society, the *History, Rules, Bye-Laws, and List of Members* (Glasgow 1910)
Callender, W.R. *The Commercial Crisis of 1857: Its Causes and Results* (London 1858)
Census of Canada, 1870-71 IV (Ottawa 1876)
Chapman, H.S. *A Statistical Sketch of the Corn Trade of Canada* (London 1832)
Cruikshank, E.A. 'A Country Merchant in Upper Canada, 1800-1812,' *OHSPR*, XXV (192) 145-90
Dent, J.C. *The Last Forty Years: Canada since the Union of 1841*, 2 vols. (Toronto 1881)

Evans, D.M. *The City; or the Physiology of London Business: With Sketches on 'Change, and at the Coffee Houses* (London 1845)
- *The Commercial Crisis, 1847-1848*, 2nd ed. (London 1849)
- *The History of the Commercial Crisis, 1857-58, and the Stock Exchange Panic of 1859* (London 1859)
Fox, William S., ed. *Letters of William Davies, Toronto, 1854-1861* (Toronto 1945)
Keefer, T.C. *Philosophy of Railroads and Other Essays*, H.V. Nelles, ed. (Toronto 1972)
List of Members of the Merchants House of Glasgow (Glasgow 1891)
The Mercantile Agency Reference Book for the British Provinces ... 1866, The (Montreal and Toronto 1866)
Morgan, H.J., ed. *The Dominion Annual Register and Review, 1883* (Toronto 1884)
- *Sketches of Celebrated Canadians and Persons Connected with Canada...* (Quebec 1862)
Notman, W. and F. Taylor *Portraits of British Americans with Biographical Sketches*, I (Montreal 1865)
Office of the Mercantile Agency, 'To Our Subscribers, Jan. 1858,' printed as 'Business Failures in the Panic of 1857,' *BAR*, XXXVII (1963) 437-43
Poole, Braithwaite *The Commerce of Liverpool* (London 1854)
Rattray, W.J. *The Scot in British North America*, 4 vols. (Toronto 1880-3)
Reid, Colin D. *Our City Government and Our City Member* (Hamilton 1861)
Reid, R. *Glasgow Past and Present*, 3 vols. (Glasgow 1884)
Sanderson, C.R., ed. *The Arthur Papers*, 3 vols. (Toronto 1957-9)
Smith, W.H. *Canada, Past, Present and Future*, 2 vols. (Toronto 1851)
- *Canadian Gazetteer; Comprising Statistical and General Information Respecting All Parts of the Upper Province, or Canada West* (Toronto 1846)
Stewart, George *Progress of Glasgow ... As Shown in the Records of the Glasgow Chamber of Commerce* (Glasgow 1883)
Strang, John *Statistics of Glasgow, for the Years 1850, 51, and 52* (Glasgow 1853)
Wiman, E. *Annual Report of the Board of Trade with a Review of the Commerce of Toronto for 1860* (Toronto 1861)

SECONDARY SOURCES

Books and theses

Aitken, H.G.J. *The Welland Canal Company* (Cambridge, MA 1954)
Albion, R.G. *The Rise of New York Port, 1815-1860* (New York 1939)
Armstrong, F.H. 'Toronto in Transition: The Emergence of a City, 1828-1838,' PHD thesis, University of Toronto, 1965

Bailey, T.M. *Traces, Places and Faces: Links between Canada and Scotland* (Hamilton 1957)

Barger, Harold *Distribution's Place in the American Economy since 1869* (Princeton 1955)

Baskerville, P. 'The Boardroom and Beyond: Aspects of the Upper Canadian Railroad Community,' PHD thesis, Queen's University, 1973

Bliss, Michael *A Living Profit: Studies in the Social History of Canadian Business, 1883-1911* (Toronto 1974)

Breckenridge, R.M. *The Canadian Banking System 1817-1890* (Toronto 1894)

Bridgman, H.J. 'Isaac Buchanan and Religion, 1810-1883,' MA thesis, Queen's University, 1969

Buchanan, R.M. *Notes on the Members of the Buchanan Society, Numbers 1 to 366* (Glasgow 1931)

Buck, N.S. *The Development of the Organization of Anglo-American Trade, 1800-1850* (New Haven 1925)

Cameron, R.E. *et al., Banking in the Early Stages of Industrialization* (New York 1967)

Campbell, M.F. *A Mountain and a City: The Story of Hamilton* (Toronto 1966)

Campbell, R.H. 'The Growth and Fluctuations of the Scottish Pig Iron Trade, 1828-1873,' PHD thesis, University of Aberdeen, 1956

– *Scotland since 1707: The Rise of an Industrial Society* (Oxford 1965)

Careless, J.M.S. *The Union of the Canadas* (Toronto 1967)

Caves, R.E. and R.H. Holton, *The Canadian Economy: Prospect and Retrospect* (Cambridge, MA 1961)

Checkland, S.G. *The Rise of Industrial Society in England* (London 1964)

– *Scottish Banking: A History, 1695-1973* (Glasgow 1975)

– *The Upas Tree: Glasgow 1875-1975* (Glasgow 1976)

Clapham, J.H. *An Economic History of Modern Britain*, I, *The Early Railway Age, 1820-1850* (Cambridge 1926)

– *An Economic History of Modern Britain*, II, *Free Trade and Steel 1850-1886* (Cambridge 1932)

Clapp, B.W. *John Owens, Manchester Merchant* (Manchester 1965)

Clark, John G. *The Grain Trade in the Old Northwest* (Urbana 1966)

Creighton, D.G. *British North America at Confederation* (Ottawa 1939)

– *The Commercial Empire of the St Lawrence, 1760-1850* (Toronto 1937)

– *John A. Macdonald: The Young Politician* (Toronto 1952)

Cross, Michael S. 'The Dark Druidical Groves: The Lumber Community and the Commercial Frontier in British North America, to 1854,' PHD thesis, University of Toronto, 1968

Crouzet, F. *Capital Formation in the Industrial Revolution* (London 1972)

Currie, A.W. *The Grand Trunk Railway of Canada* (Toronto 1957)

Dales, J.H. *The Protective Tariff in Canada's Development* (Toronto 1966)

Devine, T.M. *The Tobacco Lords* (Edinburgh 1975)

Dictionary of Canadian Biography, IX and X (Toronto 1976 and 1972)

Easterbrook, W.T. *Farm Credit in Canada* (Toronto 1938)

– and H.G.J. Aitken *Canadian Economic History* (Toronto 1956)

Edwards, M.M. *The Growth of the British Cotton Trade, 1780-1815* (Manchester 1967)

Firth, E.G. *The Town of York, 1815-1834* (Toronto 1966)

Fowke, V.C. *Canadian Agricultural Policy: The Historical Pattern* (Toronto 1947)

Gayer, A.D., W.W. Rostow, and Anna J. Schwartz *The Growth and Fluctuation of the British Economy 1790-1850*, 2 vols. (Oxford 1953)

Greenberg, Michael *British Trade and The Opening of China 1800-42* (Cambridge 1951)

Goodstein, Anita S. *Biography of a Businessman: Henry W. Sage, 1814-1897* (Ithaca 1962)

Hammond, Bray *Banks and Politics in America from the Revolution to the Civil War* (Princeton 1957)

Harris, R.C. and J. Warkentin *Canada before Confederation: A Study in Historical Geography* (New York 1974)

Hidy, R.W. *The House of Baring in American Trade and Finance* (Cambridge, MA 1949)

Hughes, J.R.T. *Fluctuations in Trade, Industry and Finance: A Study of British Economic Development 1850-1860* (Oxford 1960)

Hyde, F.E. *Cunard and the North Atlantic 1840-1973* (London 1975)

– *Liverpool and the Mersey: An Economic History of a Port 1700-1970* (Newton Abbot 1971)

– *Shipping Enterprise and Management, 1830-1939: Harrisons of Liverpool* (Liverpool 1967)

Innis, H.A. *Essays in Canadian Economic History* (Toronto 1956)

– and A.R.M. Lower, eds. *Select Documents in Canadian Economic History, 1783-1885* (Toronto 1933)

James Finlay & Company Limited, Manufacturers and East India Merchants, 1750-1950 (Glasgow 1951)

Jenks, L.H. *The Migration of British Capital to 1875*, 2nd ed. (London 1963)

John, A.H. *A Liverpool Merchant House* (London 1959)

Johnson, Arthur M. *Boston Capitalists and Western Railroads* (Cambridge, MA 1967)

Johnston, C.M. *The Head of the Lake: A History of Wentworth County* (Hamilton 1958)

Jones, Fred Mitchell *Middlemen in the Domestic Trade of the United States 1800-60* (Urbana 1937)

Jones, R.L. *History of Agriculture in Ontario, 1613-1880* (Toronto 1946)

Katz, Michael *The People of Hamilton, Canada West: Family and Class in a Mid-Nineteenth-Century City* (Cambridge, MA 1975)

Lebhor, G.M. *Chain Stores in America, 1859-1959* (New York 1959)

Lee, C.H. *A Cotton Enterprise, 1795-1840: A History of M'Connell & Kennedy, Fine Cotton Spinners* (Manchester 1972)

Lister, Herbert, comp. *Hamilton, Canada: Its History, Commerce, Industries, Resources...* (Hamilton 1913)

Lower, A.R.M. *Great Britain's Woodyard: British America and the Timber Trade, 1763-1867* (Montreal 1973)

Macgeorge, A. *The Bairds of Gartsherrie* (Glasgow 1875)

Macmillan, D.S., ed. *Canadian Business History: Selected Studies, 1497-1971* (Toronto 1972)

– *Scotland and Australia, 1788-1850* (Oxford 1967)

MacRae, M. and A. Adamson, *The Ancestral Roof* (Toronto 1963)

Marriner, Sheila *Rathbones of Liverpool 1845-73* (Liverpool 1961)

Masters, D.C. *The Rise of Toronto, 1850-1890* (Toronto 1947)

Matthews, R.C.O. *A Study in Trade Cycle History: Economic Fluctuations in Great Britain, 1833-1842* (Cambridge 1954)

McGrane, R.C. *The Panic of 1837* (Chicago 1924)

McIlwraith, T.F. 'The Logistical Geography of the Great Lakes Grain Trade, 1820-1850,' PHD thesis, University of Wisconsin, 1973

McKelvey, Blake *Rochester, the Water Power City, 1812-1854* (Cambridge, MA 1945)

Middleton, J.E. *The Municipality of Toronto: A History*, 3 vols. (Toronto 1923)

Miller, Orlo *A Century of Western Ontario: The Story of London, 'The Free Press,' and Western Ontario, 1849-1949* (Toronto 1949)

Morton, W.L. *The Critical Years: The Union of British North America, 1857-1873* (Toronto 1964)

Naylor, T. *The History of Canadian Business 1867-1914*, 2 vols. (Toronto 1975)

Neu, Irene D. *Erastus Corning, Merchant and Financier, 1794-1872* (Ithaca 1960)

Neufeld, E.P. *The Financial System of Canada: Its Growth and Development* (Toronto 1972)

Neutel, Walter 'From "Southern" Concept to Canada Southern Railway 1835-1873,' MA thesis, University of Western Ontario, 1968

Oakley, C.A. *The Second City* (London 1946)

Ouellet, F. *Histoire économique et sociale du Québec, 1760-1850* (Montreal 1966)

Pares, Richard *Merchants and Planters*, Economic History Review Supplements 4 (Cambridge 1960)

Payne P.L. *British Entrepreneurship in the Nineteenth Century* (London 1974)

Perkins, E.J. *Financing Anglo-American Trade: The House of Brown, 1800-1880* (Cambridge, MA 1975)

Platt, D.C.M. *Latin America and British Trade, 1806-1914* (London 1972)

Porter, Glenn and R. Cuff, eds. *Enterprise and National Development* (Toronto 1973)

Porter, Glenn and H. Livesay, *Merchants and Manufacturers: Studies in the Changing Structure of Nineteenth-Century Marketing* (Baltimore 1971)

Pred, Alan *Urban Growth and the Circulation of Information: The United States System of Cities, 1790-1840* (Cambridge, MA 1973)

Preston, R. *Kingston before the War of 1812* (Toronto 1959)

Price, Jacob M. *France and the Chesapeake: A History of the French Tobacco Monopoly, 1674-1791, and of Its Relationship to the British and American Tobacco Trades*, 2 vols. (Ann Arbor 1973)

Ragatz, L.J. *The Fall of the Planter Class in the British Caribbean, 1763-1833* (New York 1928)

Rait, Robert S. *The History of the Union Bank of Scotland* (Glasgow 1930)

Rankin, J. *A History of Our Firm* (Liverpool 1921)

Robertson, J. Ross *Landmarks of Toronto*, 6 vols. (Toronto 1894-1914)

Ross, V. *A History of the Canadian Bank Commerce* I (Toronto 1920)

Slaven, A. *The Development of the West of Scotland: 1750-1960* (London 1975)

Smith, W.B. and A.H. Cole, *Fluctuations in American Business 1790-1860* (Cambridge, MA 1935)

Spelt, Jacob M. *Urban Development in South-Central Ontario* (Assen, The Netherlands 1955)

Stephenson, W. *The Store that Timothy Built* (Toronto 1969)

Stevens, G.R. *Canadian National Railways*, 2 vols. (Toronto 1960)

Teeple, G., ed. *Capitalism and the National Question in Canada* (Toronto 1972)

Thorp, W.L. *Business Annals* (New York 1926)

Tucker, G.N. *The Canadian Commercial Revolution, 1845-1851* (Toronto 1964)

Tulchinsky, G.J.J. *The River Barons: Montreal Businessmen and the Growth of Industry and Transportation, 1837-53* (Toronto 1977)

Urquhart, M.C. and K.A. Buckley, eds. *Historical Statistics of Canada* (Cambridge 1965)

Van Vleck, G.W. *The Panic of 1857: An Analytical Study* (New York 1943)

Wilson, Alan *John Northway: A Blue Serge Canadian* (Toronto 1965)

Wilson, R.G. *Gentlemen Merchants: The Merchant Community in Leeds, 1700-1830* (Manchester 1971)

Wood, J.D., ed. *Perspectives on Landscape and Settlement in Nineteenth Century Ontario* (Toronto 1975)

Articles

Abella, I.M. 'The "Sydenham Election" of 1841,' *CHR* XLVII (1966) 326-43

Acheson, T.W. 'The Nature and Structure of York Commerce in the 1820s,' *CHR* L (1969) 406-28

Aitken, H.G.J. 'Government and Business in Canada: An Interpretation,' *BHR* XXXVIII (1964) 4-21
- 'A New Way to Pay Old Debts' in W. Miller, ed. *Men in Business* (New York 1952) 71-90
Albion, R.G. 'New York Port and Its Disappointed Rivals, 1815-1860,' *Journal of Economic and Business History* III (1930-1) 602-29
Anonymous, 'Glyns and the Bank of Upper Canada,' *Three Banks Review* LV (Sept. 1962) 43-52
- 'The Rise of Glasgow's West Indian Trade, 1793-1818,' *Three Banks Review* LI (Sept. 1961) 34-44
Armstrong, F.H. 'Metropolitanism and Toronto Re-examined, 1825-1850,' CHA *Annual Report* (1966) 29-40
Bailyn, Bernard ' "Hedges" *Browns*: Some Thoughts on the New England Merchants in the Colonial Period,' *Explorations in Entrepreneurial History* IV (1951-2) 229-33
Barnett, J.D. 'An Election without Politics – 1857 – I. Buchanan,' *OHSPR* XIV (1916) 153-62
Baskerville, P. 'Donald Bethune's Steamboat Business: A Study of Upper Canadian Commercial and Financial Practice,' *OH* LXVII (1975) 135-49
Brown, G.W. 'The Durham Report and the Upper Canadian Scene,' *CHR* XX (1939) 136-60
Bruchey, Stuart 'Success and Failure Factors: American Merchants in Foreign Trade in the Eighteenth and Early Nineteenth Centuries,' *BHR* (1958) 272-92
Burton, F.W. 'Wheat in Canadian History,' *CJEPS* III (1937) 210-17
Campbell, R.H. 'The Anglo-Scottish Union of 1707, II, The Economic Consequences,' *EcHR*, 2nd ser. XVI (1963-4) 468-77
- 'Developments in the Scottish Pig Iron Trade, 1844-1848,' *JEH* XV (1955) 209-26
- 'Edinburgh Bankers and the Western Bank of Scotland,' *SJPE* II (1955) 233-48
Careless, J.M.S. 'Somewhat Narrow Horizons,' CHA *Historical Papers* (1968) 1-10
Chambers, E.J. and G.W. Bertram, 'Urbanization and Manufacturing in Central Canada, 1870-1890,' in Canadian Political Science Association, *Conference on Statistics* (1964) 225-58
Checkland, S.G. 'Two Scottish West Indian Liquidations after 1793,' *SJPE* IV (1957) 127-43
Cohen, I. 'The Auction System in the Port of New York, 1817-1837,' *BHR* XLV (1971) 488-510
Coleman, D.C. 'Textile Growth' in N.B. Harte and K.G. Ponting, eds. *Textile History and Economic History: Essays in Honour of Miss Julia de Lacy Mann* (Manchester 1973) 1-21
Davis, L.E. and J.R.T. Hughes, 'A Dollar-Sterling Exchange, 1803-1895,' *EcHR*, 2nd ser. XIII (1960-1) 52-78

Devine, T.M. 'Glasgow Colonial Merchants and Land, 1770-1815' in J.T. Ward and R.G. Wilson, eds. *Land and Industry: The Landed Estate and the Industrial Revolution* (Newton Abbot 1971) 205-44

– 'Glasgow Merchants and the Collapse of the Tobacco Trade, 1775-1783,' *SHR* LII (1973) 50-74

– 'Sources of Capital for the Glasgow Tobacco Trade, c. 1740-1780,' *BH* XVI (1974) 113-29

Firestone, O.J. 'Development of Canada's Economy, 1850-1900' in *Trends in the American Economy in the Nineteenth Century*, Studies in Income and Wealth, XXIV (Princeton 1960) 217-52

Fowke, V.C. 'The Myth of the Self-Sufficient Canadian Pioneer,' Royal Society of Canada, *Transactions* LVI, ser. III (1962) sec. II, 23-37

Gardiner, H.F. 'The Hamiltons of Queenston, Kingston and Hamilton,' *OHSPR* VIII (1907) 24-33

Habakkuk, H.J. 'Fluctuations and Growth in the Nineteenth Century' in M. Kooy, ed. *Studies in Economics and Economic History: Essays in Honour of Professor H.M. Robertson* (London 1972) 259-79

Hartland, P. 'Factors in Economic Growth in Canada,' *JEH* XV (1955) 13-22

Heaton, Herbert 'Benjamin Gott and the Anglo-American Cloth Trade,' *Journal of Economic and Business History* II (1929-30) 146-62

Hughes, J.R.T. 'The Commercial Crisis of 1857,' *Oxford Economic Papers* (ns) VIII (1956) 194-222

Hyde, F.E. and S. Marriner, 'The Economic Functions of the Export Merchant,' *The Manchester School* XX (1952) 215-26

'Jacob Jay Vandergrift,' *Dictionary of American Biography* X, part I, (New York 1959) 179

'James Isaac Buchanan,' *Who Was Who in America*, I, *1897-1942* (Chicago 1943) 159-60

Johnson, J.K. 'John A. Macdonald: The Young Non-Politician,' CHA *Historical Papers* (1971) 138-53

Jones, R.L. 'The Canadian Agricultural Tariff of 1843,' *CJEPS* VII (1941) 528-37

Kellett, J.R. 'Property Speculators and the Building of Glasgow, 1780-1830,' *SJPE* VIII (1961) 211-32

Kelly, Kenneth 'Wheat Farming in Simcoe County in the Mid-Nineteenth Century,' *Canadian Geographer* XV (1971) 95-112

Kennedy, G.G.C. 'The Union Bank of Scotland Ltd.: Its Contribution to Scottish Banking,' *Scottish Bankers' Magazine* XLVII (1955) 17-23

Killick, J. 'Risk, Specialization and Profit in the Mercantile Sector of the Nineteenth Century Cotton Trade: Alexander Brown and Sons, 1820-80,' *BH* XVI (1974) 1-16

Le Goff, T.J.A. 'The Agricultural Crisis in Lower Canada, 1802-12: A Review of a Controversy,' *CHR* LV (1974) 1-31

Lee, G.A. 'The Concept of Profit in British Accounting, 1760-1900,' *BHR* XLIX (1975) 6-36

Lower, A.R.M. 'The Assault on the Laurentian Barrier, 1850-1870,' *CHR* X (1929) 294-307

MacDermott, T.W.L., ed. 'Some Opinions of a Tory in the 1830's,' *CHR* XI (1930) 232-7

MacDonald, L.R. 'Merchants against Industry: An Idea and Its Origins,' *CHR* LVI (1975) 263-81

Marwick, W.H. 'The Cotton Industry and the Industrial Revolution in Scotland,' *SHR* XXI (1923-4) 207-18

McCalla, D. 'The Canadian Grain Trade in the 1840's: The Buchanans' Case,' CHA *Historical Papers* (1974) 95-114

– 'The Commercial Politics of the Toronto Board of Trade, 1850-1860,' *CHR* L (1969) 51-67

– 'The Decline of Hamilton as a Wholesale Centre,' *OH* LXV (1973) 247-54

McDougall, D.M. 'Immigration into Canada, 1851-1920,' *CJEPS* XXVII (1961) 162-75

Miller, Orlo 'The Fat Years and the Lean: London (Canada) in Boom and Depression, 1851-1861,' *OH* LIII (1961) 73-80

Michell, H. 'Statistics of Prices' in H. Michell and K.W. Taylor, *Statistical Contributions to Canadian Economic History*, II, *Statistics of Foreign Trade and Statistics of Prices* (Toronto 1931)

Mitchell, G.M. 'English and Scottish Cotton Industries,' *SHR* XXII (1924-5) 101-14

North, D.C. 'Ocean Freight Rates and Economic Development 1750-1913,' *JEH* XVIII (1958) 537-55

Ouellet, F. and J. Hamelin, 'La Crise agricole dans le Bas-Canada, 1802-1837,' CHA *Annual Report* (1962) 17-33

Parker, W.H. 'The Towns of Lower Canada in the 1830's' in R.B. Beckinsale and J.M. Houston, eds. *Urbanization and Its Problems* (Oxford 1968) 391-425

Pentland, H.C. 'Further Observations on Canadian Development,' *CJEPS* XIX (1953) 403-10

– 'The Role of Capital in Canadian Economic Development before 1875,' *CJEPS* XVI (1950) 457-74

Pollard, S. 'Fixed Capital in the Industrial Revolution in Britain,' *JEH* XXIV (1964) 299-314

Potter, J. 'Atlantic Economy, 1815-60: The U.S.A. and the Industrial Revolution in Britain' in L.S. Pressnell, ed. *Studies in the Industrial Revolution* (London 1960) 236-80

Price, Jacob M. 'The Rise of Glasgow in the Chesapeake Tobacco Trade, 1707-1775,' *William and Mary Quarterly*, 3rd ser. XI (1954) 179-99

– 'Who Was John Norton? A Note on the Historical Character of Some Eighteenth-Century London Virginia Firms,' *William and Mary Quarterly*, 3rd ser. XIX (1962) 400-7

Risk, R.C.B. 'The Nineteenth-Century Foundations of the Business Corporation in Ontario,' *University of Toronto Law Journal* XXIII (1973) 270-306

Robertson, A.J. 'The Decline of the Scottish Cotton Industry 1860-1914,' *BH* XII (1970) 116-28

Robertson, M.L. 'Scottish Commerce and the American War of Independence,' *EcHR* 2nd ser. IX (1956-7) 123-31

Smout, T.C. 'The Development and Enterprise of Glasgow, 1556-1707,' *SJPE* VII (1960) 194-212

Soltow, J.H. 'Scottish Traders in Virginia, 1750-1775,' *EcHR* 2nd ser. XII (1959-60) 83-98

Swainson, Donald 'Business and Politics: The Career of John Willoughby Crawford,' *OH* LXI (1969) 225-36

Waite, P.B. 'The Edge of the Forest,' CHA *Historical Papers* (1969) 1-13

Ward-Perkins, C.N. 'The Commercial Crisis of 1847,' *Oxford Economic Papers* (ns) II (1950) 75-94

Williams, D.M. 'Liverpool Merchants and the Cotton Trade, 1820-1850' in J.R. Harris, ed. *Liverpool and Merseyside: Essays in the Economic and Social History of a Port and Its Hinterland* (London 1969) 182-211

– 'Merchanting in the First half of the Nineteenth Century: The Liverpool Timber Trade,' *BH* VIII (1966) 103-21

Wilson, Charles 'The Entrepreneur in the Industrial Revolution in Britain,' *Explorations in Entrepreneurial History* VII (1955) 129-45

Index